Soviet and Post-Soviet Politics and Socie[
ISSN 1614-3515

General Editor: Andreas Umland,
Stockholm Centre for Eastern European Studies, andreas.umland@ui.se

Commi
London, [

Soviet and Post-Soviet Politics and Society (SPPS)

ISSN 1614-3515

Founded in 2004 and refereed since 2007, SPPS makes available affordable English-, German-, and Russian-language studies on the history of the countries of the former Soviet bloc from the late Tsarist period to today. It publishes between 5 and 20 volumes per year and focuses on issues in transitions to and from democracy such as economic crisis, identity formation, civil society development, and constitutional reform in CEE and the NIS. SPPS also aims to highlight so far understudied themes in East European studies such as right-wing radicalism, religious life, higher education, or human rights protection. The authors and titles of all previously published volumes are listed at the end of this book. For a full description of the series and reviews of its books, see www.ibidem-verlag.de/red/spps.

Editorial correspondence & manuscripts should be sent to: Dr. Andreas Umland, Department of Political Science, Kyiv-Mohyla Academy, vul. Voloska 8/5, UA-04070 Kyiv, UKRAINE; andreas.umland@cantab.net

Business correspondence & review copy requests should be sent to: *ibidem* Press, Leuschnerstr. 40, 30457 Hannover, Germany; tel.: +49 511 2622200; fax: +49 511 2622201; spps@ibidem.eu.

Authors, reviewers, referees, and editors for (as well as all other persons sympathetic to) SPPS are invited to join its networks at www.facebook.com/group.php?gid=52638198614 www.linkedin.com/groups?about=&gid=103012 www.xing.com/net/spps-ibidem-verlag/

Recent Volumes

Vladimir Dubrovskiy, Kálmán Mizsei, and
Kateryna Ivashchenko-Stadnik
in collaboration with Mychailo Wynnyckyj

EIGHT YEARS AFTER THE
REVOLUTION OF DIGNITY
What Has Changed in Ukraine during 2013–2021?

With a foreword by Yaroslav Hrytsak

ibidem
Verlag

Bibliografische Information der Deutschen Nationalbibliothek

Die Deutsche Nationalbibliothek verzeichnet diese Publikation in der Deutschen Nationalbibliografie; detaillierte bibliografische Daten sind im Internet über http://dnb.d-nb.de abrufbar.

Bibliographic information published by the Deutsche Nationalbibliothek

Die Deutsche Nationalbibliothek lists this publication in the Deutsche Nationalbibliografie; detailed bibliographic data are available in the Internet at http://dnb.d-nb.de.

English editor: William Golovaha-Hicks
Cover picture: *Paving Stones*. © copyright 2021 by Petro Chekal

ISBN-13: 978-3-8382-1560-0
© *ibidem*-Verlag, Stuttgart 2024
Alle Rechte vorbehalten

Printed in the EU

Contents

List of Figures and Tables

Figures

Tables

List of Abbreviations

ABCA	Annual Business Cost Assessment
ACC	Anti-Corruption Court
ATO	Anti-Terrorism Operation
BPP	Block Petro Poroshenko
CIPE	Center for International Private Enterprise
CIS	Commonwealth of Independent States
CoE	Council of Europe
DCFTA	Deep and Comprehensive Free Trade Agreement
EBRD	European Bank for Reconstruction and Development
ESBU	Economic Security Bureau of Ukraine
ESS	European Social Survey
EU	European Union
EUAM	European Union Advisory Mission
FDI	Foreign Direct Investment
GDN	Global Research Network
GDP	Gross Domestic Product
HQCJ	High Qualification Commission of Judges of Ukraine
ICT	Information and Communication Technology
IER	Institute for Economic Research and Policy Consulting
IFI	international financial institution
IMF	International Monetary Fund
IT	Informational Technology
KGB	Committee for State Security
LAO	limited access order
MBA	Master of Business Administration
MP	Member of Parliament
NABU	National Anti-corruption Bureau of Ukraine
NAS, NASU	National Academy of Science of Ukraine
NATO	North Atlantic Treaty Organization
NGO	Non-governmental organization
NKVD	People's Commissariat for Internal Affairs

OAO	open access order
PF	Peoples' Front party
PGO	Prosecutor General's Office
PIC	Public Integrity Council
PIT	Personal Income Tax
PM	Prime Minister
PPO	Public Prosecutor Office
PR	public relations
PhD	Doctor of Philosophy
RoL	Rule-of-Law
RPR	Reanimation Package of Reforms
R&D	Research and development
SAP	Special Anti-Corruption Prosecution (bureau)
SBI	State Bureau of Investigations
SBU	Security Service of Ukraine
SME	small and medium-sized enterprise
SME Platform	small and medium-sized enterprise platform
SOEs	state-owned enterprises
SUP	Union of Ukrainian Entrepreneurs
SWP	Stiftung Wissenschaft und Politi
UkrSSR	Ukrainian Soviet Socialist Republic
URB	Ukrainian Council of Business
US	United States
USSR	Union of Soviet Socialist Republics
WGI	Worldwide Governance Indicators
WVS	World Values Survey
WW2	Second World War

Foreword

The book that the reader holds in their hands analyzes Ukraine's recent transformation on the eve of the full-scale Russo-Ukrainian war. It is not the only book of its kind but certainly one of the best. It possesses a scope and depth of analysis not present in other books on the same subject for a number of reasons. Firstly, instead of treating various social, economic, and political processes as *disjecta membra*, it proposes a holistic approach. Secondly, it focuses on processes that have gone largely ignored by other observers. Finally, it combines the short-term and the long-term perspective. Taken together, these characteristics make the book the best in the field, a must-read for anybody wishing to understand present-day Ukraine, especially in the context of Ukraine's current heroic and effective resistance against Russian aggression.

Ukraine has experienced several turning points since the break-up of the Soviet Union: the first was the proclamation of Ukrainian independence in 1991, which radically transformed modern geopolitics. Next was the 1993-1994 political crisis that started a regular rotation of ruling elites in the new Ukrainian state. After that came the first "Maidan" (the Orange Revolution of 2004) and the second "Euromaidan" (the 2013 Revolution of Dignity), which put Ukraine on a path of sustainable democracy. Following this was the Russian annexation of Crimea and the Donbas along with the ensuing and protracted war, and now, since February 24, 2022, the full-scale Russian invasion. Each of these points may be considered crucial, and it makes little sense to discuss which one was most important. Instead of treating them as separate events, perhaps we ought to consider the history of Ukrainian independence as "thirty years of revolutions and wars". In a sense, it may be compared to the thirty years comprising the two World Wars and the tumultuous interwar period (1914-1945). These radically transformed the traditional and overwhelmingly agrarian Ukrainian society into a modern Soviet Ukraine, with dramatic and often tragic consequences. This poses a general question: can any systematic transition occur without wars and revolutions?

The answer this book suggests is that "it takes at least one revolution for this change to happen, because a transition from one system to another based on opposing principles can never be fully evolutionary".

The authors focus on the most revolutionary eight years (2014-2022), from the Euromaidan protests to the full-scale war. Based on sociological data and evidence-supported observations, they conclude that the Euromaidan was both an effect and a cause of fundamental changes that Ukraine underwent in the 2010s. At the core of these changes is an emergence of what they call an "urban creative class", represented by journalists, academics, entrepreneurs, qualified professionals, managers, specialists, programmers, and others employed in service sector jobs. These formed a critical mass in the protests that mobilized against the authoritarian regime of Viktor Yanukovych during the Euromaidan, and became the main drivers of reform in their wake. Even the fate of these reforms remained unclear until the eve of the war — the authors describe a "one-step-forward-one-step-back" pattern — still, these processes appear overwhelming and irreversible.

The book was completed on the eve of the war. This war, like any other deep crisis, focuses our vision. Even though some hypotheses and conclusions of this book seem to not be relevant anymore, we may confidently state that the authors were essentially correct in their cautious optimism. What, to unfamiliar eyes, may appear like a "Ukrainian miracle", is instead an accumulation of processes that started long before the war.

As a historian, I am particularly pleased that the authors put their analysis in a global historical context. To the best of my abilities, I have tried to do the same in my recent *Global History of Ukraine*. The similarity of our approaches partially explains why our conclusions concur. However, there is one point of disagreement. I believe that the authors may be too harsh in their condemnation of President Petro Poroshenko for his reliance on a "Ukrainian ethnolinguistic identity". In January 2018, in his address to Parliament he proclaimed the slogan "Army, Language, Faith" as a new formula of Ukrainian identity. As I had once been close to his political advisors, I can confidently state that this was a pragmatic formula, rather than a strategic one. Poroshenko made his statement within the context of the upcoming 2019 presidential election campaign. His camp was expecting his main rival to be Yulia Tymoshenko, and the decisive fight to take place in western Ukraine, where an ethnolinguistic Ukrainian identity was particularly strong. His slogans were thus intentionally tailored for these circumstances. At the time, Volodymyr Zelensky had not yet announced his decision to run for president. Once he did, Poroshenko's plans failed—but it was too late to revise them.

One irony is that since the beginning of the full-scale war, Zelensky has increasingly relied on the "Army, Language, Faith" formula. In a sense, he might be considered a Poroshenko 2.0. This raises a more general question: which formula of national identity—a civic or an ethnic one—better fits the challenges of modernization? One answer would be to suggest that it may be a false dichotomy. With few exceptions, there are no purely ethnic and no purely civic nations—each nation is to some extent both ethnic and civic. The real question, then, is what should be the ethnic core of the civic nation? In the Ukrainian case, the tentative answer is along the lines implied by the authors: the core is largely made up by the creative urban middle class—to which Zelensky definitely belongs, and which he represents.

My wish would be that once the war ends with Ukraine's victory, the authors write a new book about the prospects and challenges of Ukraine's transition to a liberal democracy and market economy. Without any doubt, war is the worst disaster that can happen to any country. But this war also creates opportunities that cannot be missed. It accelerates processes and makes possible things that had seemed impossible. Hopefully, unlike the failed Soviet modernization that was fostered by the wars and revolution from 1914 to 1945, this time Ukraine's transition will be genuinely successful. Still, as the authors rightly state, the chances of success depend on whether fragmented reforms can be replaced with a clear strategic vision. That remains to be seen. However, the sober and systematic analysis offered in the present book may serve as a good example for future strategists to emulate. The authors did the best they could; let their successors do better.

Yaroslav Hrytsak, historian, professor, and Vice-Rector
of the Ukrainian Catholic University,
author of "Overcome the Past: The Global History of Ukraine"

Authors' Preface

The idea to analyze the reforms (and overall developments) that took place in Ukraine since Maidan's victory at the end of February 2014 first came to Kalman Mizsei in 2018. By that time a number of "scorecard"-like analyses had been published, but all of them were devoted to "inputs" in the form of reforms and policy measures, while the main question was "by how much and in which direction has the country changed as a result?" He shared this idea with Vladimir Dubrovskiy, who, in turn, involved Mychailo Wynnyckyj, a sociologist who had just finished writing his book "Ukraine's Maidan, Russia's War: A Chronicle and Analysis of the Revolution of Dignity". The project was arranged by CASE Ukraine (with special acknowledgments going to Dmytro Boyarchuk, Executive Director, Konstantin Latsyba, Administrative Director, and Rostislav Kulish, Financial Director), with the financial support of the International Renaissance Foundation (special thanks to Olexander Sushko, Executive Director), to which the authors wish to express their deep appreciation. The whole report is now available at CASE Ukraine's web site.[1]

Vladimir Dubrovskiy was the Team Leader, and the principal author of most of the text. Kalman Mizsei is the main author of Section 2, which covers the rule of law (with acknowledgment going to Mychailo Zhernakov for the factual input into the analysis of the judicial reform), and Mychailo Wynnyckyj was responsible for the societal analysis, although he has also made substantial contributions to the general concept. Unfortunately for the project, after a few months he was appointed to a government assignment as Secretary of the National Agency for Higher Education Quality Assurance, and had to discontinue his participation in the further work, so his textual contributions were used without their author's control. Kateryna Ivaschenko-Stadnik successfully

---

1   Dubrovskiy, V., Mizsei, K., Ivashchenko-Stadnik, K., and Wynnyckyj, M. *Six years of the Revolution of Dignity: what has changed?* CASE Ukraine, 2020, 19-20. Available at: https://case-ukraine.com.ua/content/uploads/2020/06/6-years-of-the-Revolution-of-Dignity_ENG.pdf

took over his role and became the principal author of the sociological Section 5, and other pieces of the text where we analyze sociological data (special thanks to Evgenii Golovakha for his endorsement of using the Institute of Sociology (NAS Ukraine) longitudinal data in this volume). Additional thanks to Nestor Cheryba for his valuable help and advice on the aggregated survey data analysis.

When it was eventually published in 2020, Andreas Umland, founder and editor of the Ibidem Press book series "Soviet and Post-Soviet Politics and Society" (SPPS), invited the authors to make a book out of it for publishing in this series. We have substantially amended the initial report. Yaroslav Hrytsak and Balint Magyar provided highly appreciated, excellent and extremely beneficial reviews to the earlier version that largely helped us in writing this volume. The manuscript was ready by the end of January 2022.[2] But while the technical finalization was in progress, Russia invaded Ukraine again, this time in a full-scale invasion.

Of course, the biggest war in Europe since WW2 is a much bigger shock than even the Revolution of Dignity and the first, limited wave of Russian aggression in 2014. This war will certainly produce major shifts in all the dimensions studied in this book, and so will the EU candidate status that was granted to Ukraine in support of its resilience in the war. But it is too early to assess these shifts, and especially to forecast them, so amending our manuscript with further events at this moment would not make much sense.

However, although Ukraine will never return to the state described in this book, we believe that our study can still be valuable as a historical document shedding light on the roots of Ukraine's surprising resilience. The book happened to embrace the epoch of exactly eight years from the victory of Maidan to the full-scale invasion. It was a special and important period in the reframing, reforming, and solidifying of Ukraine. Despite widespread disap-

---

2   We extend our sincere gratitude to William Golovaha-Hicks for his editing and proofreading contributions to the book, ensuring its readiness for publication in June 2023.

pointments, many important things changed, as we describe. Huge systemic shifts occurred that actually prepared the country to face future shocks. We think we have analyzed most of them, with the notable exception of the army. We are sure, however, that defense analysts will soon fill this gap.

Still, this is not just a historical document. Most of the recommendations we have derived from our analysis still hold. In particular, we hope that Ukraine's international partners and civil society will learn the lessons of the successes and failures of those eight years, and will not repeat the mistakes they made in that period. The relative success of the reforms in 2014-22 was largely due to the lessons learned from the mostly missed window of opportunity in 2005-09, after the Orange Revolution. We hope that this book will help to make the next such window, which should be wide open after Ukraine's victory, ultimately successful. (The views, thoughts, and opinions expressed in the text belong solely to the authors and contributors of this volume, and not necessarily to the authors' employers, organizations, committees, or other associated groups or individuals.)

KYIV, UKRAINE
2023

Introduction

We embarked on writing this book amidst the backdrop of the Revolution of Dignity and the subsequent first phase of Russia's war against Ukraine (2014-2015). These dramatic events, although they posed significant challenges to the stability of institutions and society, triggered complex transformations. The primary objective of this volume was to examine whether Ukraine has undergone systemic changes that are either irreversible or nearly irreversible due to the Revolution of Dignity. Additionally, we sought to identify concrete measures that can be taken in the foreseeable future to further advance these changes.

Obviously, the all-out war that Russia unleashed on this nation on February 24, 2022, with the aim of annihilating it, has shaped and influenced new realities and circumstances for those systemic changes that are our primary concern in this volume. Yet we are convinced that this volume has not lost its topicality; on the contrary, with Ukraine's EU candidate status the analysis only gained in importance. Most analysts, quite legitimately, focus on the military aspects and potential outcomes of this horrible war. We, however, try to analyze the institutional and societal conditions created by the Revolution of Dignity and the reform efforts of its aftermath. We do this so that those efforts can be accomplished after the hopefully victorious end of the current war. This is particularly so since the methodology of this volume focuses on a strategy of change grounded in reality, rather than simply a laundry list of "tasks". In our view, this is crucial if we want to successfully and irreversibly reform and modernize Ukraine towards a liberal state order after the war.

We consider these changes from the perspective of a systemic transition that begins at a state that North et al. call a "limited access order" (LAO)[3] governed by a "natural state". Hale incorporates Acemoglu and Robinson's concept of "extractive institu-

---

3 North, D., Wallis, J., and Weingast, B. Violence and Social Orders: A Conceptual Framework for Interpreting Recorded Human History. Cambridge: Cambridge University Press, 2009.

tions"[4] and Hale's notion of "patronal politics".[5] The aforementioned transition moves in the direction of an "open access order" (OAO) that includes aspects such as "liberal democracy", "free entrepreneurship", "open society", etc. We use the concept of "systemic transition" as outlined by North et al. because it appears to us the most general and encompassing of all other definitions used in Economics and Political Science. "Modernization" is an even broader term for this transition, however, that also includes societal processes, which are normally far slower than economic and institutional changes.

The kind of systemic transition we consider should not be confused with the rather primitive concept of the "post-communist transition", which assumes rigid motion from planned to free-market economy and from dictatorship to democracy along economic and political axes, and was popular in the 1990s. As Magyar and Madlovics[6] rightly point out, only a few of the post-communist countries have reached the endpoint of this transition, becoming genuine liberal democracies with predominantly market economies. Others, including Ukraine, reached different intermediate stable or quasi-stable equilibrium states — in the case of Ukraine it is a "patronal democracy" that implies more or less free competition between the patronal "political clans" (or "pyramids" in Hale's terms), a type of regime the country has had since the mid-1990s.

However, from a broader historical perspective this quasi-equilibrium seems to also be transitional, because a democracy cannot be stable without rule-of-law (RoL), which is, in turn, inconsistent with patronalism. This is because routinely and permanently changing the people in power, which is inherent to democracy, disrupts the personal connections that are at the core of pa-

---

4   Acemoğlu, D., Robinson, J. Why Nations Fail: The Origins of Power, Prosperity, and Poverty. Crown Publishers, 2012.

5   Hale, H. "Patronal Politics: Eurasian Regime Dynamics" in Comparative Perspective (Problems of International Politics). Cambridge: Cambridge University Press, 2014.

6   Magyar B., Madlovics B. The Anatomy of Post-Communist Regimes. A Conceptual Framework. Budapest: Central European University Press, 2020.

tronalism. This makes the patronal aspect of the system less effective and generates demand for stable, impersonal "rules of the game". Thus, depending on how successfully RoL is established, a patronal democracy is likely to evolve into either a liberal democracy, should the RoL squeeze out patronalism, or into a patronal autocracy otherwise. The latter is also unlikely to be stable in Ukraine (see further for a specific discussion on this matter), while the former requires a systemic transition to an OAO. This is the internal driver for the systemic transition that we believe justifies our use of this word.[7] The geopolitical constellation also seems to be favorable for further evolution towards an OAO, and ultimately towards liberal democracy. However, none of this is guaranteed—so well-designed nurturing and well-targeted aid (admittedly, this is usually in scarce supply) can make a big difference.

Ukraine's systemic transition (commonly called "reforms") has been a subject of great interest both in and outside the country, given how crucial these changes are to the survival of Ukraine.[8] However, most of these analyses lack two crucial components. First, almost nobody addresses the issue of "change strategy". Here, in the introductory chapter, we address this issue head-on in a methodological sense and try to analyze the changes not as a laundry list of necessary tasks (as many others do), but in how these changes affect one another and have the potential to bring about the systemic transition in Ukraine. We see this approach as more intellectually ambitious and potentially more useful than simple checklists of the recent changes in Ukraine that do not clarify the connections between the different areas of reform. Our approach also demands establishing priorities of reform, which is usually missing in the "laundry list" approach that has been so prevalent during the 2014-19 period. Second, most analyses of the reforms fail to consider the constraints inherent in the

---

7   For more details see: Dubrovskiy, V. "The Main Driving Forces for De-Patronalization of Ukraine: The Role of Ukrainian business" in *Ukraine. Patronal Democracy and the Russian Invasion: The Russia-Ukraine War, Volume One*, edited by Madlovics, B. and Magyar, B. Budapest–Vienna–New York: CEU Press, 2023.

8   This is in itself a highly debated issue that we will later address in detail.

deeply entrenched system that has developed in Ukraine during 30 years of independence, as well as those more broadly inherent to an LAO.

The Ukrainians, who are struggling to modernize their country, rightly call the setup that evolved in the last 30 years "The System". It is indeed a well-established socio/politico/economic system. In this introductory chapter we present our brief theoretical analysis of, and methodological approach to, "The System" and the resulting implications for our further analysis.

This volume is based on an analysis of primary and secondary sources (mainly thematic literature review, analysis of available government records, and relevant longitudinal survey data). We can only collect limited empirical evidence in favor of our propositions, but hope other scholars will follow up with their own empirical testing. So far, we have had to largely rely on logically grounded hypotheses.

Theoretical inference: the System's logic[9]

To enhance the introduction of our approach, we begin by presenting our comprehensive vision of "The System." We have observed that many analyses of the Ukrainian reforms tend to operate within a limited conceptual framework. They often label the existing socio-politico-economic structure as "a system" and describe its primary features, but fail to delve deeper. By addressing this limitation, we aim to provide a more thorough and nuanced exploration of "The System" in our approach.

By definition, a system implies not just a combination of parts into a whole, but also the interactions between them. A system is sustainable and resilient to external shocks because its interlinkages form series of positive and negative feedback mechanisms that allow the system to react to such shocks while main-

---

9   For more details see: Dubrovskiy, V. "Patronalism and the Limited Access Social Order: The Case of Ukraine" in *Ukraine. Patronal Democracy and the Russian Invasion: The Russia-Ukraine War, Volume One,* edited by Madlovics, B. and Magyar, B. Budapest–Vienna–New York: CEU Press, 2023.

taining homeostasis.[10] In other words, certain critical components of a system form vicious cycles that allow them to be self-supporting and self-propagating and therefore able to compensate for any incremental changes brought on by external shocks without altering the nature of the system as a whole. In turn, almost all of these components are themselves sub-systems. This results in a complex web of interlinkages that is rooted in a few fundamental phenomena.

Dismantling "The System" requires breaking these vicious cycles or transforming them into virtuous ones in a new system that would replace the present one. However, in certain cases breaking or altering the interlinkages within the system can cause a chain reaction that almost inevitably leads to systemic change,[11] while in some other cases such incremental changes can be reversed by the system's aforementioned mechanisms. The idea behind our approach is that even incremental changes can culminate into a broader systemic effect on the fundamental factors that underlie the system, altering the critical systemic balances (described below), which, in turn, change the vicious cycles into virtuous ones. Respectively, one can derive conclusions about the depth and irreversibility of systemic changes from studying the current state of these balances and their change throughout the transition process.

Zero-sum vs. win-win thinking

Numerous losers in the LAO fail to fight it properly, mostly due to *zero-sum thinking,* also known as "the perception of the limited good".

First, it prevents them from distinguishing rent-seeking from normal profit-seeking business. This shifts natural economic balance from profit-seeking to rent-seeking as (a) there is no way to

---

10   We are referring here to the so-called Le Chatelier's principle. Available at: htt ps://courses.lumenlearning.com/introchem/chapter/le-chateliers-principle/

11   In fact, exactly this happened after the collapse of the Soviet Union and its institutions, ideology, and economy. Nobody planned the new system, it happened in a way that is analyzed in the next chapter.

really distinguish between them at the legal level, (b) there is no incentive for businesses to abstain from rent-seeking as their property rights are equally illegitimate whatever they do, (c) raiding is not perceived as a dangerous crime, since both sides are equally illegitimate. As a result, rent-seeking dominates, further reinforcing zero-sum thinking. This, in our view, is the most fundamental element of the vicious, socioeconomic cycle.

Second, this kind of thinking prevents people from engaging in collective action because other people are perceived as competitors for limited resources, rather than partners in a common win-win deal. But collective actions are necessary for overcoming the natural state's extractive institutions and establishing, in their place, "inclusive institutions" that serve the public. As long as institutions remain extractive and hostile to the people, the latter feel insecure. This feeling restrains peoples' time horizons and creates a permanent sense that they are struggling to survive — which, in turn, reinforces zero-sum thinking. When people endowed with "survival values" assume power, they tend to replicate and support the same behavior that sustains extractive institutions. This vicious cycle represents the sociopolitical dimension of "The System".

Third, people trapped in zero-sum thinking struggle for redistribution rather than opportunities. This makes them rent-seekers themselves, although as a collective rather than as individual actors ("oligarchs"), because even when they perform a collective action (like a strike, street rally, or even a revolt), they strive only for "fair redistribution", not for systemic change — "for a fish, not a rod". Therefore, social capital, even if accumulated, results in what Mancur Olson calls "distributional coalitions"[12] that only partly redistribute rents without changing the system. To the extent they pose a threat of violent action, they are pacified by allocating to them certain rents — a natural state just incorporates them into the system by sharing a slice of pie with them but without changing the LAO's fundamental principles. Their suc-

---

12   Olson, M. The Rise and Decline of Nations: Economic Growth, Stagflation, and Social Rigidities. New Haven: Yale University Press, 1982.

cess then supports not only their acquisition of social capital, but also zero-sum thinking, because it demonstrates a feasible way of getting certain benefits within the system through redistribution.

Therefore, this vicious cycle is also characterized by the following observable fundamental balances:

– *rent-seeking vs. profit-seeking.*

– *insecurity vs. sense of confidence/long time horizon (or "survival values" vs. "self-realization" and "self-reliance").*

Vertical of power vs. checks and balances

Rent seeking – like, for instance, lobbying for government subsidies or other privileges – is by definition a zero- or negative-sum game. As such, it requires external control and coordination, otherwise unrestrained competition for the sources of rents will result in their exhaustion ("the tragedy of the commons").[13] In some cases, this problem can be solved through collective action, but it is complicated and incurs high transaction costs.[14] Much easier, though less beneficial for the actors, is the emergence of an external arbiter – a "violence specialist" (in North et al. terms) that imposes quotas on all actors or helps them in restraining competition.

For instance, this can happen when one of the actors invites a violence specialist to force out all competitors so the two alone can share the rent. However, the violence specialist may soon realize that his negotiation power vis-a-vis a single rent seeker will be lower than if he betrays his ally and becomes an arbiter over all the rent extractors, just auctioning the quotas between them. In such a way he can theoretically extract the whole rent due to his own monopoly on coercion. Or, rather, the arbiter leaves a part of the rent to the actors on his own volition in exchange for loyalty –

---

13   In the case of natural resources, normally the best solution is private ownership – see Demsetz, H. "Toward a Theory of Property Rights." The American Economic Review, 1967, 374-359.

14   See, for example, Ostrom, E. Governing the Commons: The Evolution of Institutions for Collective Action. Cambridge: Cambridge University Press, 1990.

thereby turning them into his clients. We (after Dubrovskiy et al., 2010[15]) call this form of LAO the "arbiter-client model".

Rent seeking is intimately connected to authoritarianism. As long as an arbiter's legitimacy and power are largely based on his role in preventing the tragedy of the commons as described above, he has a vested interest in weakening alternatives to this role, namely property rights and social capital, as well as potential personal competitors. However, democracy is commonly believed to be even more threatening to property rights so long as people are trapped in zero-sum thinking, because if they get a voice they will demand redistribution, and hence expropriation. This becomes yet another reason why rent-seekers might support an arbiter as opposed to democracy. But the arbiter may realize this too and become interested in further undermining other actors' legitimacy. He may do this, for instance, by presenting all conflicts with them in terms of "good Tsar, bad boyars". The stronger the arbiter, the more danger there is for the rest of the actors to try and remove him. This problem is more acute in countries with a tradition of strong centralized power and capable bureaucracy, like Russia, and less in ones with traditionally stronger informal checks and balances, like Ukraine.

As long as a ruler's power relies on societal legitimacy, there is another critical balance in this context:

identification with a leader vs. imaginable community – tendency to personify vs. admittance of impersonal principles, phenomena, and institutions.

Personal rule vs. the rule-of-law (RoL)

The issue of power and the political regime's nature is intimately connected to one of the most fundamental differences in the social order. Politically, the power of an authoritarian leader is grounded in the self-fulfilling expectations of his or her subordinates (as

---

15   Dubrovskiy, V., Szyrmer, J., Graves, W., Golovakha, E., Haran', O., and Pavlenko, R. *The Driving Forces for Unwanted Reforms: Lessons from the Ukrainian Transition,* edited by Dubrovskiy V., Szyrmer J., and Graves W. CASE Ukraine, 2010.

described by Hale[16]) about his future ability to reward and punish arbitrarily, at his own discretion, not restrained by enforceable formal rules. As long as such expectations persist, his orders (including the ones rewarding loyalty and punishing traitors) are fulfilled. But the RoL cannot be established as long as none of the leaders want it for obvious reasons, nor if the people do not aspire to it—since they may not really believe in the protecting power and benevolence of independent institutions and instead identify themselves with a leader rather than with an imagined community. Hale stops there, but we could also add peoples' tendency to personalize any kind of communities and phenomena inherited in their mythological consciousness.[17]

According to North, et al., an LAO is defined by a system of power in which personal rule as a principle spreads across all spheres and types of organizations, including enforcement. Under patronalism, as described by Hale, this rule is predominantly grounded in self-fulfilling expectations that the same ruler will remain in power long enough to have the ability to punish disloyalty and reward loyalty at his discretion. Consequently, disobeying a ruler's orders, including those pertaining to punishment or rewards, would inevitably lead to negative consequences. This type of order stands in stark contrast to the principles of the rule of law. Simultaneously, in the absence of the rule of law, individuals are compelled to seek protection from a patron who can offer a certain degree of security and justice. This forms arguably the most fundamental vicious cycle at the institutional level. There are three necessary (but not sufficient) preconditions for a transition to an OAO. North et al. describe them as (a) the rule of law, at least for the elites, (b) political control over the use of force, and (c) perpetual organizations.[18] None of this can be fully achieved within an LAO, but transition further reinforces these preconditions.

---

16   Hale, H. "Patronal Politics: Eurasian Regime Dynamics" in *Comparative Perspective (Problems of International Politics)*. Cambridge: Cambridge University Press, 2014.

17   As, for instance, ancient Greeks interpreted a sea storm as Poseidon's anger.

18   A perpetual organization is one whose existence is not dependent on one person. "Perpetually lived organizations must have an impersonal identity".

In the case of Ukraine and other patronal democracies, this balance is even more important, because it is also critical for the direction of the further evolution that a patronal democracy takes, as described above.

Extent of corruption

Ukraine, like most developing countries (and like all post-Soviet ones) *formally* has all the institutions of the RoL. But they are mitigated and emasculated by discretional implementation of law by dependent police, prosecution, and courts, precisely as described by Magyar and Madlovics. This situation provides the officials and other (often even informal) decision-makers with personal power almost totally unconstrained by formal rules. The rulers and other beneficiaries use their power for various purposes, including personal enrichment (corruption), unconstrained power, and replication, if not amplification, of the impracticability of the law. Thus, another vicious cycle is *legislation (impracticable) – discretion (inevitable) – corruption*. It can be broken mainly by making legislation practicable, which includes but is not limited to deregulation, streamlining of norms and procedures, tax reform (towards easier implementation), administrative procedure reform, party reform, reform of election financing, etc.

The respective balance can be best characterized by the *extent of corruption*. This means real corruption, not the "corruption perception" that is usually referred to in public discourse (in our view, this perception is usually shaped by mass awareness of corruption, which is more contingent upon freedom of media than personal experience). However, in light of the description above, the first problem is that only one specific sort of corruption – namely collusion in circumventing impracticable[19] law – should be

---

19   That is, a law that cannot be impartially implemented because it contains either internal contradictions or contradiction with other regulatory acts. In most cases, this is done purposefully to create room for extracting illegal revenues. In other cases, it contradicts widespread practice and common sense so that it gets mostly violated; or it contains vast opportunities for personal discretion of the implementers (e.g. inspectors), which makes the law nothing but a cover for personal arbitrary decisions.

assessed for the purpose of a systemic analysis like ours, but this category includes not only bribes but also patronalism/favoritism, the informal exchange of favors, etc.

The second problem is that as a component of an LAO, corruption matters a lot when it comes to business and political opportunities, whereas opinion polls address lay citizens. These people not only have to collude with officials in order to circumvent an impracticable law much less often than political activists and businesspeople, but the price they pay is much smaller than the involuntary contributions of businesses. Benchmarking here is also complicated because, on the one hand, corruption of this sort is present to some extent in any country; on the other hand, it never pervades all business operations or contacts with government authorities. Therefore, in practice we cannot observe the "balance" simply because there is no benchmark for comparison with certain types of corruption that cannot be quantified. Unfortunately, as of now we cannot offer a tangible proxy for this kind of corruption, hence we provide no assessment for this balance.[20]

From the perspective of the conceptual framework of Magyar and Madlovics, "The System" in its Ukrainian version can be characterized as a "patronal democracy" political regime with a mostly "relational economy". This is in contrast to "patronal autocracies" (a "basic" LAO in North et al. terms) with the same kind of economies characteristic of most post-Soviet countries on the one hand, and liberal democracies with more or less free market economies on the other. A patronal democracy is, in turn, one of the forms of a "mature" limited access order[21] that Ukraine features. This is due to its strong tradition of plurality and relatively more inclusive political culture with informal veto rights of minorities, represented by the "arbiter-clients" model described above[22] rather than a

---

20   For analysis of the anti-corruption reforms see Lough, J., Dubrovskiy, V. *Are Ukraine's Anti-corruption Reforms Working?* Chatham House, 2018.

21   According to the definition (see North et al.), "mature" refers to the kind of LAO in which numerous organizations not related directly to the State and, respectively, the dominant coalition, may exist, unlike in a "basic" LAO in which they are repressed.

22   "Arbiter-client model" refers to the framework offered for the description of the Ukrainian politico-economic model of the 1990s. This framework is briefly

strong single-pyramid vertical, as explained in more detail below. Still, like any kind of patronal regime, it is based on personal rule (*vlast*) and corruption, both exercised mostly through the discretionary use of largely impracticable law. And all of this is, in turn, grounded on a transitional public consciousness, meaning that it is not a traditional (patrimonial) public consciousness anymore in many respects, but not yet a modern one either.

These factors shape the peculiarities of The System's transition process in many ways, as will be described in this study.

Post-colonial context and nation-building

Transitions historically often went hand-in-hand with nation-building, because the subject and object of transformation should be an independent state as opposed to a semi-autonomous part of a former empire. For the transition from LAO to OAO to be commonly accepted, understood, and supported as a common goal—a national project, based on either identity or values,[23] should serve

---

described above. It did not gain broad recognition yet, but nevertheless seems to be quite fruitful. In a way, it describes, although from a different perspective (political-economic rather than socio-political), how a certain kind of "pyramid" emerges and whose interests keep the participants together. Precisely speaking, this model refers to the modus operandi of a single level of a pyramid (of this kind), explaining why the players of different sorts (immediate rent-seekers and the "violence specialists") are getting together but not going into details of operations, as Hale does. "Competing pyramids" is hence a different story. However, not all of the pyramids can be described as "arbiter-client" ones: if the rent-seekers are totally dependent on a leader on the top of a pyramid (or, for the same token, if he owns the rent sources, formally or informally), then the rent-seekers work as employed "managers" rather than independent players. The "arbiter-client" model therefore refers to a more "feudal" organization of the society, whereas the other model is "oriental". See more details in Dubrovskiy, V., Szyrmer, J., Graves, W., Golovakha, E., Haran', O., and Pavlenko, R. *The Driving Forces for Unwanted Reforms: Lessons from the Ukrainian Transition,* edited by Dubrovskiy V., Szyrmer J., and Graves W. CASE Ukraine, 2010.

23   See Fukuyama, F. "Against Identity Politics. The New Tribalism and the Crisis of Democracy." *Foreign Affairs,* 2018. Available at: https://www.foreignaffairs.com/articles/americas/2018-08-14/against-identity-politics-tribalism-francis-fukuyama

as a clue for integrating the "holy trinity"[24] of state, market, and society in the most effective way for inclusive participation and empowerment.

According to one of the conventional understandings of integration, "true integration is achieved through the implementation of a promise" by leaders, actors, or parties "to engage in a particular course of action over a period of time"; this "entails a lengthy process of establishing common rules, regulations, and policies".[25] Is this an applicable logic for a modern Ukraine? A widespread understanding of Ukraine has been informed by the view that, for the largest country in Europe in terms of territory, with a population that is linguistically, ethnically, culturally, and religiously heterogeneous, the integrative principles behind common development are too complex to remain indisputable. Still, we suggest that the recent developments of the context (historical, geopolitical, social), within and around Ukraine, require that debates and disputes around 'common principles' that bring Ukraine together are situated with a different agenda. This agenda is about functionality, resilience capacities and, eventually, developmental success.

On the cultural/ideological level, the definition of the Ukrainian nation can pivot around a narrower "ethnolinguistic" pillar that refers primarily to the unity based on a unique ethnicity and language; and a broader "political" one that prioritizes sociopolitical peculiarities and informal economic institutions that have emerged as a result of a common historical experience and is not necessarily ethnic-bound. Both 'forms' of Ukraine juxtapose Ukraine against the Russian Empire in all of its incarnations, but along different axes: many ethnolinguistic nationalists dream

---

24 Civil society is seen by development theorists and practitioners as a "counterweight to vested interest that promotes accountability between state, market, and society". For more discussion, see Forsyth, T., Green, E., and Lunn, J. *Introduction to International Development*. University of London, London School of Economics and Political Sciences, 2011, 45-55; Leach, M. "Introduction: States, Markets and Society — Looking Back to Look Forward." IDS Bulletin 47, N 2A, 2016, 1-17.

25 See Mattli W. *The Logic of Regional Integration: Europe and Beyond*. Cambridge: Cambridge University Press, 1999, 3, 12.

about a statist, centralized, imperial Ukraine under a "strong hand" leader—in fact, very much resembling the hated Empire, just with a different titular nation and language; while the "political" nationalists see Ukraine as a liberal-democratic modern alternative to Russia and, of course, independent from it. The former, if given power, could produce a "conservative autocracy"[26] based on a consolidation of the LAO. The latter, on the other hand, promises rapid modernization.

Obviously, language, ethnicity, religious affiliation, and historical memory are not factors that easily unite all Ukrainian citizens[27] into one community. At the same time, identification with the Ukrainian political nation based on equal rights and common goals of the different communities and groups, as parallel or opposed[28] to local self-identifications and identities linked to the Soviet empire or its post-Soviet incarnation,[29] can serve as an instrumental principle for future OAO development. From a historical perspective, it is also important that the modern Ukrainian

26   In Magyar and Madlovics's definition, this type of political regime is featured with ideologically-based authoritarianism and mostly formal rule, in distinction to a patronal autocracy, in which an ideology serves only as a façade for a mafia-like, mostly informal, structure of the state.

27   Since the Revolution of Dignity, Ukrainian civic identity (foremost self-identification with the Ukrainian state) has dominated over all other identities (local, regional, European, Soviet, etc.) in all regions of Ukraine for the first time since Ukrainian independence and continued to rise beyond 2022. For more details, see Golovakha, E., Ivashchenko-Stadnik, K., Mikheieva, O., and Sereda, V. "From Patronalism to Civic Belonging: The Changing Dynamics of the National-Civic Identity in Ukraine." In *Ukraine: Patronal Democracy and the Russian Invasion: The Russia-Ukraine War, Volume One*, edited by Madlovics, B., and Magyar, B. Budapest–Vienna–New York: CEU Press, 2023 (forthcoming).

28   The pyramid of identities and how they affect each other require further studies. As the Ukrainian Society Survey data suggest, if the respondents are asked whom they most consider themselves, a majority of them choose "a citizen of Ukraine" (from 45% in 1992 to 63% in 2021). However, local identity remains rather stable (compare 24% in 1992 and 21% in 2021 considering themselves primarily as inhabitants of the village, region, or city where they live). Apparently, the Soviet identity is gradually decreasing (from 12% in 1992 to 3% in 2021). The dynamics of change is traced in the *Ukrainian Society Survey*, 1992-2021 by the Institute of Sociology, Kyiv. See Section 5 of this volume.

29   This issue is also discussed in Veira-Ramos, A., et al. *Ukraine in Transformation*. London: Routledge, McMillan, 2020. Available at: https://www.palgrave.com/gp/book/9783030249779.

political nation offers an attractive modernization project that would be unachievable in contemporary Russia or any other state which follows a similar development path in terms of institutions and values and, by and large, is moving away from an OAO. This is a point of unity in the critically important alliance between the "creative class" (represented by Western-oriented liberals and depicted by Richard Florida, the author of the best-selling *The Rise of the Creative Class*[30]) and the "conservatives" preoccupied with Ukrainian ethnolinguistic and cultural identity (these groups partly, but not entirely, overlap). For the former, modernization is itself a goal, which, however, requires strengthening Ukraine's independence from Russia. For the latter group, independence is the main value itself, but it cannot be sustained without modernization.[31]

Therefore, a number of indicators gauging the degree of establishment and maturity of the Ukrainian political nation (in the above sense) are also necessary for measuring the progress towards the OAO. Although the respective balance between national self-identification and other forms of self-identification does not in and of itself characterize the transformation, it assesses one of the necessary critical conditions for a successful transformation.

Nation-building as such is necessary, but definitely not sufficient for systemic transition: there are lots of well-established nations that continue living under an LAO and show few signs of such a transition yet. However, this is hardly the case in Ukraine due to its geopolitical situation and historical specificity. At the geopolitical level, breaking with the Russian Empire necessarily means drifting towards the West, which is, in turn, impossible without a systemic transition. In this regard, shifts in all kinds of economic, cultural, human, and other kinds of connections from East to West solidify and amplify the transition. Particularly, the

---

30   Florida, R. The Rise of the Creative Class: And How it's Transforming Work, Leisure, Community and Everyday Life. New York: Perseus Book Group, 2002.

31   For further discussion, see Грицак Я., Батько наш Кундера… Новое время, February 6, 2022. Available at: https://nv.ua/ukr/opinion/istoriya-ukrajini-c hogo-ukrajinci-ne-znayut-pro-banderu-gricak-novini-ukrajini-50213835.html

balance of foreign trade matters a lot, as well as, perhaps, other less easily measurable balances in the cultural sphere.

The role of the revolution(s)

North et al. describe systemic transition as a predominantly evolutionary process, emphasizing that the most fundamental changes occur in the "informal institutions" which are rooted in people's beliefs and social practices. This is true, but at the same time it takes at least one revolution for this change to happen, because a transition from one system to another based on opposing principles can never be fully evolutionary. At least one major disruption is needed in order to eliminate certain critical institutions of the "old" system (in this case the LAO) that maintain the homeostasis described earlier, which prevents new institutions from developing. Almost no country[32] that now has an OAO avoided having at least one revolution or military occupation that changed its institutions in a forceful way. In most, multiple revolutionary episodes took place. For example, France underwent four revolutions; the US, a Revolutionary War that was, at the same time, a War for Independence and then the Civil War; Japan, the Meiji Revolution followed by civil war and American occupation after the WW2; England had two; and The Netherlands was among the luckiest having only one revolution, which was tied to both independence and religion.

In terms of institutional change, the essence of a revolution, unlike a simple revolt, is subordinating the state to the nation, "shackling of the Leviathan" in Acemoglu and Robinson's[33] parable, thereby changing the state's institutional nature from "extractive" to "inclusive". A "natural state" that serves the dominant coalition originates from an ancient cartel of "stationary bandits", or from conquerors. In both cases, its main task is to extract resources

---

32   Switzerland seems to be the only exception to this rule. But this is a very specific nation formed by the self-selected people that once escaped from the LAO.

33   Acemoglu, D., and Robinson, J. *The Narrow Corridor: States, Societies, and the Fate of Liberty*. New York: Penguin Publishers, 2019.

in favor of the elites and to provide public goods only to the extent they are needed to secure those resources or for the legitimization and maintaining of power. In Magyar and Madlovics' terms it pursues the "elite interest" as opposed to the "societal interest", the latter being the mainstream approach to the state's role in liberal democracies. It is no surprise that a Leviathan desperately resists its shackling: the "natural state" actively opposes any transformations towards an OAO. It actively suppresses economic competition, persecutes counter-systemic political opposition, supports "traditional values" and the informal institutions of a traditional society, etc.

Even if some elites start thinking positively about transitioning to an OAO, there is always an important and influential faction that opposes it till the end because these beneficiaries of the LAO realize that they will lose everything in a competitive society. This raises the cost of an uprising for the elites who are interested in systemic change, since an open conflict will inevitably result in fighting that destroys many lives and wealth on their side too. Therefore, even for dissidents among the elites, it is rational not to insist on pursuing their own interests, unless they suffer severe oppression or are being repressed. If some lower-class people rebel, the elites either suppress it or share some part of their income as sops — in full accord with the LAO's logic. This system is remarkably stable — it has sustained numerous riots and wars through thousands of years without changing its essence; and OAOs still remain rare in the world now.

However strong the system's homeostasis, it may still slowly evolve in areas that do not pose an immediate threat to the dominant coalition's monopoly on power and access to economic opportunities. Some of these changes may eventually appear to have a systemic effect, as it was with the destruction of traditional society's institutions, the development of education, and the proliferation of the natural sciences, engineering, and mathematics in the USSR. Accumulation of such developments can steadily undermine the fundaments of the LAO. However, a natural state (and/or traditional society) begins to strongly resist such changes when they pose real challenges to the essential privileges of elites and their mechanisms of power — and it takes a revolution or other form of a forceful takeover to overcome this resistance.

In contrast to a natural state, a modern state, or "shackled Leviathan", is believed to pursue a "societal interest", thereby serving the people (the political nation) by providing public goods by various legitimate means. Using power for personal enrichment beyond what is legally sanctioned by citizens is considered a crime (corruption) and severely persecuted. Although not without its problems and difficulties, a modern state nevertheless can evolve towards an OAO in a mostly smooth, evolutionary manner. But it needs a revolution to change the state's nature first. Or a series of revolutions, if the first one fails to make a sufficient change that enables further evolutionary development.

Of course, not all revolutions lead to systemic changes. Hale argues that under patronalism the "color revolutions" are part of normal political dynamics because, from time to time, the incumbent "pyramid" resists the democratic change of power. He derives the necessary conditions of a successful color revolution from his expectation-based concept of power within a pyramid as follows: (a) a leader should be a "lame duck" with a finite horizon of staying in power, (b) he should be highly unpopular so that neither an extension of his term limits, nor appointing a successor can proceed smoothly. But in his framework, a revolution just changes the pyramids in power without undermining the regime's core foundations.

Magyar and Madlovics look at such revolutions from a slightly different angle, attributing them only to patronal democracies ("competing pyramids regimes" in Hale's terms). As we already mentioned above, this type of regime is inherently unstable because patronalism is incompatible with the RoL. Weak RoL allows a patronal leader to test the constitutional checks and balances, and from time-to-time attempt to establish an authoritarian regime. Then it takes a (successful) revolution to bring the country back to democracy, but as long as this democracy remains patronal (hence, still without an effective RoL), a new clan leader, when elected, can attempt to consolidate his power into an autocracy again, so the cycle repeats in a sort of dynamic equilibrium.

Magyar and Madlovics demonstrate how patronal democracies "oscillate" between attempts at establishing an authoritarian regime and "color revolutions" that oust a particular failed authoritarian ruler but fail to remove the polity's underlying patronalism. However, there is no guarantee that such a revolution will indeed occur and succeed: sooner or later there can emerge a leader able to consolidate a patronal autocracy, just as it happened in Hungary. A patronal autocracy is a highly internally consistent system, so a country trapped in such a bad equilibrium is unlikely to escape any time soon, at least without overwhelming external pressure. Suppose the revolutions change nothing except the political clans in power, and each poorly constrained but democratically elected ruler tries to weaken the RoL further. In that case, a patronal democracy is trapped in a vicious cycle that sooner or later ends in autocracy.

There is, however, another possible way out of this cycle: if the revolutions empower the civil society that—along with non-oligarchic businesses and international partners—pushes for the strengthening of the RoL, then the regime can evolve towards a liberal democracy. Progress in the RoL makes authoritarian attempts more difficult and less attractive; it also substitutes and undermines patronalism—so that eventually the country has a chance to turn a vicious cycle into a virtuous one and proceed to an OAO. Therefore, the question is whether "color revolutions" are necessarily non-systemic, or whether some of them may alter the system's nature so they can eventually culminate in a real revolution that "shackles the Leviathan".

From the socio-historical perspective, a "real" revolution follows a defined life cycle described by Crane Brinton.[34] The first phase is regime change, the second is moderate reform. Then, the country's development may follow the classic French/Soviet revolutionary path with terror as a third phase (i.e., the rise to power of a Robespierre or Stalin). The academic literature predicts a "thermidor" period after the terror phase, i.e., the cooling of social

---

34   Brinton, C. *The Anatomy of Revolution*. First ed. 1938; revised ed. New York: Vintage Books, 1965.

passions and a return to a pre-revolutionary ancien regime in an evolved form.

However, this chain of events is not necessarily pre-determined. In the US case, terror was avoided because the passion of the revolution was channeled into institution-building (enshrined in a constitution) and social discourse avoided a "leftward shift" (see Hanna Arendt's extension of this analysis[35]) from idealism to materialism. Hence, at the end of the second phase, a revolution faces a "fork", with one path representing further evolutionary development based on institutionalized achievements of the revolution, while the other promises future disturbances, in which case the changes brought about by the revolution become reversible and a 'thermidor' essentially resurrects the problems that led to this revolution.

Applying these considerations to Ukraine, we can suggest that the Orange Revolution brought to power the moderate reformer (Yushchenko) along with an economically populist radical (Tymoshenko). They partly neutralized each other so neither substantial reforms nor the terror (like "re-privatization") took place on any significant scale—but the attempts were there. This clash, along with Tymoshenko's awkward policies (especially but not only in managing the response to the economic crisis of 2008-09) eventually led to the "thermidor" election of Yanukovich in 2010 as a response against Tymoshenko. In the course of the Revolution of Dignity, Poroshenko and Yatseniuk can be qualified as "moderate reformers" (see Section 4), while Zelensky is more radical by his voluntarism and neglect of institutes and procedures, although as of now the "terror" is quite mild. Still, the cycle is not completed—this is why we are talking about the Revolution of Dignity as an ongoing process, as opposed to short-time past phenomena like the Euromaidan, or one-time events like Yanukovich's escape.

At the time of finishing of this volume (February 2022) this process is still open-ended. Ukraine faces a three-way fork: (a) falling into a patronal autocracy, like its Northern and Eastern neighbors; (b) experiencing a new revolution that would prevent

---

35   Arendt, H. *On Revolution*. Penguin, 1963.

such a fall, but given Russia's aggressive intentions, poses an existential threat to the country; and (c) continuing on the evolutionary path started in 2014 — not without dramatic conflicts, but resolving those conflicts nonviolently within the constitutional democratic procedures. We hypothesize the third option, of course, while cautioning that too little time has passed for any definite conclusions, which could only be made looking back many years from now. In this volume, we can only suggest a trend.

With regard to the systemic transformation to an OAO, whether or not the changes to the public consciousness can be reversed becomes a crucial question. Following Hrytsak's arguments drawn from European history,[36] several patterns may emerge. The pattern with the most sustainable and long-term changes is brought about by evolutionary developments such as demographic change, the development of infrastructure, and technological progress (with a national project needed as a framework for development that covers the 'holy trinity' of state, market, and society). Another pattern, in which changes to public consciousness prove irreversible, is brought about by abrupt and dramatic emergencies such as wars and "total revolutions", followed by a phase of terror. Personal solid emotions associated with such change can solidify it and produce a "hysteresis" effect. In this case, the change cannot be reversed without an equally strong emotional impact. Finally, geopolitical changes such as, for instance, joining strategic multinational unions, are hardly reversible, especially if they mean a change from one, sometimes civilizational or value-based, center of gravity to another that ultimately affects all spheres of nation's cultural and intellectual life.

In this regard, the purpose of this work is to assess if the Ukrainian Revolution of Dignity has succeeded in such difficult-to-reverse changes. We suggest (and attempt to prove below) that in Ukraine the components of the LAO still dominate over the OAO, although some of the latter are already present. It is also

---

36 Hrytsak, Y. *Selected Issues of European History.* Series of online lectures. PRO-METHEUS, 2017. Available at: https://prometheus.org.ua/

very likely, though, that the "old" system will be hard-pressed to resist the forces of change so long as it retreats (even if it puts up a fierce fight), such as in the case of the Anti-Corruption Court. However, the Revolution is still in progress, and it is a matter of balance between the forces of systemic change and the forces of systemic conservation that determines the pace of the changes, as well as its final destination. Here two questions arise: are the revolutionary forces sufficiently strong to win at this stage, and, if so, can they do it in an evolutionary way without another uprising?

Therefore, we formulate the following research questions:

- 1. Have the changes that occurred in the course of the Revolution of Dignity already put Ukraine on a smooth, evolutionary path to an OAO?
- 2. If not, then have they already created the momentum to complete the revolution process in the aforementioned direction?
- 3. If not, what further changes should occur to achieve this intended result?
- 4. Can such changes occur in an evolutionary way, or are further forceful transformations necessary?
- 5. Are the achievements listed above permanent/sustainable, or could they be rolled back?
- 6. In the worst case, will the remaining permanent changes be sufficient to serve as the groundwork for further revolutionary processes?

The working hypotheses are as follows:

1. The Revolution of Dignity so far has failed to change the nature of the State. The State is a monopolist on legitimate violence, and thus the nature of the regime is primarily about who controls the violence. The respective institutions have not changed in their nature, institutional role, and corporate culture, except for the patrol police, NABU, and, maybe, a few other exceptions. None of the three

"doorstep conditions" listed by North et al.[37] is in place yet.

2. For a majority of the population, the detachment from the Russian 'field of gravity' is irreversible, at least within the living generations the aggression of the Russian Federation in Ukraine. This may have a long-term systemic effect, although it depends on the ability of the collective West to understand the deeper nature of systemic transition, as opposed to the often-formalistic blueprinting of EU norms ("harmonization") or following the "best practices" of already-successful countries. As a parallel process, further globalization and development of free international travel will continue to steadily erode the remnants of the "Soviet mindset" in the minds of Ukrainians, bringing inevitable value changes.

3. The core of the Ukrainian political nation, consisting of proactive citizens with a largely democratic mindset, is already formed and has started modernizing.

4. In the political sphere, a "competing pyramids" regime of patronal democracy is firmly established and will sustain itself from now on — a "single pyramid" regime is unlikely to re-emerge. The system will likely become more open to political competition and further evolution. However, it is still unclear whether or not such evolution can ultimately alter the nature of the State and result in a liberal democracy.

---

37 North, Weingast, and Wallis (2009) define them as (a) rule-of-law (at least for the elites), (b) political control over use of force, and (c) perpetual organizations.

1.   Historical inference
Ukraine's transition from the LAO vs OAO perspective

Post-soviet developments in Ukraine can be viewed in three inter-twined dimensions. The broadest and deepest one is societal modernization. Ukraine underwent a substantial part of this before its independent history began. Unlike typical traditional societies, Ukrainians live mainly in urban, nuclear families, preoccupied with non-traditional work. From this perspective the Revolution of Dignity and the continuing volunteer movement are important steps in the long process of societal modernization necessary to form a political nation, increase social capital, develop civil society, etc. In this regard, Ukraine's trajectory is not unlike Georgia's since 1991, with each wave contributing further to the still-unfinished formation of the independent *and* open access state.[38]

The transition from the USSR's socialist economy and totalitarian regime to market economy and democratic rule is a stage in the transformation from an LAO towards an OAO. However important this stage was, it was not the ultimate one — contrary to optimistic expectations of mainstream economists and political scientists, but in line with contemporary institutional and political economic theory. Instead of a liberal market democracy, this transition so far has resulted in a "mature" LAO in the form of patronal democracy. In this regard, the Revolution of Dignity is potentially the next step on the trail towards an OAO.

Finally, at the political and institutional level, Ukraine has gained independence and started developing its own statehood, which it had lacked since the Mongol invasion in the 13th century. The previous two such attempts at independence in the 17th century and in 1917-19 had been, in the long run, unsuccessful.

---

38   See for this point on Georgia: Mizsei, K. "The New East European Patronal States and the Rule-of-Law." in *Stubborn Structures: Reconceptualizing Post-Communist Regimes,* edited by Magyar, B. Budapest-New York: CEU Press, 2019.

Although Ukrainians were one of the core ethnicities of the Russian Empire and later the USSR, institutionally Ukraine remained a colony and suffered from a number of policies deliberately detrimental to its further development as an independent nation — the extinction of both cultural and economic elites; the co-opting of national elites into metropolitan ones; the Holodomor; and the emasculating of its national policymaking institutions. Many structural features of Ukraine's economy, polity, and public services have developed according to Russian or imperial patterns and interests, but contradictory to Ukrainians' historically inherent fundamentals.[39] In this regard, the Revolution of Dignity is a groundbreaking event that seems to have ultimately established Ukrainian independence. The consequences would probably be somewhat less dramatic were it not for the role that the Kremlin played in the Euromaidan confrontation and the further Russian "hybrid" aggression that immediately followed Yanukovich's flight.

None of these three components (modernization, transition, or decolonization) ever proceeded smoothly anywhere, with the arguable exception of post-colonial transitions in a handful of countries that not only gained their independence peacefully, but also were lucky enough to avoid revolutions and civil wars afterward. However, none of them so far could be qualified as an OAO except for the British dominions that have undergone a systemic transition along with their empire and gained independence only then.

In Ukraine societal modernization had started as early as 1861, when serfdom was abolished in the Russian Empire. Then, along with the whole Empire, it went through the First Russian revolution of 1905-07 that resulted in a constitutional monarchy,

---

39   See an excellent popular description of these historical traditions at Plokhy, S. *The Gates of Europe: A History of Ukraine*. Basic Books, 2015.; Riabchuk, M. "Two Ukraines Reconsidered: The End of Ukrainian Ambivalence?" *Studies in Ethnicity and Nationalism*, vol. 15, no. 1, 2015; Hrytsak, Y. "Understanding Ukrainian history." Interview conducted by Yermolenko, V. Ukraine/World, 2019. Available at: https://ukraineworld.org/articles/ukraine-explained/history-h rytsak?fbclid=IwAR2DqIFafNJ96GpmQkXHWpJsryfntlKAEBoiG-u2qATiIk5L wQn-mto7AB4

and the February Revolution of 1917 that ousted the Tsar and abolished all aristocratic privileges. However, after a short and dramatic period of independence, the country was occupied by the Red Army with the support of local Bolsheviks and Ukraine became part of the USSR. In the beginning of WW2, the Soviet army also occupied Western Ukraine, including the territories which never belonged to the Russian or Soviet Empire before.

The next event in this row, which some observers call the "Revolution on the granite" occurred in 1990. This was related to the ousting of the UkrSSR's PM Masol under pressure from a student-led hunger strike at Maidan Square (still the October Revolution Square then) in Kyiv. However small, this episode was crucial for Ukraine's evolution, as it was the first time since the Bolshevik occupation that a group of activists (supported by many Kyivans) managed to force the government to yield on crucial issues. The innovative way it was organized (by occupying the main square with tents) was then replicated in all other later revolutionary episodes, successful or not, that took place in Ukraine. A number of participants then became prominent politicians, artists, and journalists. Still, in some other Soviet republics at that time protests were much louder and more resolute, sometimes involving violent confrontation with numerous casualties.

Ukraine eventually gained independence after the unsuccessful August 1991 coup in Moscow, which could also be treated as a revolutionary event for the whole former USSR. At that time the Ukrainian *nomenklatura*, however, was strong and smart enough to hijack this process and maintain its privileges, although it was transformed according to the new concepts of capitalism and democracy—just as in all other post-Soviet states (except the Baltic countries). But in Ukraine, as a rather rare example, the former *nomenklatura* never managed to restore a "basic" LAO in the form of an authoritarian regime, and even the strong ("semi-authoritarian") president Leonid Kuchma had to accommodate vigorous opposition. Although he built a kind of "single pyramid" with a working political machine (as the 1999 presidential elections proved), this Ukrainian version was much less strict than in any CIS country other than Moldova and Georgia, and maybe

Kyrgyzstan. Both regional and non-geographic "political clans" (sub-pyramids) always remained strong and partly independent. As a result, Ukraine became a patronal democracy and has remained within the frames of this kind of regime since then, in spite of at least two attempts of consolidation of a patronal autocracy. This remarkable and crucially important difference from most Eurasian countries was caused by a number of fundamental factors. We suggest that these, in turn, have largely resulted from the multiple overlapping historical legacies and transitional social and political settings in Ukraine:

1. By and large, Ukrainians have a deep tradition of plurality and no tradition of single-man rule.[40] The tradition of the Russian Empire and later the USSR was considered rather alien. Although the people more often perceive state power as vested in the President rather than in the Parliament or Cabinet, no Ukrainian President was ever overwhelmingly popular (unlike in Russia, Belarus, Kazakhstan, or almost any other post-Soviet state), and from his second year in office no president's popularity ever exceeded 35%. Kuchma, Yushchenko, and Poroshenko spent most of their tenures with ratings well below 10% (even in spite of the spectacular economic boom during Kuchma's second term and Yushchenko's first few years), and only Yanukovich was a bit luckier due to his core electorate in the Donbas—though he became so wildly disliked in the rest of the country that he was the first to be ousted by a popular uprising. Zelensky so far remains the most popular president of all his predecessors, but he struggles to keep his declining approval just slightly above 20%,[41] and net rating in the low red, which is a very modest result compared to Putin or Lukashenko. Remarkably, Ukrainians have never acquired their own inherent tradition of absolute power, even though they lived

---

40   Ibid.

41   The numbers keep changing, but as of the completion of this volume (January 2022) the rate was 23.5% among those who decided, and 17.4% among the whole sample. See: *Press-release of the Kyiv International Institute of Sociology*, January 2022. Available at: https://www.kiis.com.ua/?lang=eng&cat=reports &id=1090&page=1).

under such a system during both the Russian and Soviet occupations.

2. Against the background of strong informal vertical structures, the state institutions in Ukraine remain relatively weak and incapable of exercising tight control. For example, even Leonid Kuchma's "single pyramid" that existed for more than eight years failed (or perhaps did not even try) to achieve the degree of control that Lukashenko (elected just two years later) established within a couple of years. Note also that all attempts at restoring price controls in Ukraine in 1992-94 failed miserably. Public views on the actual distribution of power are reflected in the results of recent surveys. According to the *Ukrainian Society Survey* of 2015, oligarchs were considered the most influential actors in Ukraine (with 44.6% of respondents choosing them, compared to the 21.8% that chose state officials).[42] In 2021, as data from the Kyiv International Institute of Sociology illustrate, 92% of respondents believed that "oligarchs have a big influence on Ukrainian society".[43]

3. Sources of rents are plural and of comparable size. Although the highly concentrated industries that the country inherited from Soviet times are prone to monopolization, and as such prone to oligarchic rule, they are still plural. Unlike in Russia, where drillable hydrocarbons strongly dominate the economy over all other rent sources, in Ukraine rents of mutually comparable magnitudes can be found in many different sectors, including but not limited to power generation and distribution, natural gas drilling and trading, ferrous ore mining and processing, agriculture (which itself is diverse), and more. In addition, of course, there are common rent sources in fiscal (e.g., government subsidies) and financial spheres, as well as natural monopolies, state-owned enterprises, and procurement, not to mention large-scale organized tax evasion. All of them gave rise to numerous pyra-

42 Data of the *Ukrainian Society Survey*. See: *Українське суспільство: моніторинг соціальних змін*. Київ: Інститут соціології НАНУ, 2015, с. 620. This item was measured only once during the 2015 ad-hoc survey and is not included in the traditional scale used in the questionnaire.
43 *Press-release of the Kyiv International Institute of Sociology*, March 2021. Available at: http://kiis.com.ua/?lang=ukr&cat=reports&id=1020&page=1

mids (called "clans" in the Ukrainian political jargon), of which none have been able to dominate the rest for more than a few years. Instead, these power pyramids have appeared, disappeared, and oscillated in their degree of influence.

4. For all of the time since independence, the East-West division remained strong enough that a single leader could hardly be sufficiently popular in both parts. However, the growth of a relatively unified Ukrainian civic identity, as described in Section 5, has recently blurred this division and helped Volodymyr Zelensky and his party to win in virtually the whole of Ukraine, although his popularity and unpopularity still vary tremendously across the regions.

The USSR's meltdown launched a chain reaction of changes that led to a drastic increase in the proliferation of liberal Western values in Ukraine, in a very real case of "modernization". The abolishment of ineffective central planning and the total price control inherent to it inevitably resulted in the closing down of many inefficient Soviet "enterprises without entrepreneurs". This process was magnified by the loss of the Soviet defense industry that had once held a larger share of the industrial sector in Ukraine than in any other Soviet republic. The conjunction of delayed privatization and the extreme docility of government, even by post-Soviet standards, towards the "intermediate winners"[44] in this first stage of post-Soviet transition (mainly "red directors") led to an unprecedented volume of loans to support domestic producers, resulting in hyperinflation and, eventually, economic collapse.[45]

This, in turn, triggered further changes. At the political and policy level, the rather inert and cautious but democratic Leonid Kravchuk lost the early Presidential election to the more resolute and entrepreneurial Leonid Kuchma. The latter realized immediately after his unexpected and remarkably peaceful victory that he can hardly maintain power without an inherently unsustainable

44   Hellman, J. "Winners Take All: The Politics of Partial Reform in Post-Communist Transitions." *World Politics*, vol. 50, 1998, 203-234.
45   Babanin, O., Dubrovskiy, V. and Ivaschenko, O. "Ukraine: The Lost Decade … and a Coming Boom?" Kyiv: Alterpress, 2002.

combination of two factors. The first consisted of urgent, liberal economic reforms imposed by international financial institutions (IFIs) — meaning the "Washington consensus trinity" of financial stabilization, privatization, and further liberalization — and the other was the building of his own "single pyramid".[46] In doing both he had to betray the "red directors" who brought him to power. They had to be substituted with some other kind of subdued, or at least loyal, business supporters and, just as Yeltsin a couple of years before, Kuchma found them among the rising oligarchs. He also believed that Ukrainian tycoons would be the strongest pillars of Ukrainian statehood in its confrontation with the former empire.

In contradiction to this, because he was a stubborn industrialist Kuchma continued state support of the Ukrainian mining and manufacturing industries. Moreover, he allegedly accepted a personal stake in gas trading offered to him by the Kremlin.[47] The Ukrainian industrial sector was still heavily rooted in the former USSR and was endowed with a Soviet corporate culture that even privatization failed to wipe out. The main rent sources for newly ascendant oligarchs were also linked to the CIS, primarily Russia. The latter deliberately kept the price of natural gas low and even tolerated theft or non-equivalent barter payments in exchange for maintaining Ukrainian oligarchs' and political leaders' dependency on the Kremlin. Russia also kept its market open for Ukrainian machinery production in order to nurse dependent oligarchs. Some of these, like Igor Bakay, Dmytro Firtash, and Pavlo Laza-

---

46 We refer here to Hale's terminology.

47 Ukraine used to import up to 50 bcm of natural gas from Central Asia and Russia through highly opaque barter deals operated by intermediaries informally controlled by Russian and Ukrainian presidents. The last of these intermediaries, Dmytro Firtash's RosUkrEnergo, was explicitly co-owned by GazProm. At the first gas supply negotiations after the Orange Revolution, Russian PM Dmitry Medvedev said to Oleh Rybachuk, then Chief of Staff for President Yushchenko: "You are now in power, so here is your share in the gas deal — you will get it provided that you agree to our conditions". Evidently, before this, a corresponding share went to Leonid Kuchma. See: Interview with Oleh Rybachuk, February 2018. Available at: https://gordonua.com/pu blications/rybachuk-medvedev-skazal-mne-perestan-vse-chestno-vi-teper-vla st-vot-vasha-polovina-za-gaz-dva-milliarda-lyamov-v-god-232058.html

renko, who was later succeeded by Yulia Tymoshenko, made their fortunes on gas trading and as such immediately benefited from these Russian policies. Rinat Akhmetov and Sergey Taruta also received rents from gas trading for a long time, and then benefited from the cheap gas they used in metallurgical processes. Similarly, the "red directors" of the mostly Eastern Ukrainian machinery plants (such as Vyacheslav Boguslayev of Motor-Sich in Za-porizhia, or Georgy Skudar of Novokramatorsk Machinery Works) enjoyed ample access to the traditional Russian market. All of this was a series of time bombs with controls in the Kremlin that could be triggered at any time.

Privatization and the further tightening of the budget con-straints for Ukrainian enterprises, including the ones owned by oligarchs and the remaining red directors in the decade after Kuchma's second election, led to a dramatic shrinkage of rent sources. Competition in most sectors increased and led to the emergence of some genuinely competitive industries and firms. It resulted in a quick economic revival on the back of the global eco-nomic boom of 2000-2008.

In line with these dramatic institutional changes, equally es-sential processes occurred on the societal level. The economic meltdown of the early 1990s forced millions of people to give up paternalistic expectations and start surviving on their own. For many of them it unleashed the new opportunities that a market economy provides, but for even more of them, survival entrepre-neurship became a last resort that saved them from hunger. Of course, their opportunities were strictly limited by various formal and informal barriers, so that any kind of vertical mobility, at least above a certain very low level, remained subject to personal con-nections and patronal vassalage. This is because the relational economy emerged, and small business remained predominantly unofficial or "gray". Nevertheless, most of the new entrepreneurs had to play by these rules unwillingly.

In 1997-99 the situation for SMEs (small and medium enter-prises) significantly improved due to some limited but successful deregulation (mostly imposed by the IFIs) and, more importantly, the introduction of simplified taxation for small business (which was demanded by entrepreneurs through street rallies and strikes and was, at the time, supported by the IFIs). Simplified taxation as it appeared in Ukraine was especially effective in making small entrepreneurs' activities legalized and truly independent from the patrons. Fierce competition in the retail and wholesale markets, as well as in the service industries, swiftly eliminated transitory rents from arbitrage, and largely reduced the rents from the import of consumer goods. Leonid Kuchma in this period supported these policies because rent in the form of bribes extorted from micro-businesses (mostly open markets and street vendors) were highly dispersed and costly to control, and therefore of little interest to high-level actors, while the millions of small entrepreneurs and their family members could provide much needed political support for the 1999 elections.

Both developments resulted in a remarkable shrinking of the rent-seeking sector of the economy as a whole that elites could not prevent. The oligarchs and state officials, led by the President as their arbiter, had to withdraw from sectors that brought less concentrated rents, such as retail and services, since they required a higher cost to control and coordinate (although some forms of racketeering still remained there). They focused instead on commodity trading, metallurgy, the financial sector, large-scale real estate, etc. Simultaneously, impudent rent-seeking in the energy and fiscal spheres (particularly through opaque barter trade and financial operations) resulted in the fiscal and currency crisis of 1998 that eventually forced Kuchma to launch a new wave of reforms, this time focusing on imposing transparency and tightening "budget constraints". Soft budget constraints benefitted many firms earlier on (those mainly controlled by the "red directors" and oligarchs). These reforms were done by the Yushchenko-Tymoshenko Cabinet that Leonid Kuchma appointed and pushed through the Parliament (controlled by oligarchs and red directors) immediately after his crafty victory in the 1999 elections. However, as soon as the economy was stabilized and started to grow, this Cabinet was ousted while Kuchma remained remarkably indifferent, signaling that he was not willing to proceed any further with reforms.

As a consequence of this wave of partial reforms, the space for competitive business had widened further, and the "ceiling" above which a firm needed a patron increased, so many more SMEs remained below the radar. In other words, the islands of genuinely competitive markets expanded. At the same time, on the social level, a non-Soviet middle class emerged: small entrepreneurs finally could fully legalize, which gave them confidence; strong economic growth also quickly enriched many white-collar employees, who by this time had succeeded in getting a good education, often even in Western universities. Though these may seem like insufficient changes, they are significant both from the perspective of understanding system dynamics and when considering what the alternative situation would have been without these reforms.

Although the Orange Revolution of 2004 perfectly fits Hale's description of the dynamics of political regimes, which considers changes of power supported by massive street rallies as part of the normal political process,[48] it was nevertheless an important step in the societal and institutional transformation of Ukraine. Having started as a political technology project that was prepared and tightly controlled by its initiators,[49] the Revolution soon gained its own momentum that well-exceeded initial expectations, making it a genuine revolution, albeit with limited goals and consequences. And although politics, in full accordance with Hale's analysis, remained "patronal", the rules of the game changed substantially and irreversibly.

Before the revolution, politicians used to believe that they don't need to act as politicians, as political machinery would

---

48   By 2004 Kuchma was a deeply unpopular lame-duck president, who failed to find a compromise candidate as a successor, while Yushchenko appeared as an attractive alternative for his charisma, popularity, and support by the West. At the same time, Kuchma's political machine was still strong, as well as deeply invested in his rule, and this prevented a peaceful, democratic transition of power. Hale argues that such kinds of revolutionary alternations of leaders are normal for patronal politics, and they routinely happen across the Eurasia region, usually without any substantial effect on the system's nature.

49   Lane, D. "The Orange Revolution: 'People's Revolution' or Revolutionary Coup?" *The British Journal of Politics & International Relations*, vol. 10, 2008, 525 – 549.

achieve everything. In 1999 this belief was strong enough that President Kuchma sent a *raznoriadka* (an informal order transmitted down the hierarchy through the vertical of power) regarding how many votes in his favor should be "delivered"—by all means!—in each oblast. Governors had to obey: failure to fulfill the *raznoriadka* resulted in immediate dismissal, even between the first and second rounds of elections. The same process took place at each level below, securing the President's victory. There were neither major protests nor any serious attempts to question the results, since none of the opponents were genuine politicians. Nobody in Ukraine had the skills and political capital to create an uprising in his or her favor, and no one believed that it was possible. But after Yushchenko proved the opposite, no "machine" politicians could feel safe anymore.

At the political level, the Orange Revolution marked the limits of "machine" politics very clearly: despite all the "administrative resources" employed by Kuchma with the support of Putin, the political capital accumulated by Yushchenko and Tymoshenko prevailed. Since then, even the *"khozyaistvennyks"* (former Soviet bureaucrats in charge of economic tasks) that despised politics and politicians had to become politicians themselves, as Yanukovich had to. A portion of the elites that rebelled and split off, at least for a while, had no choice but to appeal to a broader society—and this made them accountable to the voters. When they failed to justify the expectations they created, they lost support and were replaced. Notably, the Socialist Party that once had been quite powerful and who had joined the winning Orange coalition in 2004, later lost the elections and disappeared from the political scene after they betrayed the Orange coalition and joined Yanukovich's in 2006. Later on, a similar fate happened to most of the Orange politicians themselves.

In terms of political institutions, Ukraine got a "dual" constitution that ostensibly weakened the President in favor of the Parliament. Victor Yushchenko fiercely opposed this, but had to eventually accept it as part of a broad compromise that resolved the political crisis. However, this constitution, tailored by Putin crony and semi-official resident agent Victor Medvedchuk, was actually designed in such a way that it makes a President nearly omnipotent if he is skilled in selective persecution and punishment through the Soviet means of selective justice or, rather, through discretionary enforcement of impracticable laws. The President kept control over the secret service (endowed with the authority of investigating economic crimes and corruption) and law enforcement represented by the Prosecutor General's Office (PGO), which was empowered to perform all investigations of officials, as well as the "general supervision" of the legality of their decisions. On top of this, a President had enormous control over judges. With these tools in his hands, he or she could potentially blackmail any member of the elite, so full (informal) control was only a matter of his/her willingness, skill, and impunity.

Yushchenko was known to be personally reluctant and not skilled enough to use these informal instruments of power to their full capacity—thus, he predictably appeared almost powerless and had to employ Victor Baloha, infamous for his Byzantine management as Chief of Staff (but it was too late anyway, and only further destroyed the remnants of Yushchenko's ratings). Yanukovich, by contrast, successfully employed all of these methods to gain full control over the polity,[50] and as a corollary rolled back the constitutional amendments of 2004 for the obvious formal reasons that they were adopted in a revolutionary way, with no respect for proper procedure.

---

50   The extent of his real power became clear as soon as he was elected, well before he managed to undo the constitutional amendments. Yanukovich succeeded in appointing Nikolay Azarov as PM against the interests of everyone else, including not only the Orange parties (who formally still had a majority in the Parliament), but also the oligarchs. In only a couple of months he also managed to push through the Rada (which remember was still formally dominated by the Orange MPs) the notorious Kharkiv treaties with Russia—the ones that allowed the Kremlin to deploy about 40,000 Russian troops to Crimea until 2041, which later in 2014 became instrumental for Russia's annexation of the peninsula. In doing this, he also broke the old Ukrainian tradition of political inclusivity (respecting the informal veto right of a minority) that his party broadly exploited while in opposition. For the first time in Ukrainian history, the MPs that tried to blockade the Rada's tribune were physically beaten, with a few seriously injured by their colleagues from the Party of Regions (many of them former thugs).

At the geopolitical level, as a result of the Orange Revolution Ukraine made a significant step out of the former empire by rejecting the Kremlin-backed candidate and electing the Western-oriented nationalist Victor Yushchenko instead. Although initial pro-NATO and pro-EU moves had already been made under Kuchma in the course of his two-vector foreign policy, further practical actions followed after the Orange Revolution, like start of the Association Agreement and DCFTA negotiations with the EU, and an attempt (though then unsuccessful) to join the NATO action plan. Russia reacted by hiking gas prices to above market level, thereby exploding a part of the previously mentioned "landmines". However, the Ukrainian economy sustained this, and started to adjust by decreasing natural gas consumption quickly. The ferrous metallurgy industry reacted with particularly rapid technological modernization that saved more than 60% of the natural gas that it had been consuming previously.

At the societal level, the Orange Revolution was a successful collective action that inspired millions of people, increasing their social capital by a great deal. This time most of them were eventually frustrated by the ultimate results of this Revolution, but the very fact that the people could change the regime through collective action imprinted deep in the memory of society. Their frustration also had a positive effect: people partly lost their naïve faith in the "good politicians" that make reforms in favor of the whole society without further pressure. These lessons were learned well. In 2010, when Yanukovich and Azarov tried to abolish simplified taxation (understanding that this was creating their most dangerous enemy, the middle class), small businesses organized themselves (this time without any politicians and political technologists) into the Tax Maidan,[51] and again the people were able to defeat the government. This episode convinced people further

---

51   This was a massive (tens of thousands of people) rally at Kyiv's central square that gathered in Fall of 2010. They did this in response to some provisions of the new Tax Code, prepared under the direct supervision of Prime Minister Mykola Azarov. These provisions effectively abolished simplified taxation by raising taxes and, most importantly, restoring some bookkeeping for small vendors that would make them subject to pressure and extortion by tax inspectors.

that they could win if united in a decisive action, and warned the authorities about the limits of their tyranny.

Still, Yanukovich failed to learn these lessons and sparked a new revolution that appeared remarkably different in many aspects. Unlike all similar events in the post-Soviet space, the Revolution of Dignity differs in many ways from the revolutionary patterns described by Hale. Thus, we believe that it carries the potential to break Ukraine out of the limited access order and patronal politics for the following reasons:

1. The Revolution of Dignity happened when Yanukovich was in full force—not a lame duck by any means (as he had not even finished his first constitutional term)—and still relatively popular by Ukrainian standards. Thus, both criteria for a successful revolution mentioned by Hale were missing.

2. Not only did the political opposition not prepare this uprising in advance, as they had in 2004, but they themselves were not prepared at all for such a course of events. They joined the events only hesitantly, with some resistance from the "Maidaners". Although formally the official political leaders were present and even tried to negotiate on behalf of the Euromaidan community, they were never respected and trusted, and certainly did not control the Maidan—in sharp contrast to the Orange Revolution. Particularly, the agreement signed between Yanukovich and the opposition on February 21st was never respected by the rebels. From beginning to end, the Euromaidan was organized for the most part horizontally. Actually, the protest had no strong leaders at all, and failed to form a "winning party". This is also why the revolution did not result in overwhelming political victory for the revolutionaries.

3. Unlike the Orange Revolution, the motives of "fair redistribution" were much less pronounced. Instead, the main mottos were anti-corruption (or more precisely anti-extracting), pro-Europe (that is mostly pro-market and for equal opportunities for all), and, of course, the "dignity" as opposed to patronalism for which the revolution was named. "Ukraine 2.0". was one of the most popular slogans of the uprising, implied to restart the coun-

try on the principles of an OAO, and liberal democracy in particular.

4. The Revolution of Dignity resulted, among other positive things, in the restoration of the dual constitution—this time likely permanently. Still, it predictably failed to eliminate patronalism, and in this sense remains a "color revolution" that Magyar and Madlovics believe keeps a country within a patronal democracy by preventing authoritarianism from taking firm roots.

5. Apart from changing the people in power and, partly, the nature of the power, the Revolution of Dignity ultimately changed the geopolitical orientation of Ukraine. It used to be one of the countries least economically and politically dependent on Russia among the whole CIS, and for all of that time, even in the Yanukovich era, tried to exercise "two-vector" foreign and trade policies. Nevertheless, it largely remained within the gravity of Russia, particularly by having a free-trade zone with it, plus numerous cooperation agreements, especially in the defense industry (although Ukraine was not a fully participating member of the CIS). The DCFTA was about to balance this with free trade and the Association Agreement with the EU, although with no definite obligation for eventual membership. Should Yanukovich have signed it, this would have just become yet another piecemeal step of the drift towards Europe and out of Russia's orbit, with no immediate dramatic consequences.

However, the way that Russia treated the pro-European intentions of Ukraine—from the trade war of autumn 2013 to the military invasion of 2014—triggered a revolutionary reaction that ultimately and drastically pushed Ukraine into the orbit of the EU and NATO. In Ukraine this happened perhaps to an even greater extent than in Georgia a few years earlier, as it coincided with the revolution and the war that ended in the occupation of part of the country's territory. Notably, after "exploding" its second "landmine" by erecting trade barriers against Ukrainian-made commodities and goods and by forcing Ukraine to impose sanctions on trade with Russia—the former empire utterly lost its main economic leverages over Ukraine. The post-revolutionary Ukrainian government was strongly motivated to curtail all kinds of trade relationships with Russia and did so at least partly even in the most problematic spheres, such as nuclear fuel supply.

6. Unlike in the other revolutionary episodes in Eurasia, the revolution not only changed the parties and people in power, but dramatically altered their relationships with the civil society that arose as a new and powerful player in policymaking—although of course decision-making is still vested in legitimately elected and appointed politicians. At the same time, the desperate economic situation caused mainly by Yanukovich's detrimental and irresponsible plutocratic policies, as well as by Russia's aggression, has sharply increased the influence of Western countries and international institutions. They have found powerful leverage over Ukrainian authorities like never before. Therefore, the distribution of de-facto power in Ukraine has changed substantially, at least for the moment.

7. In sharp contrast to the remarkably peaceful Orange Revolution, the Euromaidan has had to break with the tradition of non-violence that seemed to be inherent to Ukraine.[52] Although the protest started as totally peaceful, and although the protesters did not even try to install tents (in spite of the harsh weather) to avoid provoking violence, they were cruelly beaten by riot police and dozens were severely injured. Still, only some marginal radicals resorted to violence at the huge rally that followed the day after next, and they were mostly treated by the protestors as provocateurs. However, the regime instantly ratcheted up violence, and this spiral eventually ended with a massacre that killed more than a hundred people, mostly unarmed rebels. It is noteworthy that the return fire that killed a few policemen is perceived by most of Ukrainian society as justified. Thus, all in all, the Maidan has partly legitimized political violence. Along with a huge number of firearms that leaked during the dramatic events of the Euro-

---

52 To be sure, there were two events when it was not obeyed: the funeral where violence on religious grounds sparked; and the unsuccessful "Ukraine without Kuchma" revolution attempt that ended with violent confrontation between radical nationalists and police. Both left no casualties, although a few people were injured; and both were condemned by the overwhelming majority of Ukrainian society, including its most vocal members.

maidan's final days, and, to a much larger extent, the war in Donbass, this largely changes earlier expectations as to further possible upheavals.

8. As we will discuss in more detail in Section 5, devoted to societal change, the main cleavages that split Ukrainian society have, arguably, been altered: instead of an ethnolinguistic "east-west" division that used to dominate for many years, the new cleavages are more between the emerging "creative class" and the "oligarchic class" (the LAO's beneficiaries).

The events after the Revolution, particularly the Russian aggression against Ukraine, not only pushed the country towards the West and facilitated the proliferation of firearms; they had deep and far-reaching sociopolitical and economic consequences that deserve separate treatment due to their importance.

First of all, at the societal level, in spite of historical ethnolinguistic, cultural, and religious cleavages, in 2014 Ukraine emerged as a political nation. This is the most fundamental and positive consequence of the chain of events that began in late 2013. It has been suggested that this may entail a systemic risk: could the higher level of social homogeneity and unity finally bring about a "single pyramid" regime of patronal autocracy? In this respect, we remain optimistic. The diversity and strength of the regional "clans" (pyramids) along with the vibrant civil society seems to remain sufficient to uphold plurality, as the subsequent Presidential election so vividly demonstrated. Even the "Donetsk clan" still exists, although it has been largely weakened compared to its heyday and is no longer able to dominate the others. Strong and independent local elites in Dnipro, Kharkiv, Odessa, and Lviv (in each case represented by multiple pyramids), along with a number of Kyiv-based powerful pyramids, ensure sufficient competition and seem to unite only when confronting the real threat of Putin's clearly visible imperialist goals, if at all.

Second, in politics since the Euromaidan, every move has been viewed through the lens of the ongoing "hybrid" war with Russia. In particular, Poroshenko's government used to defend itself with arguments that the opposition's actions play into the enemy's hands, even if they are radically anti-Russian (for instance, calling for the forceful liberation of Donbas) or just anti-corruption. The organizers of street rallies also feel responsible for not allowing any provocations or other actions that would destabilize the country or allow one to associate these rallies with Russian influence. The main line of attack against Zelensky was his vague position on the issues of Russia and the war on the Donbas. At the same time, Russia continued to play an important implicit role in Ukrainian politics, just as it does in America and Europe, though not as overtly and intensively as in Ukraine.

Third, the war largely increased the presence of armed forces of all kinds and complicated their civic oversight. They received much better funding, higher legitimacy, and increased in number. In addition to the army, police, secret service, and the PGO, Ukraine has voluntary battalions (*dobrobats*) that formally belong to the army or the National Guard (that also has largely changed and strengthened), but are actually built on different principles and values, and gained a great deal of independence. Later on, a special anti-corruption investigative agency (NABU) was created that, though not armed, has extensive authority.

Fourth, the confrontation with Russia legitimized discrimination against Russian capital in Ukraine and the sharp shrinking of trade with the aggressor, even if this resulted in higher prices for consumers or the loss of workplaces. The political-economic positions of formerly pro-Russian oligarchs respectively weakened. However, the most notorious of them, Vadim Novinsky, was not prosecuted or expelled, as expected, but Dmirty Firtash largely lost his positions (also because of simultaneous prosecution by US authorities for bribing Indian officials), and the "Yanukovich wallets" just fled to Russia. As a result, the political-economic landscape has substantially changed: it is still dominated by oligarchs of a different caliber, but the ones whose rents originated mostly from relations with Russia have lost a lot or disappeared, while the new ones are rather tied to domestic sources, which are much less abundant.

Still, in sharp contrast to the Rose Revolution of 2003 in Georgia, the Revolution of Dignity failed to bring so many sweeping reforms that it would constitute a leap in modernization.

Among the main reasons for this was lack of genuine change strategy.

In 2014, Ukraine did not have a leader with such charisma and commitment to sweeping reform as Georgia had in Saakashvili in 2004. This is one of the critical differences between the two countries regarding reforms. One might argue that Ukraine actually had, "on paper", a better chance for reform than Georgia: Ukraine in 2014 was more reliant on the support of the West than Georgia had been in 2004. Thus, the EU and the United States had more leverage over policies in Ukraine. Of course, more leverage is only useful if international powers have a solid and detailed understanding of how to implement reforms *in the given country and specific historical situation.* They also lacked a consensus on a workable change strategy, and in many crucial instances they actually used their influence to put the brakes on reforms—like the CoE approach to judicial reform that is described below. Bendukidze in Georgia, in similar circumstances just showed them the door and did what he considered appropriate and mostly succeeded. Ukraine also had a better starting point in that its people were more inclined to law-abiding behavior than the famously rebellious Georgians. Georgia also had a much stronger tradition of organized crime than Ukraine. The fact that Georgia was a living example for Ukraine's reforms is demonstrated by the eagerness of the Ukrainian leadership in 2014 to use Georgian experts as advisors, even in high, official state functions responsible for various reforms.

However, the situation also differed in the two post-revolutionary countries. Besides a lack of genuine leadership for reforms in Ukraine, the effect of the war that began right after the revolution and the economic crisis were important factors, albeit, as we argue below, not determining ones. Also, the support for the revolution among Ukrainians was not as strong as it had been in Georgia in 2003. Ukraine lost the chance to build momentum for sweeping reforms. After events like the Euromaidan in 2013-14 (as well as the Orange Revolution), there is usually a short window of opportunity to capitalize on that momentum and initiate quick, radical changes while the public still expects them and the period of "exceptional politics"[53] lasts. Instead, Ukraine's post-Euromaidan leadership adopted processes in the most politically sensitive areas that often only pretended to make reforms.

The establishment of the reform coordination body, the National Council of Reforms in the Presidential administration[54] was a prominent and important example of this. This office, instead of setting quick and ambitious priorities, engaged in lengthy processes of creating hugely complex reform matrixes that targeted a very large number of different areas, which meant the government had no practical priorities. Thus, both the official center of reform and, later, the numerous "monitors" of reform fell into the same fallacy: their change strategy was to break down the needs for reform into many different components and hope that "many" of them would be fulfilled, achieving a critical mass. "Reform scorecards" proliferated in the whole period without much thinking about the critical mass that is needed to trigger real, fundamental systemic reform. This couldn't differ more from the very hands-on reform management in 2004 and onward in Georgia by the president himself—in a creative environment where the main focus was what next reform would lead to a real breakthrough systemic transition.

Similarly, a pseudo-reform activity was the adopted law in 2014 outlining the anti-corruption strategy, the real function of which was to placate Ukraine's foreign friends and avoid the truly painful measures that had been adopted head-on in Georgia. Similar measures adapted to Ukraine's actual situation could have also rapidly reduced the level of corruption as well. By welcoming the package of laws, the international community performed a double fallacy. It allowed the government to confuse a vague strategy and the proliferation of new institutions with two types of real action: first, against obviously corrupt people and second, targeting the systemic mechanisms of corruption in an effective manner.

---

53 The term coined by Leszek Balcerowicz to describe Poland's own period of radical reform.
54 "National Council of Reforms to be Created in Ukraine." *Kyiv Post*, July 22, 2014. Available at: https://www.kyivpost.com/article/content/ukraine-politics/national-council-of-reforms-to-be-created-in-ukraine-357333.html

Moreover, in some cases, the international actors directly blocked such kinds of reforms. For instance, an attempt to apply the "regulatory guillotine" that had been so successful in Georgia was blocked by arguing that such drastic deregulation would contradict the EU Association agreement. Instead, it embarked on a steady, costly, and poorly focused process of revising business regulations. In many cases, harmonization with the cumbersome, burdensome, and often discretionary EU norms without prior establishment of genuine Europe-conforming institutions, especially the RoL and a correspondingly high quality of bureaucracy, resulted in an enhancement of corruption opportunities. In a similar way, the IMF banned corporate tax reform, which is currently the area with the most corruption due to the inherent vulnerabilities of taxation to profiting from corruption. The second broader and more complex fallacy was the mistaking of anticorruption activities for the establishment of the institutions and real mechanisms of the rule-of-law. While the public was undoubtedly right to demand a clamping down on the people who had robbed the nation during the Yanukovich era, the government was able to partially get away with empty pretentions. This is because the international partners of Ukraine and the policy-think-tank community failed to clearly define the long-term systemic goals surrounding anti-corruption measures, RoL reforms, and their interactions.

Later, in the absence of enthusiasm for reform at the top level, concentrated "critical-mass-oriented" reform activity dissipated. Between government institutions on the one hand, and the international institutions and NGOs on the other, a kind of a game set in with the latter trying to corner President Poroshenko on reforms while he pretended that he would do it and snuck out with newer and newer tricks. This was particularly true in the reform of the judiciary and law enforcement, which is the most sensitive of all reform issues as it directly affects raw political power and the potential criminal responsibilities of high and not-so-high level politicians.

Let us also address the usual excuse for modest action that a) Ukraine has been mired in a war and b) it could not financially afford the costs of the governmental overhaul. As to the first counterargument, indeed the war required a careful approach to dealing with staff of law enforcement, particularly police. But the partial success of reforming the patrol police shows that there were ways to deal with the sector despite the war. And deep reform in the prosecution and justice system could have guaranteed firm punishment of those who turned against the state or society in the critical situation of Ukraine. After all, the elimination of the Berkut did not cause insurmountable problems either. One would assume that a great deal of caution was needed in this area, but clearly, the post-revolution president's motivation was not to soften the pain of reform, but to avoid radical systemic transition altogether. To continue the argument for radical reform even in the circumstances of the external threat in 2014, a functional law enforcement and judicial system (from the point of view of a ruleof-law state) would have been a strong safeguard against the infiltration of the system by hostile powers. Plus, it could have galvanized patriotic support behind the government.

As to the second argument, a leadership that believed in the critical importance of reforms could and should have engaged the international community to help cover the costs of such an overhaul. The opposite happened: even when reforms did take place, such as the initial, modest steps towards reforms of the prosecution, the national budget did not allocate as many funds as had been approved by the law, effectively sabotaging the reforms.

This strategy-less strategy could have worked here like it did in the new EU-member states if Ukraine's challenges in its transition were similar to theirs, and if the "carrot" encouraging the transition was EU membership. In the case of the new member states, particularly the "Visegrad" countries, the transformative power of the EU was formidable, even if its interventions and influences were often bureaucratic and formalistic, interested mainly in legislation and much less in actual processes. But in those countries, the initial consensus about reforms was solid, so when the EU became very influential such a broad strategy without a clear hierarchy of goals was acceptable. Also, implementing the law according to its letter and spirit was historically a known concept in those countries. Thus, the reward was powerful.

Ukraine's more challenging and difficult situation requires a much deeper understanding of the viable change strategies that were clearly lacking in 2014. When the window of opportunity finally arrived, there was obviously no time to study Ukraine and its reform opportunities thoroughly; the friends of Ukraine were not well prepared to assist the reforms in a truly effective and tailor-made manner. The key personalities of the government, on the other hand, were preoccupied with optimizing their own short-term positions of power in the political arena, which was not perceived as being consistent with driving radical reforms. However, this situation still allowed some modest and controlled reforms. The results, and the balance of these main vectors shaped what we have gotten in Ukraine over the past 8 years.

2. Rule-of-law vs discretionary justice

An honest, competent government and a fair judiciary/law enforcement based on the rule of law are two of the most important predictors of long-term developmental success. Looking back on the last 8 years, one can conclude that progress towards both in Ukraine has been modest, albeit certainly present, and may have been cumulative. In this chapter, we try to establish what the state of affairs is in Ukraine in the area of the rule-of-law, and what has brought it about so that we can, in the last chapter, suggest further practical ways to move the country forward towards an effective and efficient rule-of-law based state.

The issue of the RoL and its respective institutions is so important because, as we described in the introduction, the success or failure of its implementation largely determines whether a patronal democracy will evolve into a patronal autocracy or a liberal democracy. In fact, they are even more fundamental because legitimized coercion is the core of a state, and it can be legitimate only if it is perceived as "just". The directions and methods of such coercion determine the regime's nature, so when it comes to the revolution (as the process in which the people overtake the state, or "shackle the Leviathan" as described in the Introduction), the main issue is who takes actual control over the state apparatus of organized violence. Note that political control over the use of force is one of three "doorstep conditions" for a systemic transition to an OAO, named by North et al. In the case of dismantling a patronal system that is largely based on informal relationships, such control cannot be fully effective without re-staffing the respective state agencies that are necessary for the destruction of the informal networks. Above all, the personnel selected (or self-selected) by a patronal system and used for corruption is different from the one needed for honest and impersonal enforcement of the law. It is hard to expect a police officer or a judge that used to live on lofty bribes (and take the respective risks) to rest on a salary, however high it is. It is the institutional culture that is so critical and, at the same time, so difficult to change. Last but not least, the very law that the new agencies are expected to enforce should be made practical, with minimal corruption opportunities in order to minimize the temptations for new staff. All of this was mostly done in Georgia after the Rose Revolution and proved to be successful, but only some relatively modest steps were taken in Ukraine.

The main concern of the public during and immediately after the Euromaidan was the rampant and gigantic corruption of public officials, including gross embezzlement, raiding, tax fraud, gas arbitrage, and other practices by Yanukovich and his entourage. These became very visible as the revolution opened up his Mezhyhirya palace and uncovered many other excesses. The mass public movement appropriately acquired the name 'The Revolution of Dignity'. Public desire was similar to that of Georgia during the Rose Revolution, which had triggered there sweeping reforms. Georgia's success in systemic transition was spectacular in the years of the Rose Revolution, even if not conclusive in that Georgia has never established a fully independent judiciary and some of the reforms seem to prove not sustainable; also, at the top level of government arbitrariness remained part of the repertoire. But even considering these factors, Georgia's reforms served as a useful point of reference in the years immediately after the Euromaidan.

Georgia wiped out most corruption during the Rose Revolution in a country that was not only famous for corruption, but also was a former home and incubator of organized crime for the entire Soviet and post-Soviet region. Crucially, in the years of the Rose Revolution Georgia radically deregulated its economy, eliminating many of the opportunities for corruption. It also reformed public administration and much of the judicial sector, though without eliminating the dependence of the latter on the executive branch. Georgia, as a consequence of its reforms, has since seen superior economic growth relative to its peers, Ukraine and Moldova, despite the war in 2008 waged against it by Russia. There have been shortcomings in the Georgian reforms other than failing to grant independence to the judiciary or prosecution, mostly connected to the still overly powerful office of the president during Saakashvili's time. These include a degree of arbitrariness, exceptions for the president from certain rules, and an excessive degree of informality in the day-to-day functioning of the government.

Given that Ukraine had better human resource conditions before the revolution and that the revolution was more dramatic than in Georgia, it should have implemented even deeper reforms. Ideally, the judicial system and law enforcement, especially the prosecution, should have been severely reformed along four lines:

- Changing legislation to functionally secure the integrity and independence of both the courts and the prosecution.
- Thorough re-staffing based on the state's new principles, and strict attestation/vetting criteria under the control of an independent body, made up of reputable members of civil society and international experts, to apply the principle of transparency to its fullest.
- Drastically reducing the power of prosecution and greatly increasing the power and prestige of judges.
- A radical increase in the remuneration for these professions, including investigators and police officers, to a level that corresponds to the high social importance of ethical integrity in these state services.

We shall see below what happened relative to these expectations.

Partial reforms

Looking back to the Poroshenko years, overly gloomy evaluations may cloud some important and potentially positive, albeit incomplete, systemic developments, analyzed also by John Lough and Vladimir Dubrovskiy.[55] Their report suggests that, though punitive anti-corruption measures fell short of their ambitious promises, some important shrinkages in corruption opportunities occurred, particularly regarding deregulation, natural gas supply,

---

55   Lough, John, and Dubrovskiy, Vladimir. "Are Ukraine's Anti-corruption Reforms Working?". *Royal Institute of International Affairs (Chatham House)*, 2018. Available at: https://reader.chathamhouse.org/are-ukraines-anti-corruption-reforms-working#

tax administration, and some other spheres. For instance, the Annual Business Cost Assessment (ABCA) survey demonstrates a decrease in the total cost of compliance with non-tax regulations for the SME by 8% in absolute numbers, not corrected for inflation, in the single year of 2016[56] (other economic effects are analyzed in the section devoted to rent-seeking), and a national opinion poll's respondents admit some decrease in the frequency of bribes,[57] which can likely be associated with the reform of administrative services. The reforms — where they took place — also managed to create reasonably trusted government bodies, like the new patrol police and the NABU. However, such successful reforms were rare in that period elsewhere, especially in other parts of the judiciary and law enforcement.

To understand why this has been the case, we first need to scrutinize what happened and didn't happen in those sectors. While no change strategy outlined specific priorities among the different subsystems of these sectors, a number of initial actions proved to be of modest but significant value over the first years of the revolution. Initial action took place in 2014 in each of the large subsectors: the judiciary, prosecution/police, and, as we mentioned, the anti-corruption sphere, which given its perceived importance also gained the status of a "quasi-sector". In three of the main sectors for the rule-of-law the main responsibility belonged to the Presidency: the judiciary, prosecution, and secret services. Responsibility for police reform also belonged to the government in the sense that the Minister of Internal Affairs was a key member of the junior coalition party. Naturally, there have been overlaps and disputes over jurisdiction, such as the distribution of investigative functions among different agencies.

---

56   Although we cannot directly compare to previous years, since this survey was conducted only in 2015-17, the respondents admitted that the situation improved compared to 2013. Note that Ukrainians generally tend to be rather negative (for instance, in the same period of 2015-2016 the balance between those perceiving improvements and no improvements was −7.2% in spite of an actual decrease in the cost of compliance).

57   "Socio-political moods of the Ukrainians: new challenges". *Rating Group*, 2018. Available at: http://ratinggroup.ua/en/research/ukraine/obschestvenno-pol iticheskie_nastroeniya_ukraincev_novye_vyzovy.html

In the absence of overall understanding and genuine desire, and thus leadership, of reforms at the top of the executive branch, each of these actions were the result of particular tugs-of-war among sectors of government (mainly presidency) on one hand, and major donors (the US and the European Union) together with think tankers and civil society activists on the other. The latter gathered mainly in the Reanimation Package of Reforms, a unique organization that pushes for reforms for any post-socialist country. This *fragmentation* of reform actions was compounded by the earlier-mentioned checklist approach of the reformist public, and also by the reform center of the presidential administration. The Renaissance Foundation, together with the EBRD, supported the reform process by financing a large number of experts in different ministries. This happened without a clear view of a desirable change strategy that could have been a good selection criterion for placing people into these ministries and could have helped prioritize talent and attention.

Various change strategies could have been imagined back in 2014 in the rule-of-law area, which was probably the most critical domain for breakthrough systemic reforms. In other words, we think that there was more than one such path to achieve this breakthrough. Clearly, the final check on disputes and crime belongs to the judges. Therefore, court reform had the appeal of fixing the independent position of the ultimate gatekeeper—and in a liberal order, indeed, their power would clearly overwhelm that of prosecutors, police officers, and secret service officers. However, a different argument could be made for focusing on prosecution reform: since prosecutors are such a pillar of both the patronal state and the creation of local and national monopolies (even with competing oligarchs), reform here could have triggered such a vacuum in *oligarchic power* that it would have opened the road to the open-access order. The power and level of corruption among the prosecutors was so overwhelming that it cried for action to weaken the anti-reform camp and the organized corruption networks. Finally, the somewhat marginal patrol police reform could have been seen, in the generally reluctant reform environment, as a first, "morale boosting" step, visible to the public, which could have then been followed by other, more complex and ambitious reforms overseen by the Minister of Internal Affairs. But as it happens, these initiatives remained fragmented, without strong political support (with the initial exception of the "patrol police reform" that helped the PR of the president and Minister of Internal Affairs and placated donors and civil society for a while).

In well-established democratic societies there is a large variety of regulations in the justice sector. One axiom is that "the courts should be independent", but even this sits somewhat oddly in Georgia, the only successful site of anti-corruption reform in the (former) CIS-space, where in the initial phase of the Saakashvili reforms, justice was so centralized that the president personally presided over the council of the judges.[58] Obviously, there should be no debate that the courts must ultimately become independent. However, Saakashvili's route was not only self-serving, it was also a response to the local reality of massive organized crime and rampant judicial corruption. Regarding the prosecution, the necessity of independence from executive power is equivocal. This is true to such an extent that in many countries with deep democratic checks-and-balances the norm is for the prosecution to be subordinated to the executive branch to various degrees (mainly in the form of a minister of justice) — of course without the institutional *history* prevalent in Ukraine.[59] Georgia, again as the closest success example to Ukraine, did not make the prosecution independent in the Saakashvili period and this ultimately became the source of significant abuses of power. There, the prosecution

---

58   See a detailed comparative analysis in Mizsei, K. "The New East European Patronal States and the Rule-of-Law." In *Stubborn Structures: Reconceptualizing Post-Communist Regimes,* edited by Magyar, B. Central European University Press, 2019.

59   "…the exercise of public interest functions (including criminal prosecution) should not be combined or confused with the function of protecting the interests of the current Government, the interests of other institutions of state, or even the interests of a political party. The functioning of such a system however depends on legal culture, and especially in younger democracies, where there is a history of abuse of prosecution for political goals, special precautions are needed." See: "The Independence of Judges and Prosecutors: perspectives and challenges". *European Commission for Democracy Through Law (Venice Commission)*, Strasbourg, 15 March 2011.

modernized very intensely and underwent deep reforms of its organization, budget, internal organizational, and salaries, but still remained under the executive branch with a large propensity for arbitrary action.

Anti-corruption institutions

The creation of a separate or partially separate anti-corruption chain in Ukraine was an immediate response to outrage at the gross and rampant corruption that was especially flourishing under Yanukovich. This approach was predicated on the vaguely articulated philosophy that since one of the core characteristics of the current system is rent seeking via extra-legal means, and because the radical overhaul of the whole system was not politically feasible in 2014-15, reformers had to fight corruption separately.

There were three unspoken interpretations of what that fight against corruption meant. For many in the general public it simply meant putting corrupt politicians and businesspeople behind bars (not to mention the perpetrators of the murders and beatings during the Euromaidan). The second interpretation was wiping out corruption through repressive measures, while the third was to reduce the scope of corruption via radical deregulation, privatization, and positive incentives for lawful behavior. The third approach never got much exposure among reform professionals, such as those in the RPR and in the international support community. A notable minority, however, like the authors of this paper, Alexander Danilyuk, and a few others, have advocated for such a complex and more positive incentive-oriented approach but haven't so far gained strong political backing. One of the main reasons for this, other than the very understandable populist line of thinking that corruption should be "fought" exclusively by punishing it, is a professional one: lawyers are (a) more inclined to treat corruption not as a social practice that plays a critical systemic role, but as "simply a crime that should be punished, that's it"; and (b) generally less likely to advocate for radical shrinking of the role of the state as part of their understandable professional bias. At best, they do not have a (usually unspoken) belief in the unlimited capacity of the state to regulate and enforce. Often the question is not even asked, but state capacity is, erroneously, assumed. It is more likely liberal-minded economists who conclude that the role of the state should be reduced, like in Georgia under Saakashvili, which was helped by Bendukidze's enormous charisma and focus on reducing the state's role. Diplomats in the support community also lack the kind of structural reform expertise that would equip them with the way of thinking that we advocate. They also rarely have a sufficient understanding of state organization.

Naturally, our point is not exclusivist: we do recognize the importance of using the rigor of law enforcement. However, critically, we do not believe it is enough. Also, in a situation where practically the whole higher echelon of the political class, in government and in opposition alike, is part of the system of extra-legal practices, it is very likely the "rigor of the law" will mean selective justice of the holders of power against their political or economic competitors. Anyway, the inevitability of punishment for lawbreaking, the core principle of justice, cannot be implemented if the percentage of lawbreakers is not in the low single digits, as is the case in a normal situation. This is certainly not true of corruption as a "simple crime" in Ukraine. Thus, before punishment can become effective in fighting corruption, some other reforms should narrow the scope for its application to a few percentages of public servants and politicians. Until then, the best use of punishment would be to scare or remove the staunchest opponents of such reforms.

After the failure to radically overhaul the system, legal professionals' main focus was to find alternative routes to create independent state capacity to prosecute corruption, seeing it as one of the gravest ills of the state. While, again, we maintain a certain distance from this approach, we do not necessarily disagree with it. We do, however, consider it an open question of what policy approach would be most likely to ultimately establish an open-access society in Ukraine with a firm RoL, and we are particularly interested in how that course would affect the country's relationship with its largest neighbor, a permanent existential threat.[60]

What Ukraine has found itself in is the **proliferation of new institutions without eliminating or seriously shrinking any of the old ones**. First, on the basis of the 2014 legislation, NABU was established. Then, the institution of anti-corruption prosecution (SAPO) was created. Just as is currently going on in the anti-corruption court, there has been public controversy surrounding the appointment of the head of the anti-corruption prosecution. Later, ferocious and very public inter-agency fighting ensued between the anti-corruption investigative agency, the prosecutor's office, and the state security services. Rather than siding with any one side, we simply want to point out that this proliferation of different agencies around corruption has been one of the reasons for such infighting. Like with the establishment of NABU and of the anti-corruption prosecutor's office, the establishment of the courts has also been part of the IMF's conditions for the new stand-by loan facility, which is vital to Ukraine's financial sustainability. The founding of each of these institutions was based on the hope of Ukrainian think-tanks, NGOs, and international supporters for one day creating a liberal, European state.

The very same anti-corruption law also established a new special indirect anti-corruption mechanism of punishment for "illegal enrichment". All public officials and several other categories of public servants were obliged to fill in publicly available e-declarations of their incomes and ownership of valuable assets, such as real estate, securities, vehicles, watches, antique and fine arts artifacts, etc. Failure to declare assets of significant value is subject to criminal punishment. And yet another new anti-corruption body — the National Agency on Corruption Prevention (NACP) was created for two major tasks: (a) screening prospective legislation for possible corruption vulnerabilities; and (b) checking

---

60 "Activists say prospects of anti-graft court look bleak." Kyiv Post, October 23, 2014. Available at: https://www.kyivpost.com/ukraine-politics/activists-say-prospects-of-anti-graft-court-look-bleak.html?utm_source=traqli&utm_mediu m=email&utm_campaign=traqli_daily_editors&tqid=nfOzaiR9H00BU8Zw6.c V9PTKjrSf1xqnARoue24%24

the e-declarations for validity and their correspondence to legal incomes. In theory, this should allow for indirect detection of illegal (corruption-related) incomes if the difference in amassed wealth for a certain period of time did not match the legal income earned during the same period.

However, in the patronal system, this mechanism has so far never worked as intended. To our knowledge, as of now (in the 5 years since the legislation was enacted) nobody was convicted for illegal enrichment. Instead, the public e-declarations became a sort of collective coming-out for the corrupt political class that, on the one hand, has largely undermined its political legitimacy—which was one of the key reasons for electing the anti-elites in 2019; on the other hand, it has underlined that "everybody is corrupt", hence anti-corruption persecution of particular persons is not so much related to corruption per se, but mostly to political or other motives behind the selective justice; not to mention the excuse it provided for petty corruption. Poroshenko greeted the e-declarations because he rightly considered it as another discretionary tool: he established firm control over the NACP and used it for political persecution, as he did, for example, in the case of Saakashvili's allies. Notably, under Poroshenko the NACP completely failed to perform its primary task of legislative screening: this critically important mission was simply abandoned.

The "re-loading" of the NACP in 2019-20 appeared to be one of the very few examples where Zelensky strengthened the institution. The Agency was staffed with competent and devoted personnel, including reputable civil society representatives with demonstrated success in the elimination of corruption opportunities (one such representative being Alexander Starodubtsev, who was previously in charge of the creation of the ProZorro digital procurement platform) or anti-corruption activists, such as Ivan Presniakov. Since then, the NACP has performed all of its tasks, including drafting a solid National Anti-Corruption Strategy, more than 200 anti-corruption expert documents for preparing legislation, and routine automated analysis of e-declarations that seems to not be politicized any more—at least we are not aware of any complaints of this sort.

The hope put into the new set of anti-corruption institutions has not yet, after 8 years, materialized, which makes it legitimate to ask whether this strategy was wise to begin with and whether it needs major correction, or at least some augmentation. NABU, however, has done some robust work, beyond what was expected of it. Yet, the ruling elites have plenty of ways to neutralize an institution if it really starts to act according to the expectations of civil society and supporting international partners. We will return to this question later in the study. A possible answer is that, while the apparatus for repressing corruption is important to establish, it is going to be a longer process in the best of circumstances; in a less fortunate scenario the different institutions can fall under the influence of powerful interests (since Ukraine does not have a single pyramid political formation, it may well be that competing politico-business interests acquire positions in different law enforcement and judicial agencies). Therefore, it is important to seek other means to reduce the scope of corruption in Ukrainian society. Yet, the costs of revisiting the establishment of the new institutions and eliminating any of them is too high, plus there is no alternative strategy so far that has been articulated in a convincing manner. If the above set of points is true, the task is to improve the institutions and design mechanisms that guarantee that they focus on well-defined mandates and that they will not fall prey to particular political and corrupt business interests.

Judiciary: interface with public vs prosecutor

The judiciary and particularly the prosecution are core elements of patronal politics because the very essence of a patronal leader's rule is, according to Hale, his right and ability to punish and reward at his own discretion. This is opposite to the rule-of-law where independent judges have the last word in punishment, which is regulated by law, and where prosecution is independent in its action from executive power, let alone oligarchic power. This makes judicial reform key to combating patronal politics, which is, in turn, a key part of the LAO. The most powerful players in

Ukrainian politics and business clearly understand this too,[61] so an independent and effective judiciary is the last thing they would allow to emerge, because by losing control over the courts and prosecution they lose much of their informal power.[62]

On the formal level, the transformation towards an OAO presupposes changing the power relationship between prosecutors and judges, with the influence of the former needing to be weakened. There are also thoughts that, for a start, at least one of the two needs to be reformed if the political determination is lacking for a complete radical overhaul in the short run. This may be a necessary position if the capacity of government to reform is very limited. However, the risk that reforms may be reversed remains high so long as either prosecutors or judges remain unreformed. The prosecution's power should ultimately be broken, its hierarchy weakened, mandate reduced, and number of prosecutors reduced, while their salaries should be seriously increased. The judiciary, meanwhile, should be professionalized, their salaries increased, and ethical standards and the authority of judges raised. This is a very complex set of tasks and, thus, will not happen overnight and inevitably will require some trial and error.

When it comes to judicial reform, an additional difficulty is that the system is highly complex. Initially it had four judicial levels (now merged into three) and many institutions. In order to make the judiciary function properly, the whole system needs to be reformed as blockages resulting from the combined effects of political pliancy and corruption can occur on different levels of the judicial hierarchy, and just one link in the chain can stop the pro-

---

61 Here we quote the informant of the Ukrainian Pravda newspaper: "Some asshole from abroad will come and tell us how to live and develop our country? They will make their manually controlled court, and this is the end. They will complete the vertical NABU - SAP - ACC. And then there will be anticorruption "trinities", like in the [Stalin's] NKVD. Because they will go after whoever they want, and whenever they want. This will be the state within the state." Another one added: "The West wants to get complete external control over us!". See: "Страшний антикорупційний суд. Чому Україна свариться з Заходом." *Українська правда*, January 23, 2018. Available at: https://www.pravda.com.ua/articles/2018/01/23/7169243/

62 Only the most recent liberal reformers pay anything close to adequate attention to the reform of the judiciary and prosecution regionwide.

cess of delivering justice. A major difference between the approach of the chief European standard setter, the Council of Europe, and the Ukrainian radical reformers is that the latter started with the proposition that it only has a chance of achieving breakthrough judicial reform if there is a near-complete overhaul of the system of corrupt judges as well as reform on *every* judicial level; while the former assumed that applying the CoE norms in every area will gradually result in more or less the same Western European system, ignoring the enormous differences in attitudes and institutional behavior. The radical reformers' rationale for their approach has been that such corrupt institutional culture dominates Ukrainian courtrooms that it can only be changed by a critical mass of new blood. It is a real dilemma as, on the one hand, there have been positive examples of systemic change the way the Council of Europe recommends it—Poland and Hungary are very good examples, despite their later reversals—but, on the other hand, these judiciaries had never been as deeply rotten and dysfunctional as the one in Ukraine (and in the majority of post-Soviet states). Ukraine has its own uncharted path, and earlier examples of judicial reform in other countries are only of limited value.[63] The Council of Europe—and in its footsteps the European Union—would be well advised to take this problem seriously and raise their expectations of what breakthrough reforms in Ukraine will take.

Similarly, the CoE principle, according to which "a majority of judges should be elected by judges", did not work well in Ukraine. Judicial governance bodies which select, appoint, discipline, and dismiss judges, gaining more independence from the

---

63   The European standards on the composition of judicial governance bodies, based on the principle of "majority of judges elected by judges, do not work in transitional democracies. Ukraine might need to change this approach, with recognition from the EU and international organizations" Zhernakov, M. "Judicial Reform in Ukraine: Mission Possible? Policy Report." *International Renaissance Foundation*, 2017. Available at: https://rpr.org.ua/wp-content/uploads/2017/02/Renaissance_A4_5JURIDICIAL-REFORM.pdf;   Popova,   M. "Ukraine's Judiciary after Euromaidan." *Comparative Politics Newsletter*, Volume 25, Issue 2, Fall. This subsection also greatly benefitted from Mykhailo Zhernakov's valuable extensive feedback.

executive and legislative branches in 2014, began abusing their powers to pressure "overly independent" judges and encourage the loyal ones. As a result, a tendency occurred to punish judges of high integrity and reward the corrupt. Thus, the phenomenon of a mutual guarantee of impunity and joint opposition to any further reform was formed. To sum up the above, "independence" of the mostly corrupt judiciary brings only consolidation of corruption. Here "quantity turns into quality" in the sense that the instruments that are good at fighting corruption when it is rather minor fail when corruption is systemic and overwhelming. When most judges are free of corruption, then independence and self-governance would allow the clean majority to get rid of the corrupt minority. Meanwhile, if the balance is the opposite, as in Ukraine, the very same mechanisms allow the corrupt majority to successfully get rid of the clean minority. Unfortunately, the Council of Europe was not driven by this recognition.

Reform of the judiciary has been tried via many avenues in the last 8 years. The process of firing all the presidents of district courts and reappointing them by votes from the local judges illustrated perfectly the fear of the radical reformers: 80 per cent of the presidents, deemed to be long hands of the previous Yanukovich government, were simply reinstated by the local judges, illustrating just how much organized crime had penetrated the courts.[64]

There was a short, naïve moment after the Euromaidan in which the main path forward seemed to be through the lustration law. Lustration was a dead end not only because of its failure to purge corrupt senior judges—though undoubtedly a worthy cause—but also because the goal of lustration could not be defined in a way that would have satisfied the requirements of "justice". Firing the leaders of the border guards—arguably the most professional segment of law enforcement at the time because of many years of intense EU assistance—exemplifies the point. They were fired on the basis of having been trained in the old KGB academy. However, it had earlier been a strict formal requirement for them to attend it! The other problem was that such purges are only fea-

---

64   Ibid.

sible in a situation where the leaders of the revolution take over the state apparatus, and only so long as they work according to their professed goals. Here the revolution did not result in a take-over of the political leadership, thus there was no strong interest in managing the process in an honest way other than from NGOs and international actors, so it lacked the critical political mass needed to support it. In certain segments of government the lustration process was manipulated in various ways by the people already in power.[65] On top of this, lots of law enforcement officials and servicemen lustrated or screened out by attestation commissions in the course of these reforms eventually managed to return to the same positions or to similar ones through court decisions — this fact further reinforces the primacy of the judicial reform.

In the 2014-15 period the strong position of non-governmental reform experts gathered in the Reanimation Package of Reforms which, combined with the Council of Europe's advocacy, pushed the presidency towards declaring a reform strategy and even constitutional amendments to create an independent judiciary. The country's vital dependence on Western aid meant that such a strong reform push could not go unanswered. However, afterwards the leadership of the country lacked the guts to do what was necessary to completely renew the judicial corps, or rather was not willing to for the reasons explained above. In each step brakes got built in and the incumbents got the upper hand. At the same time, the judiciary was not left unchanged; modest positive change did occur too. In the Supreme Court, thanks to the involvement of the Public Integrity Council (PIC) from 2017-18, a number of notorious judges were disqualified from the competition, and new blood, some representatives of academia and practicing lawyers who had never been judges, were co-opted into the system, even if the opinion of the PIC was often disregarded. According to the PIC, the integrity of about half

---

65   "Lustration law faces sabotage, legal hurdles." *Kyiv Post*, October 23, 2014. Available at: https://www.kyivpost.com/article/content/reform-watch/lustration-law-faces-sabotage-legal-hurdles-369135.html

of the 193 judges in the new Supreme Court is questionable, and at least 44 (22.5%) definitely did not meet the integrity criteria.

The most successful case of judicial reform in Ukraine though was the creation of the High Anti-Corruption Court (HACC) in 2018. This success was made possible by the involvement of international experts in the selection of judges for the HACC, which was a unique experience for Ukraine's judicial reform. To establish the HACC, a new subsidiary body, the Public Council of International Experts (PCIE), was created, consisting of six members, delegated by reputable international organizations who assisted Ukraine in the anti-corruption sphere to select judges for the HACC. The idea of involving international experts was also supported by the Venice Commission. The PCIE screened the candidates and could veto those whose integrity was doubtful. The results of the PCIE's work were significant—not a single judge with severe reservations regarding integrity was appointed. The establishment of the HACC has set a precedent and demonstrated that the involvement of independent international experts in the selection of judges could break the vicious circle of judges and contribute significantly to the reform.

These efforts, combined with the substantial increase in judges' salaries, make it more feasible for them to live professionally honest lives without bribes. Salaries at the low-level courts are still very low though, while even in the upper levels they are hardly comparable with the honoraria of lawyers with similar credentials. However, the above reforms, as well as the impact of free media, bode well for the prospect of the emergence of islands of honesty in the judicial corps that can, over time, show a positive example of judicial ethos to the whole profession. Such an evolution happened in other post-communist countries earlier. But in those countries, the reforms were supported by an intense adjustment and monitoring process under the supervision of the European Commission, were reinforced by reforms in other areas relevant to the rule-of-law, and also took place in a period of rapid economic growth that certainly contributed to the emergence of an honest rule-of-law ethos. In those countries, the gap between their governance culture and that of the West was not as deep as in Ukraine.

After the 2019 elections, as a result of which Volodymyr Zelensky became President and his Servant of the People party won a majority in Parliament, the issue of judicial reform gained a new twist. Society remained dissatisfied with the progress of reform in 2014-2019, while the main problems of the judiciary – the political dependence of the judiciary and the great number of judges of low integrity – remained unresolved. The new President was expected to give a new and decisive push to judicial reform, because unlike Poroshenko he lacked his own political clan, and, respectively, did not have the conflict of interests described above: he could exercise his power without a discretionary rule, especially given the Parliament majority he enjoys. However, so far, his record is highly mixed, because it rather looks like Zelensky is trying to stick with traditional patronal methods of rule and tries to catch up with building his own clan instead.

In the Fall of 2019, the Parliament adopted Presidential law № 193-IX, which was designed to reform the two main judicial governance bodies – the High Qualification Commission of Justice in Ukraine (HQCJ), which is responsible for the qualification assessment and selection of judges, and the High Council of Justice (hereinafter the HCJ), which is responsible for the appointment and dismissal of judges. The law provided for the dissolution of the HQCJ and the establishment of an Ethics Commission, consisting of three representative judges and three international experts, to check the integrity of HCJ members and dismiss the corrupt ones. However, the HCJ, which became a kind of "core" of judicial corruption and reciprocity, sabotaged the creation of the Ethics Commission and blocked reform. In March 2020, the Constitutional Court declared a number of key provisions of Law № 193-IX unconstitutional, thus burying this critical segment of judicial reform.

In 2020, the requirement for the HCJ reform was included in the memorandum of Ukraine with the IMF, and the requirement for the restart of the HQCJ and reform of the HCJ was included in the memorandum of Ukraine with the EU. Additionally, according to the World Justice Project Ukraine ranked[66] 72nd out of 182 countries on rule of law in 2020. Thus, the authorities received a clear external and internal message that judicial reform needed to be completed. Indeed, the survey of the European Business Association found that still in 2020 the biggest obstacle to foreign investment in the country was the malfunctioning of the judiciary and that the situation had not become better during all these years of reform efforts.[67]

In July 2021, the Parliament passed two important laws (№ 1635-IX and № 1629-IX), which provided for the reform of the HCJ and the reboot of the HQCJ. The main purpose of these laws was to provide for the cleansing of the key judicial governance bodies, which can then, in turn, oversee a deeper cleansing of the judiciary as a whole. The importance of these laws was also increased by the fact that the HQCJ has not functioned since 2019, when it was dissolved under Law № 193-IX, resulting in a judicial staff shortage - almost 2,500 vacancies were open (almost 30% of all judges in Ukraine). This staff shortage was also caused by the introduction of the "e-declarations": a large number of judges simply resigned rather than fill out the wealth declarations.

Thus, the reboot of the HQCJ with decent composition would fill 2,500 vacancies in the long run with trustworthy judges and continue the qualification assessment of about 2,000 judges. At the same time, the reform of the HCJ would permanently eradicate the circular bail of judges.

According to the laws of July 2021, two bodies were created - the Ethics Council to verify the integrity of current members and candidates for the HCJ and the Selection Commission to form the new composition of the HQCJ. Each body consists of six members - three representatives from judges and three independent international experts delegated by international organizations that pro-

---

66   "Ukraine—2020 WJP Rule of Law Index Country Press Release." *World Justice Project*, 2020. Available at: https://worldjusticeproject.org/sites/default/files/documents/Ukraine%20-%202020%20WJP%20Rule%20of%20Law%20Index%20Country%20Press%20Release.pdf.

67   "Lack of trust in the judiciary is the major obstacle to foreign investment in Ukraine." *European Business Association*, September 11, 2020.

vided support to Ukraine in the fight against corruption. A key achievement of these laws was that international experts were given a casting vote in commissions if the vote on the candidate was divided three against three. Given the deep corruption of the HCJ, this provision gave a chance for a real reform of this body and a decent composition of the HQCJ.

By analogy, during president Zelensky's first failed attempt to reform the courts in 2019, the HCJ members, all of whom were of notably poor integrity, began to sabotage the implementation of the reform, in particular the formation of the Ethics Council. Through their influence on other judicial bodies, the HCJ members aimed to sabotage the delegation of judges to the Ethics Council in order to invalidate it. Only due to fierce pressure from civil society, leading NGOs, and international partners, especially the G7 Ambassadors, was the process able to break the deadlock in 2021 and prevent a repeat of the 2019 scenario. The Ethics Council is currently screening the candidates to the HCJ and is preparing to start the screening of current members. The Selection Commission will soon hold its first meeting and start selecting candidates for the HQCJ.

This approach to judicial reform may perhaps become successful because it has some chance to break the current vicious circle of corrupt judges electing their corrupt colleagues into the HCJ and HQCJ that, in turn, select and promote poor candidates with low integrity but good ties to the judicial mafia. Should the new governing bodies of the court system be staffed with real professionals, clean and competent, they will be steadily restaffing the courts with similar kinds of personnel.

In general, the attention of international partners to judicial and anti-corruption reforms in Ukraine in 2021 reached its historical maximum. It was recognized as a top priority at the first meeting of presidents Zelensky and Biden at the White House in autumn 2021,[68] as a result of which the Ukrainian president pledged

---

68   "Joint Statement on the U.S.-Ukraine Strategic Partnership." *The White House*, September 1, 2021. Available at: https://www.whitehouse.gov/briefing-room /statements-releases/2021/09/01/joint-statement-on-the-u-s-ukraine-strategi c-partnership/.

to reform the courts in accordance with international practices. Also, in a joint statement with the President of the European Council, Charles Michel, and President of the European Commission, Ursula von der Leyen, following the 23rd Ukraine-EU Summit in October 2021, the president of Ukraine called judicial reform vital to strengthening Ukraine's resilience and future success.[69] The increased attention both domestically and of international partners played key roles in the progress in judicial reform in Ukraine. It is clear that the deeply corrupt judiciary will continue to use all possible levers to further sabotage the reform, so the close attention of international partners to its course may be crucial for its successful implementation.

One of the most vivid symbols of judicial corruption in the years after the Revolution of Dignity was the District Administrative Court of Kyiv (DACK). In 2019, NABU, together with investigators of the Department of Special Investigations of the Prosecutor General's Office (hereinafter PGO), conducted searches of the premises of the court. According to the investigation, the Head of the DACK, Pavlo Vovk, together with other judges of the administrative court, were involved in making illegal judgments and influenced the HQCJ in order to avoid passing the qualification assessment. NABU soon released recordings of conversations in Judge Vovk's office, which confirmed his and other DACK judges' involvement in mass corruption. NABU detectives reported documented cases of illegal influence of the DACK judges on the State Bureau of Investigation, the Security Service of Ukraine, judges of the Constitutional Court and the Administrative Court of Appeal, as well as members of the HCJ. Such influence became possible through the excessive authority of the DACK, which is the first court in almost all cases against national authorities.

After the publication of recordings of judge Vovk's conversations, civil society demanded that President Zelensky liquidate the DACK, as a result of which he introduced a corresponding draft

---

69   "Joint Statement Following the 23rd EU-Ukraine Summit." Official website of the President of Ukraine, October 12, 2021. Available at: https://www. presid ent.gov.ua/en/news/spilna-zayava-za-pidsumkami-23-go-samitu-ukrayina-y evropejsk-71037

law (№ 5369). However, according to leading Ukrainian NGOs, the liquidation of the court will not solve the problem of its excessive authority. To solve the problem comprehensively, it is necessary to also transfer the excessive powers of the DACK to hear high-profile administrative cases to a newly established High Administrative Court (with a selection procedure similar to that of the HACC). The situation is complicated by the fact that, despite pressure from civil society, Volodymyr Zelensky and his Servant of the People party do not have enough political will to liquidate the court altogether. According to civil society watchdogs, like former President Poroshenko, the current presidency also uses the DACK and its excessive powers for political purposes. That is why draft law № 5369, which the President once called "urgent", has been gathering dust for nine months in the Parliamentary Committee on Legal Policy, headed by a People's Servant MP.

The recent example of the use of the DACK powers by the President is the competition for the position of the Head of the SAPO, which has been going on for about a year and a half. Transparent competition and the appointment of an independent Head of the SAPO were part of Ukraine's international commitments with the EU and the IMF, and its importance was stressed in a joint statement after the meeting of the presidents of Ukraine and the United States in September. However, throughout the competition, the president's office tried in every way to influence it. When it became clear that an "overly independent" candidate was winning the competition, the President's Office decided to use the DACK to create legal barriers. As a result, the DACK ruled that the Rules of Procedure of the competition were illegal, which delayed the process indefinitely. Amid the growing threat of a full-scale Russian invasion of Ukraine, President Zelensky's failure to meet expectations of strategic partners was counterproductive.

Constitutional crisis and reform of the Constitutional Court

In October 2020, the Constitutional Court of Ukraine (hereinafter the CCU) issued a decision abolishing criminal liability of civil servants for non-declaration or incorrect declaration of their assets. By its decision, the Constitutional Court also deprived the National Agency on Corruption Prevention, which implements state anti-corruption policy, of some of its crucial powers. This decision not only made the fight against corruption more difficult but also affected Ukraine's relations with the EU and the West in general, one of the cornerstones of which is the fight against corruption. President Zelensky called the CCU decision "a plot of the old elites and oligarchs", and National Security and Defense Council of Ukraine Secretary Oleksiy Danilov stated that the CCU judges were influenced by the Russian Federation.

The CCU's decision provoked protests in society, to which it had become clear that the current composition of the court posed a threat to state security. President Zelensky introduced a draft law to dissolve the entire Constitutional Court, without actually having the authority to do so, because, according to the Ukrainian Constitution, the President cannot dismiss judges of the Constitutional Court. This draft law was immediately criticized by the Venice Commission.

It became more complicated when in December 2020 journalists revealed the recordings of President of the CCU Oleksandr Tupytsky's phone conversations, showing his involvement in mass corruption. In response, President Zelensky revoked decrees appointing Oleksandr Tupytsky and another judge of the Constitutional Court, Oleksandr Kasminin. However, such decrees have no legal force, as only the CCU can dismiss CCU judges, and the revoke-of-appointment decrees do not entail dismissal. Irrespective of Zelensky's real intentions, the dismissal of Constitutional Court judges in such a manner was not a good solution for overcoming the constitutional crisis and strengthening the rule of law.

This crisis highlighted the importance of reforming the Constitutional Court, in particular the procedure for selecting its judges, who may be subject to political pressure due to the imperfections of the current procedure. Currently, in Ukraine, CCU judges are appointed by three bodies according to their quotas - the All-Ukrainian Congress of Judges, the Parliament, and the President. Candidates for these appointing bodies are selected by the Council of Judges, the Parliamentary Committee on Legal Policy, and the Presidential Selection Committee, respectively. This procedure makes judges possible targets of political influences. The new procedure, recommended by the Venice Commission and supported by civil society, should provide for the establishment of a single Selection Commission for all CCU judges composed of representatives of civil society and independent international experts. The Venice Commission also stressed that filling the vacancies before such a procedure is implemented would be undesirable. Similar recommendations followed from the G7 countries.

The draft law № 4533 "On the Constitutional Procedure" could have resolved the situation if adopted by the Verkhovna Rada, but the Parliamentary Committee on Legal Policy rejected amendments to provide for a single commission to select judges for the Constitutional Court. This shows that the President does not want to lose influence over the selection of judges of the Constitutional Court, who would perhaps help him to win decisions that benefit his political agenda in the future. In the autumn of 2021, the Presidential Selection Commission held a competition for the Constitutional Court, during which the Commission recommended the appointment of two new judges to replace Tupytsky and Kasminin. As stated above, the President does not have the power to dismiss judges of the Constitutional Court, thus, legally judges Tupytsky and Kasminin continue to hold office until the end of their terms (May and September 2022, respectively). The appointment of two new judges of the Constitutional court would lead to a situation where four judges hold two positions. Such a situation would undermine the legitimacy of the institution and any of its decisions. Despite appeals and joint statements from leading NGOs, Volodymyr Zelensky appointed new judges, but the CCU itself refused to swear them in, thus maintaining its own legitimacy. However, this is only a temporary solution to the problem, as a comprehensive one requires legislative changes to eliminate the possibility of political influence on judges by introducing a new selection procedure, as recommended by the Venice Commission.

Prosecution — a core institutional battlefield between the existing patronal system and fundamental systemic reform

If the prosecution is a core institution in preserving the patronal state, then reforming it is necessary to fix the system as a whole irreversibly. As analyzed earlier in this section, the prosecution has a very bad institutional history in post-Soviet societies. In the Soviet Union, by Stalin's design, it was a core institution to secure general repression and fear. Subsequent post-Soviet Ukrainian regimes failed to dismantle this horrible organization and its excessive mandate to investigate, i.e., to harass arbitrarily. Thus, its control has remained a key issue in the political fight for power. Crucially, the Ukrainian state in the Yushchenko period missed a uniquely favorable opportunity to cut the prosecution's strong ties to the Donetsk clan (controlled by Yanukovich and Akhmetov), thereby weakening the clan's institutional position. Because of this missed opportunity, when Yanukovich became president, the prosecution remained a powerful ready-made tool, a de facto criminal organization, which in his hands was used to exert monopolistic control over potential rivals, i.e., to establish a single power pyramid. And, like Kuchma, he tried but ultimately failed to consolidate it.

The reform of the prosecution in the post-Euromaidan situation thus became critical, but also more difficult because by now its new role in the mafia-like political and business elites became much more deeply entrenched than it would have been if the core reforms had come right after Ukraine had gained independence, or even after the Orange Revolution. As much as Timoshenko at the time was responsible for the economic mismanagement, in this area reform should clearly have been initiated by the president, which he critically failed to do. We should also note that the international and NGO pressure at the time was also much weaker than in 2014, as people's understanding of the *real* systemic features was more limited than it is in the current period.[70]

In 2014, the pressure on the leadership to dismantle the powerful prosecution increased, in part because of the very ostentatious role that Pshonka, the prosecutor general under Yanukovich, had played. The normative knowledge of how prosecution should be structured in a liberal state was mainly on the side of the Council of Europe, which runs its largest field operation in Ukraine. In the Parliament, the President's junior coalition partner, *Samopomich,* as well as RPR in civil society, were strong partners in this endeavor. The EUAM and European Commission's capacity concerning the design and execution of prosecutorial reform was modest in this period, but later it gradually grew. One of the authors of this paper, at that time head of EUAM, strongly advocated for there to be a primary focus and radical reform in this area, but at the time EU institutional support was insufficient. US Ambassador Geoffrey Pyatt, with the strong backing of US Vice President Joe Biden, was perhaps the strongest political advocate for prosecution reform.

For President Poroshenko the risks were high in this situation, as he must have clearly remembered the consequences of leaving the prosecution in the hands of the gang of Yanukovich during the Yushchenko era. His response was similar to his handling of the judicial reform: try to yield enough to satisfy the donors, coalition partners, and civil society while not to such an extent that he would lose control over this critical institution in the fight for political power as well as losing his own "pyramid". Legislation thus moved in the right direction, but his appointments

---

70 We also are due self-criticism on this, since the Blue Ribbon Commission that I set up also missed advocating for dismantling the excessive power of the prosecution and establishing a balance with the judiciary in our recommendations in 2004-5. Nobody else whom we could recall pointed out the critical importance of the rule-of-law reforms at the time. See: "A New Wave of Reform: proposal for the President." *Blue Ribbon Commission.* UNDP Ukraine, 2005. Available at: https://www.researchgate.net/publication/284189647_Pr oposal_for_the_President_A_New_Wave_of_Reform/link/564f92e008ae1ef92 96eaee8/download and "Ukraine must reform fast. UN Team says." *The Guardian,* January 13. Available at: https://www.theguardian.com/world/20 05/jan/13/ukraine.iantraynor?CMP=gu_com.

were such that he would not lose personal control over the prosecutor general, effectively safeguarding against any radical changes in the organization of the prosecution. His first appointments were not successful, and he had to fire them eventually due to pressure from the reformers listed above, but he did gain critical time. His first two prosecutor generals did as much as possible to delay the reforms outlined by law. By the time Yuriy Lutsenko was appointed, Poroshenko's room to maneuver domestically and internationally was large enough to be able to appoint his core political confidante without even the legally necessary preconditions.[71]

In this situation, although reform proved to be mostly cosmetic, it did open the door to further, more substantial changes. Perhaps most importantly, the constitutional provision about the *general oversight* power of the prosecutors was eliminated and its role was reduced to managing—thus not actually conducting— investigations. Although research shows that this was not immediately put into practice[72] and the excessive power of the prosecutor remained in place in criminal proceedings, legal change now enables reformers to closely monitor the implementation of the new legal provisions and push for real improvements. The legal changes opened the door to dismantling the system over time.

Four other important elements of the reform have been tried that, together with the aforementioned reduction of the roles of prosecutors, could have prepared the ground for radically altering the system over time. They have all been successfully neutralized by entrenched interests, but the door is still open for further change.

First, the *excessive centralization* of the institution of prosecution needs to be dismantled in order to make the system less prone to top level political or corrupt interventions, as well as

---

71 For Lutsenko's lack of formal qualifications for the job it was necessary to change the law. "Ukraine appoints Poroshenko ally with no legal experience as top prosecutor." *Reuters*, May 12, 2016.

72 Romanov, R. *Study Report: The Role of the Public Prosecutor at the Pre-Trial Stage of Criminal Proceedings*. The Renaissance Foundation, 2015.

interventions of local strong interests. Here, progress has been very minor and inconsequential.

Second, Ukraine's prosecutorial force, thanks to its Soviet heritage, is excessively large. Legislation has reduced this force from 18,000 to 10,000. Only a small part of this reduction was implemented during the Poroshenko presidency. The initial progress was lukewarm. Simultaneously, in an attempt to shake up the system Deputy Prosecutor General David Sakvarelidze, a close long-term associate of Saakashvili from Georgia, initiated a revamping of the organization's structure that aimed to create larger territorial units and simultaneously *reduce the number of prosecutors*. He also launched a new appointment system. The active resistance of the prosecutor general at the time, as well as the failure of the government to allocate the funds necessary for the salary increases envisaged by the Law on the Office of the Public Prosecutor, caused this effort to only very partially succeed. The number of prosecutors has, over time, decreased, but the system was not cleaned up, partly because the extremely low salaries at the time only attracted either the incompetent or those who had the aim of enriching themselves through the abuse of their station. This happened despite the strong participation of civil society in monitoring the selection process.

Salary reform for prosecutors was delayed in this period, causing serious damage to the reform in the critical period of the bottom-up cadre renewal. The 2015 salary adjustments mentioned earlier were only allotted funding in 2017.[73] While the delay can, to some extent, be justified by the tough budgetary situation in those difficult times, not abiding by the law and not providing the necessary funds critically slowed down the personnel changes in the prosecution, thus reducing what should have been a radical reform of prosecutorial culture to a barely significant minimum.

The elimination of *general oversight,* the loosening of centralization, the half-hearted reorganization (including cadre change),

---

73   See: Governmental Decree №657 dated August 30, 2017 "On amendments to some decrees of the Cabinet of Ministers of Ukraine concerning payment of work of the prosecution employees."

salary reform, and the newly introduced — but so far timid —
internal controls are changes that have not yet resulted in a defini-
tive altering of the role of the prosecution in Ukraine towards one
that resembles liberal democracies. Yet, these are leakages in the
system that not only leave hope for further gradual change, but
may have actually prepared the ground for it, and perhaps even
for a radical change, if and when the political constellation becomes favorable. The above-quoted study by Roman Romanov
and his team at the Renaissance Foundation also shed light on the
fact that changing such an enormous, entrenched organization,
which is critical to maintaining the existing system of governance,
is a really difficult job if it is not done as a radical overhaul. At the
same time, the legal changes that we are mentioning here are likely contributing to the gradual erosion of the excessive power of
prosecution. Also, citizens' awareness of how the system is supposed to function, and accordingly their expectations, also contribute to a slow change of the system.[74] And as we discuss in the
subsequent sub-sections, the appearance of investigative functions
in NABU as well as in the SBI are also pushing the prosecutors
towards a slow change in their factual roles to catch up with the
ones written in the law.

During Zelensky's presidency, the international pressure to
move ahead with prosecutorial reform remained intense. Also, he
first appointed a prosecutor general, Rouslan Ryaboshapka,
whose determination to move ahead with reforms was strong.
Ryaboshapka addressed some of the key issues listed here, such as
the incompetent, corrupted, and oversized army of prosecutors.
His key method was starting with a complete overhaul of the staff
of the Office of Prosecutor General, then repeating the process
with the regional and local offices.[75] It is noteworthy that, unlike
the earlier attempts of Sakvarelidze, he tried to address the problem of the organization "head-on" from the center. His first phase
of reform was indeed sweeping, but after barely half a year, he

---

74   Point emphasized by Roman Romanov in a conversation with the author.
75   "Rule of Law Reform After Zelenskyi's First Year. A Return to Business as
Usual in Ukraine." *DGAP Analysis*, May 26, 2020. Available at: https://dgap.o
rg/en/research/publications/rule-law-reform-after-zelenskyis-first-year

was voted out in the parliament from office.[76] It is unclear if this was because of his reforms, his reluctance to pursue Poroshenko's (undoubtedly political) case, or the unfortunate situation of Ukraine being pressured by US President Trump to investigate presidential candidate Joe Biden's son. It was likely a combination of all of these that contributed to his dismissal.

Where Ryaboshapka has been criticized by the expert community is that he did not show strong intention to decentralize the system internally. One can, however, be sympathetic to his dilemma: if he, as a reformist Prosecutor General could have prevailed, he would have been more effective in a rather more centralized system. And ideally, decentralization could have come in the next phase of reform. This is admittedly a very fragile strategy, because who knows if an entrenched PG would be willing to give up part of his power even after successful initial reforms. This belongs to the sequencing question of reforms, which has no one-size-fits-all solution; both successful and unsuccessful reforms have had different sequencing configurations. This is not to deny that there is a critical difference between political leaderships that are committed to reforms with a clear vision of attainable goals, and those whose aim is only to muddle through and maintain and increase their personal power.

His successor has been much more of a secure hand without reform ambitions. Nevertheless, some much less radical changes continued, such as the attestation process. A very large number of prosecutions got through the attestation/vetting process.[77] The numbers are not clear, but certainly more than 2,000 of them failed some of the levels of competence testing and some have resigned. Some prosecutors didn't even try to meet the test. However, illustrating the incredibly organized nature of the unlawful web in the law enforcement and justice area, a very large number of prosecu-

---

76 "Ukraine prosecutor gets sacked, raising Europe concerns." *Euractiv*, March 6, 2020. Available at: https://www.euractiv.com/section/europe-s-east/news/ukraine-prosecutor-gets-sacked-raising-european-concerns/

77 Venedictova, I. "A New Vision for Ukraine's Prosecution Service." Atlantic Council. May 13, 2021. Available at: https://www.atlanticcouncil.org/blogs/ukrainealert/a-new-vision-for-ukraines-prosecution-service/

tors challenged the decisions at the courts and the early indication is that many are winning the cases. Thus, it is so far hard to say how much the reorganization and attestation will ultimately change the nature of the institutions.

The donors and activists are pushing to introduce the so-called "e-case management system", and it is now in the pipeline. This could erode the excessive hierarchy and centralization of the system, prone to strengthening corrupt networks.

One can hope that all the elements of change mentioned in this sub-section, plus the fact that prosecutors' salaries were, if not overhauled, at least significantly corrected, will slowly erode the excessive power of the prosecutors — but not without a new wave of deliberate institutional rearrangements. Without very precise further reforming interventions, the logic of the old system will likely prevail and get restored. A positive in the situation is that, since Ukraine is exposed to Western assistance, the influence of reform-minded donors remains large. However, as we have argued in many parts of this volume, reforms need to be applied in a smart way. And again, one can trust the learning process of the citizens themselves, that they will gradually expect more from the courts and about the road leading to them.

However, the know-how is there to make changes in each of the five areas mentioned in this section to pave the way for radical reforms that would change the balance of the criminal process, as well as tear apart the dense web of prosecutorial and judicial corruption.

State Bureau of Investigations

The need to establish an independent investigative state body first officially surfaced in the very first year of the independent history of Ukraine. A combination of the need to balance political power in the higher echelons of society, the fear that such an organ could be abused by the already powerful for political purposes, and bureaucratic and professional ineptitude, prevented the creation of such an office for a long time. Also, the excessive power of prosecution, central to the oligarchic state, could have been challenged by reconfiguring investigative roles. Finally, and perhaps ironically, in 2012 its establishment was decided in the Criminal Procedural Code, a quite high-quality legal document from the Yanukovich era that was greatly assisted by international expertise, particularly from the Council of Europe. The Council of Europe, at that time, was pushing for the State Bureau of Investigations to be established within five years. The extinguishing of the investigative functions of the Office of Public Prosecutor, at least by law from 2016, made the fulfillment of this function more urgent. However, the question loomed as to what its exact functions were, given that the task of investigation primarily rests with the police under the supervision of the Ministry of Internal Affairs.

The SBI was established to investigate crimes committed by public officials that do not fall under the jurisdiction of NABU.[78] Concerning questions related to clashes/overlaps of jurisdictions and the use of organizations for political gains also apply to the SBI, which has a large staffing ceiling of up to 1500 investigators.[79] On the one hand, if done well, creating this new institution is an opportunity to break with the Soviet (and post-Soviet) past and create institutions that conform to Western standards. On the other hand, there are again risks in the proliferation of large, overlapping institutions that can be misused for political purposes. Creating a good institution ultimately depends on leadership and honest effort.

The original selection of the leadership of SBI was already marred with controversy.[80] This was unsurprising as in the sys-

---

78 "Whereas NABU focuses on high-level corruption cases, the SBI will be mostly responsible for investigating those crimes by public officials not covered by NABU. For example, if a judge is implicated in a traffic hit-and-run or a high-ranking official orders election fraud, they must be investigated by the SBI". See: "The SBI: Ukraine's Civilian Security Sector reform will not be complete without it. Interview with EUAM national experts Vadym Chovgan and Ievgen Vorobiov." *EUAM Ukraine*, March 15, 2018. Available at: http://www.eu am-ukraine.eu/news/the-sbi-ukraine-s-civilian-security-sector-reform-will-no t-be-complete-without-it/

79 Ibid.

80 See: "Who will lead the State Bureau of Investigations?". *Antac*, November 17, 2017. Available at: https://antac.org.ua/en/analytics/who-will-lead-the-state -bureau-of-investigations/ and Petrenko, I. "State Bureau of Investigations:

temic environment of Ukraine, any executive would try to ensure the pliancy of the key law enforcement institutions, including this one. The same thing happened again in 2020 when the officially competitive selection process was basically fully manipulated.[81] The building up of the SBI in such an environment couldn't have been ideal. However, in spite of the controversies, donors and international supporters generally assess that SBI is not on a bad track as it becomes an important player of the law enforcement landscape of Ukraine. Whether over time they will become genuinely independent and not biased by the power-seeking aspirations of politicians remains to be seen.

Economic Security Bureau of Ukraine (ESBU)

One of the IMF's current conditions following the long-term struggle of the civil society and business community has been to establish this law enforcement agency. This would take away investigative mandates in the economic crime area from the tax police, SBI, prosecution, National Police, and SBU. The issues with this new agency demonstrate the whole kaleidoscope of other challenges described in this chapter. As it was envisaged, it was to become "an umbrella body to investigate all manner of economic crimes and serve as a platform for constructive dialog between the state and the business community".[82] The legislation also establishes a large personnel, without corresponding legislation reducing the functions and personnel of redundant agencies. As in the case of other agencies discussed here, the appointment of the head

will it be possible to create an independent and transparent authority?" in *Inside Ukraine*. Independent Centre for Policy Studies, January 31, 2018. Available at: http://icps.com.ua/assets/uploads/files/IU_75_ENG_2018_01_31_col%20(1)_2103.pdf

81   Sukhov, O. "Anti-corruption activists say head of Ukraine's 'FBI' appointed after fake contest." *Kyiv Independent*. January 1, 2022. Available at: https://kyivindependent.com/hot-topic/anti-corruption-activists-say-head-of-ukraines-fbi-appointed-after-fake-contest/

82   Tregubov, V. "Old problems threaten Ukraine's new Bureau for Economic Security." *Atlantic Council. Ukraine Alert,* October 14, 2021. Available at: https://www.atlanticcouncil.org/blogs/ukrainealert/old-problems-threaten-ukraines-new-bureau-of-economic-security/

of this one was again manipulated, and an old hand was appointed to build it up from the old and infamous State Fiscal Service (actually the tax police) — which leaves few chances for building a genuinely new corporate culture free of corruption and politicization. The Bureau's Civil Supervisory Board was also established in a way that was sharply criticized by civil society representatives. At the same time, the very establishment of such an organ may, over time, generate a useful supervisory function.

Security Service of Ukraine (SBU)

The issue of reforming the SBU received less public attention in the first period of the Revolution of Dignity than that of the public prosecution, although the misuse of the secret services has been another massive pillar of presidential patronal power in Ukraine and elsewhere in the former Soviet space. As part of the "silovik" sector was left with the minor coalition party after the Euromaidan, the presidential political camp felt that the "checks and balances in relation to the Ministry of Interior" necessitated that they not only keep this organization, but also maintain a wide mandate for it, causing it to overlap with the jurisdiction of other institutions. This broad mandate means the president of Ukraine essentially has the ability to collect "*kompromat*" on his potential political opponents or anyone else who falls under suspicion.

Gradually, the attention of reformers and foreign supporters got directed to depriving the SBU of functions such as anti-corruption investigations and fighting economic crimes. This is crucial for dismantling the patronal state and for establishing real checks and balances and the separation of powers. In addition, this is one of the conditions for the NATO accession plan. But such a reform will be as difficult to accomplish as the judicial one.

The international community has been arguing that the functions of the SBU should be clearly delineated, narrowing its jurisdiction to counterintelligence, counterterrorism, and the protection of state secrets. This found its way into the Law on National Security in June 2018. However, like in the case of the prosecutorial reform, as well as the fight against corruption, the law lacks proper implementation mechanisms that, absurdly, the SBU itself is supposed to draft. It is particularly important that the SBU's functions in anticorruption, organized crime fighting, and economic crimes investigation be clearly separated, but it is hard to do so if the organization itself is left to decide how the law should be implemented and when the president himself is interested in maintaining unduly broad mandates.

The new president had better chances of implementing such reforms earlier in his term rather than later, when the vested interests of his administration and the logic of power struggles will make it more difficult. Blueprints for reform are available, but since dealing with economic crime is the most lucrative criminal activity within the state apparatus, with the largest opportunity for extortion, the transfer of this power to another agency needs to be directed externally. However, two and a half years passed, and this important piece of rule-of-law reform is still not finalized. There is a new draft law on the SBU in the parliament that is supposed to clear the way to narrowing its mandate, but the chances for achieving this are not high, because currently the SBU, led by the president's close friend, is one of the main pillars not only in Zelensky's discretionary power, but also in the system of personal checks and balances that each patronal ruler has to build in his close circle.[83]

Moreover, new problems appeared on the horizon as the service tried to expand its surveillance-type powers through new legislation that invited harsh reactions from civil society, concerned with human rights.[84]

---

83   "The Security Committee finalized the text of the 'SBU-reform': key amendments are postponed until the new draft law." *Antac*, September 23, 2021. Available at: https://antac.org.ua/en/news/finalized-text-of-sbu-reform/

84   Coynash, H. "New bill on the Security Service is in breach of Ukraine's Constitution and human rights standards." *Kharkiv Human Rights Protection Group*, September 28, 2021. Available at: https://khpg.org/en/1608809587

Police

In 2014-15, police reform was exaggeratedly seen as the bright spot of the broader reform picture in Ukraine. However, the creation of the patrol police was mistakenly sold to the public as a major reform of the whole system. It followed in the footsteps of the Georgian patrol police reform, but with big differences. In Georgia the patrol police, in a very short time, replaced the road police and, mainly due to the completely new workforce and better pay, radically improved service. This reform was then followed by the less glamorous but important professional reforms. The Ukrainian police reform shared the PR part—it hired new, young, good-looking police, including women, and with better pay. But this was only very gradually introduced. This, in and of itself, would not have been a problem, since Ukraine is in a war and is a much larger country than Georgia, so the operation was inevitably more complex. However, it also took a very long time to replace the road police, so the two worked side-by-side for a long time—the new and modern next to the low paid and corrupt, but also in some areas more competent. Finally, the bigger problem was that this partial but still meaningful reform was not followed by any robust changes in other, more complex parts of the police system and the giant Ministry of Internal Affairs.[85] In Georgia, police were also dramatically downsized and IT staff systematically employed, but in Ukraine this process was also much more timid.

So, while patrol police in Georgia was the skillful opening salvo of a very radical and thorough reformation in policing, which gained popular support for reform, in Ukraine it has re-

---

85 This concerns the whole law enforcement area, including those parts that do not belong under the Ministry of Internal Affairs. See: Interview with Kęstutis Lančinkas, the Head of the EU Advisory Mission in Ukraine, December 13, 2018. Available at: https://www.radiosvoboda.org/a/29652816.html?fbclid=I wAR30YHVZ6mTgTHBj-leGsEmcO7rwc1Ilhulitf-uuwexruW1OUc85ERNxoA We quote: "Of course, we conduct analysis for our own purposes. We also utilize data from publicly available sources. And yes, we have some grounds for concern, observing a significant decrease in the level of trust among Ukrainian citizens towards the law enforcement system."

mained a PR exercise without depth. Some results of the reform have so far been maintained, such as a lower level of corruption in the new patrol police, who have over time acquired basic policing skills, though there is some anecdotal evidence that some in their ranks are in fact steadily growing more corrupt. Also, the EUAM mission has contributed to certain changes such as rationalization of police structure in rural areas in order to become less bureaucratic and more service oriented. The EUAM's assistance in police training and building connections to European colleagues may also have a long-term impact on police attitudes and organization.

Another fault of the Ukrainian reforms is that most officers who had been lustrated or screened out by attestation commissions soon managed to be restored by the courts – either because the latter are also corrupt, or because the process of firing was not duly arranged and supported legally. As we saw, this fighting back of the old has now also resurfaced in the case of fired prosecutors. Some other fired police officers also found new opportunities at business-managing agencies or other places with high opportunities for extortion.

Anti-oligarch legislation

In the autumn of 2021, the Parliament of Ukraine adopted the so-called "Law on De-Oligarchization", which was presented to society as the main tool in the fight against the oligarchs. The latter have a significant influence on Ukrainian politics – for example, most of the highest-rated TV channels are owned by oligarchs, and oligarchs' funding of political parties is a key part of the Ukrainian political system.

The law provides four criteria for determining who an oligarch is. To qualify as an oligarch, one must meet at least three of the following criteria: (1) active involvement in politics, (2) significant influence over media outlets, (3) being the ultimate beneficiary of a corporate entity, and (4) possessing proven assets exceeding $85 million (this threshold is subject to change as it aligns with the minimum subsistence level in Ukraine). Also, the law provides for the creation of a register of oligarchs and gives the president-led National Security and Defense Council the authority to establish and maintain this register. If a person is recognized as an oligarch, he will not be able to financially support political parties directly or through other individuals, or participate in the purchase of large-scale privatization objects. In addition, oligarchs must file the same declarations as civil servants under the Anti-Corruption Law. Most importantly, the law stipulates very broad and rather vague criteria for naming a person "an oligarch" that are currently met by lots of wealthy people, but only some of them will be picked on, so the process as a whole will be inevitably discretional.

The law had an immediate effect: ex-President Petro Poroshenko said he sold shares of his TV channels, and Rinat Akhmetov, who ranks first among the richest Ukrainians, said he was not an oligarch but an investor, and his highest priority was a fair competition and equal rules of the game for all market participants. The reluctance to be included in the register of oligarchs is understandable—it is very bad PR, which significantly damages reputation and has a lasting negative effect. However, this is as far as the law goes in its fight. It was criticized by civil society, which stated that it was not sound enough; it is difficult to fight the oligarchs with a law consisting of eleven articles. Instead, in order to truly fight the oligarchs, it is necessary to develop and strengthen appropriate state institutions, particularly the Antimonopoly Committee of Ukraine (hereinafter the AMCU), and introduce judicial reform, as the oligarchs use primarily corrupt courts to protect their monopolies. Former Speaker of Parliament Dmytro Razumkov also stated that it was possible to fight the oligarchs without a special law by improving antitrust and anti-corruption legislation.

Shortly after, the government developed a plan of "20 steps to combat the influence of oligarchs". Among the first steps presented in the plan is the implementation of the Strategy for the Development of Judiciary and Constitutional Justice for 2021—2023 (hereinafter the Strategy). However, Ukrainian NGOs working in the field of judicial reform state that the Strategy in its current form will not solve any problems of the judiciary and may even increase the influence of judicial officials of low integrity. It is also reported that the Strategy does not contain any clear criteria for achieving any of its goals, which could indicate its successful or unsuccessful implementation, but is richly dotted with the classical Ukrainian bureaucratic cliches such as "improvement", "expansion", "compliance", "optimization", etc. Among the main shortcomings of the presented document is that it provides for the limitation of the powers of public councils (PIC and PCIE), further strengthens the influence of judges of the unreformed judicial corporation, and expands the list of powers of the as-yet-unreformed HCJ.

Even more importantly, "fighting the oligarchs" is as bad a slogan as "fighting the corrupt officials (*korruptsionery*)" and for the same reasons: neither the LAO and patronalism, nor corruption, are vested in particular persons. Both are much broader and deep-rooted social phenomena that Magyar and Madlovics explain mostly with a lack of separation of spheres of social action — the political and market activities in the case of the oligarchs, and the political and communal ones in the case of corrupt officials. This phenomenon seems to be stubborn, so in order to get rid of the oligarchs, or rather turn them into normal business owners, a genuine reform should, first of all, establish sound and resilient institutional mechanisms compensating for the culture-grounded lack of separation, so that gradually it erodes this cultural inertia. The most general features of such mechanisms are transparency and straightforwardness, as opposed to the opaqueness and vagueness ("flexibility") that allow for discretion.[86] In this sense, the above-described legislation is a step back because, to the extent it really fights the oligarchs, it does so by strengthening the president's discretionary rule and by reinforcing the personal nature of systemic relationships characteristic of an LAO. Moreover, pluralism of oligarchs is, arguably, the essence of patronal democ-

---

86   Also pointed out by: Dzamukashvili, S. "Why is Ukraine's anti-oligarch bill so problematic?". *Emerging Europe*, November 21, 2021.; "With Russian troops massing on the border, Ukraine's Zelensky focuses instead on internal foes". *The Washington Post*. December 22, 2021; Rudik, K. "Ukraine's Anti-Oligarch Law: President Zelenskyy's populist power grab?". *Atlantic Council*. November 15, 2021.

racy, at least in the case of Ukraine. Elimination of independent oligarchs, not accompanied by the establishment of powerful, genuinely ideological and democratically organized political parties, may result in a patronal autocracy, as happened in Russia after 2000 (see Section 4 for further discussion on this important matter).

So, in the first political cycle since the Reform of Dignity, Ukraine has failed to make an ultimate turn towards a rule-of-law state. On the other hand, partial reforms serve as a useful basis for further reforms in case the political will emerges in the current cycle. Ukraine's international friends and think tanks should take stock of why the breakthrough reforms have not yet happened, and formulate with greater clarity their expectations towards the holders of power.

In the two-and-a-half years of Zelensky's presidency, fundamentally we have been witnessing the same "one-step-forward-one-step-back" pattern. The new presidential team does not have a clear change (systemic, long-term reform) strategy and acts reactively: wherever the international partners and reform-minded think-tank crowd pushes, they try to satisfy expectations. At the same time, they are eager not to act in a way that may weaken their power in the short term. In that sense, the Zelenskiy presidency is similar to the administration of his predecessor. Certainly, neither of the two has linked the question of reform to the long-term resilience of Ukraine against external threat as much as national interests should have dictated.

The main causes of these disappointing results were already described above: (a) the conflict of interests of the country's leader(s), (b) lack of strategy, and (c) wrong prioritization.

This is not to say that the international community can be completely exonerated for the lack of breakthrough reforms in the rule-of-law sectors. True, the most important international partners had, by 2014, learned a lot about the nature of the system in Ukraine, and thus concentrated on issues pertaining to the RoL. This has been a very positive development that needs to be recognized. However, implanting the RoL culture is a complex endeavor, and against this admittedly enormous challenge the international community has, for the most part, failed. Particularly regrettable is that the International Monetary Fund—a critical player for a country that was in desperate need of liquidity financing in 2014-15—has largely ignored dedicated professional expertise when establishing conditionality in the area of the RoL. It is positive that they wanted to apply conditionality in this area, but due to the lack of expertise they chose a rather formalistic approach by simply demanding the creation of the National Anti-Corruption Bureau. True, with the hindsight of eight (!) years, the international community's insistence yielded first in the creation of the Specialized Anti-Corruption Prosecutor's Office at the end of 2015, and then the High Anti-Corruption Court in 2019. At the very least, one should realize that it was never asked if it is the right thing to resort to a proliferation of law-enforcement organizations rather than exert pressure to radically overhaul the existing system of prosecution and delivery of justice. The situation also tended more towards proliferation because the holders of power rightly believed that at the very least they could gain time, if not fully neutralize the new anti-corruption institutions. Thanks to the Sisyphean efforts of the international community and justice-oriented civil society organizations, the above-mentioned organizations still have the chance, after 8 years of wrestling, to finally become functional.[87] Still, the question remains if the Ukrainian society and its supporters were not better off if they concentrated on the reform of the existing institutions, rather than creating brand new ones, because those old institutions remain important pockets of resistance to reforms.

---

87   HACC has so far brought about convictions with an actual effect of imprisonment and confiscation of property in only 11 cases, involving 14 people. See: "Whom and for what the High Anti-Corruption Court sentenced in two years of work?". *Antac*, September 7, 2021. Available at: https://antac.org.ua/en/news/whom-and-for-what-the-high-anti-corruption-court-sentenced-in-two-years-of-work/

3. The Economy
Rent seeking versus profit seeking;
Eurasia versus Europe;
post-industrial versus industrial

In the last eight years, the Ukrainian economy underwent deep structural change. It has been a continuation of trends that can be traced back to the 1990s. However, after the Euromaidan, structural changes sped up, and in many cases (especially in the geographical mix of foreign trade) the fundamental systemic balances were triggered. In any case, we cannot yet state that profit-seeking overshadows rent-seeking: although substantial changes took place, the overall Ukrainian balance between these sectors described in the Introduction is likely to remain in the red.

Rent seeking versus profit seeking

By "profit", we refer to a kind of net income that is received in relation to creating a value recognized by a competitive market or a transparent public procedure ("value-adding rent"). This is posed in opposition to "rent", which is defined as net income generated by explicit (e.g., through subsidies) or implicit (e.g., through limitations on competition) redistribution of value ("value-subtracting rent"). In a political-economic sense, the former is rather associated with the open access order (OAO) that is based on competition, whereas the latter is characteristic of a limited access order (LAO) in which rents in the aforementioned meaning play a critically important role. Although, of course, some mode of rent-seeking can always be found under an OAO and, conversely, some competition (or, at least, value creation) is always present under a LAO. The hypothesis here is that the balance between the two activities matters.

Under an LAO, the rent-oriented business that is based on (formal or informal) privileges rightly fears that it will fail if deprived of them, therefore that business would support the status-

107

quo. Furthermore, it also upholds existing limitations on political competition too, because such a business would normally be connected to certain politicians and/or have its own political wings in the form of parties or factions. Under an OAO, the profit-seeking business feels more competitive in open markets, and thereby fears a rent-seeking one that could outperform it in a "competition" for privileges. Of course, no business would mind having privilege itself, but there is always a risk that once that privilege is given, that same privilege can eventually go to a competitor. Besides, unlike rent seeking, value-adding business is a positive-sum game, in which a win-win mutual agreement about the rules of the game is normally reachable and can be made self-enforceable or be enforced by the participants without an "arbiter".

For these reasons, a certain balance between rent-seeking and profit-seeking can be self-sustainable or even self-propelling, and, therefore, not only characterize the existing social order, but also be one of the predictors of that social order's further evolution. Namely, if profit seeking already prevails under an LAO, that aspect of economic life can become one of the driving forces for the entire system's opening.

Unfortunately, estimating the balance between rent and profit seeking in a given system is not a routine exercise in contemporary economic literature. To the best of our knowledge, nobody has tried to undertake this type of research before. Therefore, the methodology discussed and used below is tentative.

Of course, much depends on the ability of businesses to organize in collective action in support of their best interests: history is full of examples of small but well-organized groups able to mobilize large resources and win privileges at the expense of others, even under a mature OAO (the metallurgical industry in the United States is but one recent example). Unfortunately, this ability is hard to assess empirically.[88]

---

88 Industry concentration (measured by the Herfindahl-Hirschman index, or otherwise) can serve as a proxy, if considered with other data such as the past experience of the respective sector.

The resources at the disposal of rent-seekers can be approximated by the volume of rents, or by the total value added (formal) by the respective industries. The former may be more precise in the sense that it captures the actual amounts in question — it can be assumed that motivation for rent-seeking is roughly "proportional" to them. However, these amounts are hard to estimate, and the low precision of these estimates can cancel out the precision of the whole method. At the same time, the second gauge approximates the relative influence of an industry, which that industry can then use (or, rather, abuse) for rent-seeking activities. Ideally, one should probably take a product of both, although such a number can hardly have any meaning in itself.

The resources available for profit seeking could be best approximated by cash flows (and then compared to rents) or, similarly, the value added. Another problem is, however, that small businesses only report their total sales.

Unfortunately, available data are scarce and scattered. The World Bank has performed a useful exercise concerning "crony capitalism" in Ukraine that estimated the share of politically connected firms in the country at about 20%.[89] This means that their share in the total amount of firms' true profits can be several times more, despite poorer reported performance analyzed in that paper. As anecdotal evidence suggests (and the report itself admits), their real profits are much more likely to be concealed in tax havens. Normally, such firms are monopolies or close to it. They also receive favorable regulations, state procurement orders, etc., hence their profitability should be higher than the average, politically unconnected firm. However, all of these considerations are much too vague for any concrete conclusions and estimations.

Another study, performed by the Institute for Economic Research and Policy Consulting (IER), is devoted to the shrinkage of major rent sources in Ukraine that resulted from post-Maidan reforms. Particularly in the natural gas sector, the elimination of

---

89 "Crony capitalism in Ukraine: impact on economic outcomes." Washington, D.C.: *World Bank Group*, 2018. Available at: http://documents.worldbank.org/curated/en/125111521811080792/Crony-capitalism-in-Ukraine-impact-on-economic-outcomes.

price arbitrage and production-share agreements with crony firms reduced rents to about 0.3% of GDP; in public procurement, between 0.3% and 0.8%. Table 1 below presents an estimated overview of some major rent sources from before the Revolution of Dignity and in 2018 (which should not constitute a major difference with the present moment because no major reforms were implemented and could bring results since then), which we managed to collect from various sources footnoted at the end of the table (unless specified, the source is the author's calculation based on government statistics from State Statistics Committee or the Treasury).

Table 1. Evolution of some major sources of rents in the Ukrainian economy

Source of Rent	Value at End of 1990s (or earliest available year)	Value Before the Revolution of Dignity (2013, if not dated)	Current Value (2018, if not dated)	Comment
State subsidies to firms (as % of GDP)	20%[90] (direct and indirect)	8% (including quasi-fiscal hidden subsidies)	0.9%	By now, hidden subsidies are largely eliminated
"Tax pit holes" own income (as % of GDP)	No data	2.2%[91]	~0.2%[92]	
Kickbacks in VAT refund (assuming	No data	1.0%	0%	Fully eliminated for law-obeying

90   Lunina, I., and Vincetz, V., "The Subsidisation of Ukraine's Enterprises." In *Ukraine at the Crossroads: Economics Reforms in International Perspective*, edited by Axel Siedenberg and Lutz Hoffmann, 118–32. Berlin–Heidelberg: Springer-Verlag, 1999.

91   According to the government's claims, Yanukovich's "licensed platforms" for tax evasion had a turnover of 300 billion UAH in 2013, or about 20% of GDP. Лямець С., "Арсеній Яценюк: Усі схеми попередньої влади ліквідуються". *Економічна правда*, May 14, 2014. Available at: https://www.epravda.com.ua /publications/2014/05/14/452304/ .

92   For 2017, based on an assessment of annual turnover at about 60 billion UAH. Дубровський В., Черкашин В., *Порівняльний аналіз фіскального ефекту від застосування інструментів ухилення/уникнення оподаткування в Україні*. Київ, Інститут соціально-економічної трансформації, 2017. Available at: ht tps://rpr.org.ua/wp-content/uploads/2018/02/Instrumenty-uhylyannya-vi d-splaty-podatkiv-2017-1.pdf .

Source of Rent	Value at End of 1990s (or earliest available year)	Value Before the Revolution of Dignity (2013, if not dated)	Current Value (2018, if not dated)	Comment
30% rate, as % of GDP)				firms
Share of the SOEs in total sales	Close to 100% in 1991	10.4%	7.3%	
Share of competitive markets (% of total sales)[93]	No data	42.7% (by 2014)	43.4% (by 2016[94])	

As one can see, the sources of rents, although substantially reduced, still remain vibrant, and those rents, especially from market power, probably still politically dominate over profits. The markets where rent-seeking is substantial still prevail in the economy; the shadow economy (represented mostly by the unregistered and concealed incomes of large businesses) persists; and corruption remains rampant. For example, while the subsidies to coal mining that used to be one of the main rent sources for Rinat Akhmetov's business empire were officially abolished (in fact, partly remaining), they were soon substituted by setting the inflated administrative price for Ukrainian coal using the formula "Rotterdam's exchange price + transportation cost to Ukraine", known as "Rotterdam+". In this way the energy market regulator bailed out Akhmetov's DTEK vertically integrated energy monopoly by imposing a high price burden on domestic commercial energy consumers (household prices remained regulated).

There is not yet any sign that vested interests have lost their political connections in such a way that their ability to influence the rules of the game for maximizing rents has been substantially restricted. It did happen in a few particular and important cases: tax authorities are no longer drafting tax legislation (although here

93 *Звіт Антимонопольного комітету України за 2015 рік.* Available at: http://www.amc.gov.ua/amku/doccatalog/document?id=122547 & *Звіт Антимонопольного комітету України за 2016 рік.* Available at: https://amcu.gov.ua/storage/app/sites/1/Docs/zvity/2016/AMCU_2016.pdf. Later data are not available.

94 Unfortunately, since this year the AMKU has discontinued publication of this important indicator.

we have an unfortunate partial reversal since 2019), the management of state procurements has become much more transparent (with the important exemption of military procurement, which, however, was recently reformed too—although other gaps appeared, notably in road construction) and largely unified, and a number of notoriously corrupt government bodies were eliminated or dramatically re-organized. A few dozen presumably clean and benevolent civil activists entered the legislature in 2014, and even more appeared in the new Rada of 2019.

However, the vast majority of MPs remain connected to business interests and/or are dependent on the leaders of engaged factions. Certain private firms and SOEs still keep strong connections to the executive branch, law enforcement, police, and secret service, which allow them to influence the enforcement and application of laws, by-laws, and informal rules. In 2021, two notorious rent-seeking initiatives that were lobbied for by the domestic industrialists for many years—privileges for the industrial parks and protectionism in state procurement—were voted into laws, although with the most odious norms screened out in the public discussion. The ruling party has adopted a semi-official ideology that panders to a mainstream desire for an active state role in economic development, opening further opportunities for rent seeking and political corruption.

Among the positive trends, we can admit some consolidation of a predominantly competitive—"non-oligarchic"—business community. At least three strong players of this sort appeared in Ukraine after the Revolution of Dignity: the Union of Ukrainian Entrepreneurs (SUP), and two "associations of associations"—the SME Platform, and the Ukrainian Council of Business (URB), not to mention informal clubs like "Business 100" or CEOclub. The National Business Platform, which has united them with the support of US-based think tank CIPE, has recently put forward ambitious goals, which, if implemented, could mostly open access to economic opportunities for all. At the same time, as usual, only some business interests are truly benevolent from the national perspective—others are ill-informed and/or harbor unrealistic expectations, or merely rent-seeking ones.

Volodymyr Zelensky's victory has brought about a number of further important reforms, including but not limited to a new, surprisingly transparent wave of privatization, and the introduction of the long-awaited land market. A number of earlier reforms have been continued and implemented, including the introduction of the natural gas and electrical power markets, implementation of the anti-BEPS[95] norms preventing aggressive tax planning, increasing transparency in defense procurement, and possible success in fighting some sophisticated VAT fraud schemes. At the same time, there is a possible backslide in the procurement sector, especially in medicine and road construction—both spheres became very important due to the COVID-19 pandemic and the "Big construction" program of Zelensky, respectively. Corporate governance of the major SOEs and the NBU became subject to several scandals that may have involved corruption. Although no signals of extortion in the VAT refund have come so far, the delays in this process have been renewed. And some of the tax legislation clearly increased the number of discretion opportunities, which could further boost corruption there. Contradictory processes are ongoing in customs reform, with fights over violations that are worth many billions of USD. However, none of these processes and actions has brought measurable effects so far.

In sum, after the beginning of the Revolution of Dignity, the balance of influence between rent-seeking and profit-seeking businesses has substantially shifted toward the latter, but has not yet triggered a fundamental change in the entire system. The post-2019 record is rather ambiguous so far, but if the current trend continues, we see a substantial threat of an increase in rent seeking related to state interventionism and dirigisme.

Socioeconomic shifts

Although immediate short-term changes in the fundamental balance look insufficient for any qualitative conclusions, the long-

---

95   BEPS refers to Base Erosion and Profit Shifting. The BEPS (precisely speaking, anti-BEPS) plan by OECD is aimed against aggressive tax planning that is used for tax avoidance by multinational corporations.

term structural trend works against the main rent-oriented industries and toward real value-adding. This issue deserves a special separate study, but we can give a few examples that illustrate this statement. Above, in Table 1, the most impressive numbers concern subsidies to firms. Two diagrams (Figure 1) illustrate the evolution of foreign trade (with goods and services taken together) during the years of independence. As one can see, the exports to CIS countries (predominantly Russia) have decreased in the post-Maidan years as sharply as it did right after gaining independence. As a result, these exports and imports are now less than half as much as the amount going to and coming from the EU. In 2018,[96] only 18% of all exports went to the successor states of the former Soviet Union. Russia, for the first time, ceased to be Ukraine's main trading partner.

Figure 1.   Export and import of the goods and services by main neighboring groups of countries

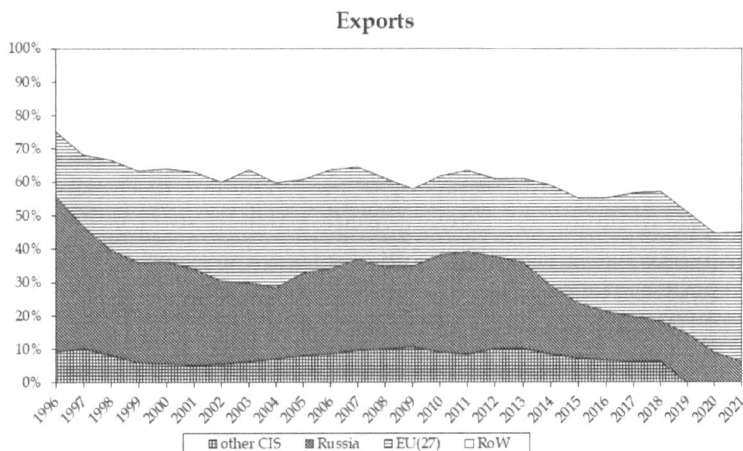

96   Unfortunately, more recent data are not available because the national statistics body has discontinued the respective series — which is, however, telling in and of itself.

Imports

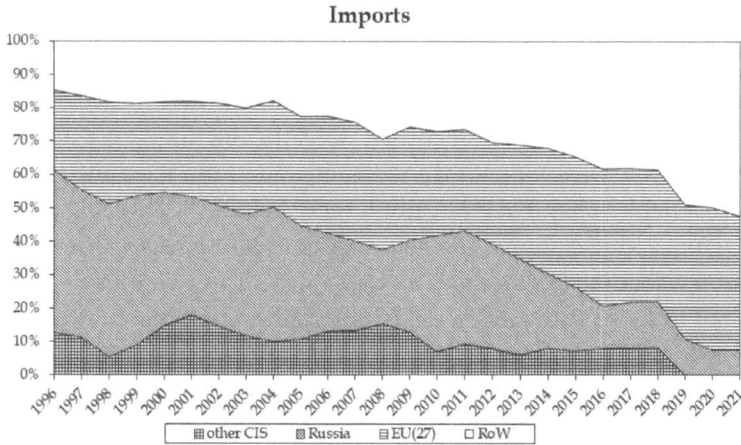

Source: author's calculations based on data from the State Statistics Service of Ukraine (DerzhComStat).

Of course, the higher share of EU exports does not, in itself, drive a country towards an OAO. However, dependence on the CIS markets often does the opposite, as access to them serves as a source of rents for obsolete and non-competitive post-Soviet firms, and further facilitates corruption, like the notorious gas-trading cartels that are mostly only possible among post-Soviet states. At the same time, firms already selling in the EU and other competitive markets abroad should, as a rule, feel less fear of opening up to competition and the impersonal application of norms, as compared to firms selling in the CIS. This rule, however, is not iron-clad, and thus should be taken cautiously. Numerous such firms actually belong to "oligarchs" and can compete mostly due to explicit subsidies (like in poultry production), privileged input prices (as in the ferrous-alloy industry), or ample opportunities for large-scale tax avoidance and evasion.

In the meantime, new sectors have emerged that work completely outside the rent-seeking "oligarchic" economy. The main — but not only one — is ICT, which already produces at least 5% of the Ukrainian GDP, more than mining, although still less than half that of manufacturing. However, unlike stagnating industrial production, the ICT sector grows by about 20% annually—so that its contribution to economic growth is already about one third.[97]

These dramatic shifts in the Ukrainian economy's structure, as well as the persistence of strong trends in the industrial mix from mining and manufacturing towards modern agriculture, services, and post-industrial sectors, are long-term ones and hardly reversible. They have already largely helped in reducing rent-seeking activities due to the very nature of post-industrial sectors, and by lending themselves to trade with OAO countries compared to those with an LAO. It is just as important that they result in gradual but inevitable demographic and social consequences that eventually have decisive impacts on electoral patterns, and, respectively, are manifested in politics and policies.

During Ukraine's first two post-Soviet decades, resource extraction and processing sectors (coal, metallurgy), as well as energy and industrial manufacturing, had become largely monopolized by business-owners who linked their wealth to direct and indirect state subsidies and to preferential tax regimes secured by lobbying the government.[98] The enterprises that these "oligarchs" controlled were generally located in Ukraine's eastern regions (Donetsk, Luhansk, Dnipropetrovsk, and Zaporizhzhia oblasts), where the country's Soviet-era heavy industries had been located. These regions generated most of Ukraine's export revenues; they were heavily populated, generally Russian-speaking, and supported the Communist Party or, later, the Party of Regions. Conversely, the Ukrainian-speaking, relatively poorer western regions voted for "Orange" parties (i.e., Yushchenko's "Our Ukraine", or Tymoshenko's "Batkivshchyna").

However, during the decade preceding Euromaidan, this stereotypical picture of Ukraine gradually changed: the economies of

---

97   The industry's analysts operate with significantly higher numbers, saying that the national statistics underestimate real proceedings that often go underreported. This is probably the case, given that immaterial exports are easily concealable. So, the numbers provided should be treated as conservative estimates.

98   Hawrylyshyn, O. *The Political Economy of Independent Ukraine: Slow Starts, False Starts, and a Last Chance?* London: Palgrave Macmillan, 2017.

several cities in the western region began to grow, benefitting from the inheritance of Soviet-era educational centers that excelled in mathematics and engineering, and (ironically) from a dearth of industrial enterprises worth privatizing. For over two decades, Lviv had not spawned a single national-level oligarch (unlike every other large Ukrainian city). This region had survived through entrepreneurship, and its "de novo" firms (primarily in the IT and tourism sectors) had developed strong horizontal networks and organizational cultures well-suited to a post-industrial economy. The "de novo" sector was first composed of small- and medium-sized businesses, and later (in select cases) included quite substantial firms (those with over one thousand employees). It was concentrated primarily in the large cities of Ukraine's western and central regions, and by the late 1990s employed up to one-third of Ukraine's workforce. Since the 2000s, the share of such companies in the overall economy has been growing.[99]

The distinguishing characteristic of the entrepreneur-founders of these "de novo" enterprises (who were interviewed by one of the contributors, Mychailo Wynnyckyj, throughout the 2000s)[100] has been their radical skepticism of the state as an institution and their contempt for other business owners who accumulated capital through insider privatization or other forms of interaction with the state. Furthermore, these owners have exhibited an ethic of social responsibility that is neither paternalistic nor patrimonial, but rather reflects civic-mindedness: they view Ukraine as the country in which they have *lived*, nor merely as a territory on which to make profit. Their entrepreneurial *ethos* has been reflect-

---

99 Wynnyckyj, M., *Institutions and Entrepreneurs: Cultural Evolution in the 'De Novo' Market Sphere in Post-Soviet Ukraine*. University of Cambridge, 2003. Available at: https://pdfs.semanticscholar.org/ac6d/d4946a2fa63fe19975f26b 80fd533857e02a.pdf.
100 In 2001, Mychailo Wynnyckyj conducted fifty-three interviews with "de novo" business founders in Kyiv, Lviv, and Donetsk as part of his dissertation research. Thereafter, beginning in 2003, Wynnyckyj taught courses at the Kyiv-Mohyla Business School, where many of his students were "de novo" business owners. He was part of the team that founded the Presidents' MBA program (exclusively for business owners) in 2007.

ed in everyday business practices: horizontal management, self-reliance, civic activism, and rules-based relations with the state.

In contrast, the cities of the east, from which Ukraine's "oligarchs" built their post-Soviet economic empires, began to shrink. Statistics are always difficult to judge in Ukraine because of its massive shadow economy (said to be almost 50% of total GDP during the Yanukovych period).[101] However, one thing is clear: individuals tend to migrate to areas where economic opportunities are prevalent and higher quality of life can be secured. It is therefore notable that, according to a UN Habitat 2012 study of the top ten fastest-shrinking cities in the world (!),[102] four were Ukrainian, and all were located in the eastern part of the country. Dnipro (formerly Dnipropetrovsk) topped the list as the city with the world's fastest rate of population shrinkage (a decline of 16.78% projected between 1990–2025); Donetsk was third, and Zaporizhzhia fourth in this global ranking. As a result of Russian aggression, Donetsk has been occupied along with the urban-industrial agglomeration around it, while the other cities in the East appeared to be risky places for investment and life. Yet, even prior to 2014, the structure of Ukraine's economy had begun to shift fundamentally. The heavy industries of the east were gradually losing both their attractiveness to the population and their significance as economic engines.

It is notable that the relative decline of the Ukrainian east, and the improvement of living standards in the western and central regions, did not magnify Ukraine's traditional geographic political cleavage as described in Section 5, devoted to societal change.

---

101 Vinnichuk, I., Ziukov, S., "Shadow Economy in Ukraine: Modelling and Analysis." *Business Systems and Economics*, No. 2, 2013, 141–152.

102 UN-Habitat's State of the World's Cities 2012/2013 ranking counts cities that had populations over 750,000 in 1990. In a similar study, with a time range of 2005–2014, two Ukrainian cities were ranked in the top ten global shrinking cities: Makeyevka (Donetsk oblast) and Dnipro. See Allen, K., "Shrinking Cities: Population Decline in the World's Rust-belt Areas." *Financial Times*. June 16, 2017. Available at: http://mirror.unhabitat.org/pmss/listItemDetails.aspx ?publicationID=3387.

Partly as a result of the sudden reorientation of Ukrainian firms' export markets from east to west, and also due to the abrupt diminution of the previous dominance of financial-industrial groups, Ukraine witnessed its second (after the late 1990s) start-up boom after the Euromaidan.[103] Three sectors may be identified as particularly entrepreneurial: export-oriented information technology, consumer product provision, and service provision for the domestic market. In the first case, programmers and managers of outsourcing companies, which had been established during the 2000s to serve North American and EU clients, used their accumulated experience and social capital to grow their businesses rapidly and to establish new companies that gradually shifted Ukraine's IT sector from project outsourcing to the provision of full-cycle technology services and (in some cases) ready products for the World market.[104]

Outside the technology sector, sparked by the drastic devaluation of the country's currency (which suddenly made imports exorbitantly expensive), Ukraine experienced an explosion of domestic consumer product and service provision. Examples include overnight delivery services, small businesses sewing clothes, manufacturing furniture, restaurants providing unique thematic ambiances, etc. For the entrepreneurs who established these businesses, and the consumers who purchased their offerings (i.e., the "creative class" employees of Ukraine's "de novo" economy), the previously entrenched system of neo-feudal rents, hierarchical government, and widespread corruption was an affront to their basic values. Self-realization, individual rights, transparency, rule-based government, and perhaps most importantly, the dignity afforded by Western social structures were principles for which they proved willing to make sacrifices in 2013–14 and thereafter.

---

103 Hulli, E. "Ukraine: The Next Startup Nation." *Medium*, August, 2017. Available at: https://medium.com/startup-grind/ukraine-the-next-startup-nation-d81e 0b7cffcc.

104 For example, see Ternovyi, D., "10 Ukrainian Startups that are Revolutionizing the Tech Industry." *Ignite*, November 29, 2018. Available at: https://igniteouts ourcing.com/publications/best-ukrainian-it-startups/.

All of this has largely contributed to the growth of the Ukrainian "creative class" as described in the Section 5.

Therefore, although we cannot accurately assess the real balance between rent seeking and profit seeking in Ukraine's contemporary economy, we can confidently state that:

1. Rent seeking has substantially shrunk, although it may still dominate in some areas.
2. The foreign trade mix has dramatically, and probably irreversibly, shifted out of the CIS and towards the EU.
3. New sectors and "de novo" firms have emerged and strengthened rapidly.
4. These factors have changed Ukraine's social structure (with the emergent creative class expanding) and economic geography (from east to west) with respective social and political consequences—these processes appear irresistible and irreversible.

4. Political institutions
Vertical of power vs. checks and balances

The balance between a vertical of power and the system of checks and balances, along with their respective trends, are of paramount importance not only from our theoretical framework's perspective, but also for the very existence of independent Ukraine. As Magyar and Madlovics rightly admit, under a patronal democracy, revolutions occur from time to time as a check against authoritarian consolidation—and from this perspective the Revolution of Dignity was not an exception. However, if it should fail laying the foundations for more institutionalized checks and balances, a new attempt at building a single-pyramid regime is likely, and would probably result in a new revolution or something alike, now with disastrous consequences because it would certainly be used by Russia for an assault on Ukrainian independence and territorial integrity.

In this section we examine the course of events, the changes that occurred, and the observed trends from the perspective of systemic processes that have or have not been brought out by the Revolution of Dignity and subsequent developments.

Brief timeline of events

Unlike after a typical "color revolution", in which the winner is an already established politician ready to power that only needs to be conceded by an incumbent predecessor, Ukraine after Yanukovich's escape had a vacuum of power, with only the Parliament remaining legitimate. After the parliamentary-presidential Constitution was restored (in a legally doubtful way, though a Parliamentary vote) on February 21st, Alexander Turchinov was elected as Speaker and, according to this version of the Constitution, acting President. Arseniy Yatseniuk was appointed Prime Minister, again according to the Constitution. Still, their legitimacy was incomplete until the early Presidential elections that were held in May and brought pro-Maidan oligarch and major politician Petro

Poroshenko to power. Yatseniuk retained his PM position until early 2016.

Together, they were a typical example of Crane Brinton's revolutionary "moderate reformers". Both were capable and experienced politicians representing the pro-Western wing of the oligarchic class (the LAO beneficiaries).

Poroshenko can be defined (in Magyar and Madlovics's terms) as an oligarch, however his main business — the confectionary company Roshen — was created and expanded without major state support in a highly competitive sector. Although his few other businesses were not so market-oriented, this is a stark difference from most other oligarchs except, arguably, Igor Kolomoisky. However, the latter, even while in conflict with the state, benefited from highly suspicious schemes, some of which are now prosecuted in the USA — this could hardly be possible without having strong political connections. Poroshenko, meanwhile, was never caught being involved in scheming of such scale.

Besides, by the time of the election Poroshenko had been a public politician for more than 15 years in a row. He started in Victor Medvedchuk's Social-Democratic Party, then unsuccessfully tried his own Solidarnost political project that eventually merged into Nikolay Azarov's Party of Regions. However, in a few years Poroshenko took a clear pro-Western stand, and then became one of Yushchenko's key supporters and an active leader of the Orange Revolution. Then, however, he served for less than a year in the position of Minister of Economy in Azarov's Cabinet during the Yanukovich era; but later he played an active part in the Revolution of Dignity. So, among the oligarchs he was (and remains) the most pro-Western and "progressive" in terms of the systemic transformation — although still remains a patronal, pragmatic, and rent-seeking clan leader.

Arseniy Yatseniuk, despite his young age (he celebrated his 40th birthday as PM) was an experienced politician in the "pyramid politics" of the patronal democracy. While lacking his own clan, Yatseniuk successfully served in a number of "pyramids" of others' and retained good relationships with a number of key persons in the Ukrainian "System". He made a career in the state apparatus, making a name for himself in 2004 when he, as acting Head of the NBU, successfully navigated the banking and monetary system through the turbulence of the Orange Revolution. After that, he took two Ministerial positions in the Orange Cabinets, then unsuccessfully ran for the presidency in 2010 (his initial success was soon undermined by an awkward campaign, allegedly sabotaged by managers imposed by the oligarch Victor Pinchuk), and remained one of the alternatives to Yanukovich since then, although with a rating in low double digits due to his insufficient personal attractiveness to the voters. Even his role as one of the formal leaders of the Euromaidan (note that they were not actual leaders, unlike during the Orange Revolution) did not help him much in gaining popularity.

Having won the Presidential election in 2014 with an overwhelming majority in the first round, Poroshenko nevertheless failed to create a pro-President majority in the Verkhovna Rada with the block of his name (Block Petro Poroshenko, BPP), and had to share power in a broad coalition with Yatseniuk, representing his own party, the Peoples' Front (PF), and a couple of smaller political forces as well as single-district MPs. Still, in the subsequent political restructuring the coalition collapsed, and Poroshenko failed to fully control even his own BPP faction, but instead managed to replace Yatseniuk, who by then became utterly unpopular, with his long-time ally Volodymyr Groysman. However, the latter, contrary to initial expectations, emancipated and distanced himself from his former patron, although, unlike the situation in the Orange era, still didn't seriously compete with the President. After Poroshenko's defeat in the 2019 election (see below), Groysman created his own political project competing with his former patron's. Finally, Poroshenko's pyramid was successfully and peacefully removed from power through democratic elections, which is at best untypical for a patronal autocracy. Hence, premature conclusions about the successful re-building of a "single pyramid system" after the Revolution of Dignity, which were made by some observers, are proven patently wrong.

In reality, a second, more informal center of power emerged in this period, according to some observers: Minister of Interior

Arsen Avakov, representing the PF, which was the second largest faction in the Rada and somewhat more disciplined than the BPP. Fully in line with Hale's predictions, the existence of two competing powerful pyramid networks allowed a plurality of other, less powerful ones to co-exist and compete without being subordinated. At the same time, clashes between the formal and informal leaders during Poroshenko's presidency never reached the degree of fierceness that had been notorious during the "Orange period". This is partly due to the external threat and dependence on the West that discipline the Ukrainian elites, and partly due to personal factors: unlike Yulia Tymoshenko, Arseniy Yatseniuk, after the 2010 defeat, seemed to have given up his Presidential ambitions. Meanwhile, Volodymyr Groysman had neither his own political party nor enough political capital to challenge his former patron—he has just recently stepped out of the latter's political shadow. Besides, Poroshenko, Yatseniuk, and Groysman were much less inclined to public fighting, not to mention Avakov, who preferred to work behind the scenes.

Ukraine has arrived at the end of the post-Maidan political cycle with this imperfect situation: checks and balances were provided not so much by real segregation of powers, as in a classical democracy (see the Section 1 for analysis of deficiencies of the Constitution), but by a balance of political powers, which is the "second best" under patronal politics. Moreover, this balance was maintained partially due to the fear of a common enemy. But on the eve of the 2019 election year, all of the "old" political forces, and their leaders checking each other, together had a rating of less than 40%. As a result, a new force emerged from nowhere that handily filled this vacuum of trust, harvested the crop of dissatisfied voters, and destroyed that fragile balance of political powers.

Many observers in Ukraine and abroad rushed to explain these events as a plot of either the oligarchs, or the Kremlin, or both. However, the vacuum of trust and Poroshenko's convincing loss of the presidential race can mainly be attributed to three intertwined factors—all relevant to the subject of this study.

First, his lukewarm attitude to reforms grossly backfired. In Section 2, we already explained in detail the reasons that made the

President unable and unwilling to provide a breakthrough in the RoL, as well as turn the oligarchs into normal businesses by cutting them off from the state and depriving them of rents. Both are among the main demands of the Revolution, no less important than the Association Agreement with the EU. Moreover, the perpetrators of the Maidan and the thieves of Yanukovich were not persecuted during this period, fundamentally for political reasons as the President was seeking support among those oligarchs that were involved in the Yanukovich era. Corruption (and the failure of fighting it) was the most visible manifestation of these shortcomings. But instead of removing the wittingly corrupt officials (including the president's cronies),[105] Poroshenko started to fight with anti-corruption activists.

The second factor was the neglect of political-economic considerations in the creation of crisis-management policies. Ukraine was in dire straits in 2014, for objective reasons. This not only led to adverse consequences, such as the dramatic devaluation of the hryvnya, accompanied by a banking crisis, but also required resolute reforms aimed at the mitigation of rent seeking at all levels. At the same time, such belt-tightening reforms, including steep price increases for household energy, would hardly be popular. Therefore, to be politically sustainable they should be implemented top-down and packed with no less dramatic "popular" reforms — that restore fairness and open opportunities. Of course, the consequences of these unpopular policies should also be mitigated.[106] The elites should receive legitimacy and trust from the public through these softening measures before implementing such reforms, or at least concurrently, as was the case in Georgia.

---

105 Indeed, punishing selected people, even in high positions, as aspired by laymen Ukrainians and some activists and donors, does not necessarily mean fighting corruption (as the Russian example certifies). Systemic corruption of the Ukrainian kind requires much more sophisticated systemic treatment. Some of the anti-corruption reforms have been quite effective (see Lough and Dubrovskiy, 2018 for detailed analysis), but still scattered and, in most cases, inconclusive.

106 For more details see Dubrovskiy, V. "Political, Economic And Institutional Aspects Of Making Cuts To The Ukrainian Budget." *Vox Ukraine,* February, 2015. Available at: https://voxukraine.org/en/political-economic-and-institutional-aspects-of-making-cuts-to-the-ukrainian-budget/

Instead, the incumbent political elites led by Poroshenko (and personified in him by the public) have done exactly the opposite. For instance, in the case of utility tariff increases, the people suffering from it could see Akhmetov's energy monopoly not only surviving, but also being bailed out by the regulator (controlled by Poroshenko) with the infamous "Rotterdam+" pricing formula. Moreover, nothing at all was done to improve the transparency and regulation of natural monopolies in the utterly inefficient/corrupt district heating and energy supply, which could have largely mitigated the bills' increase if implemented.

As a corollary to all of this came a major political mistake: Poroshenko (or his advisors) thought he could win by playing the ethnolinguistic card. In fact, the elections proved the opposite to be true, because, as we describe in more detail in Section 5, by the time of the elections (and perhaps already in 2014) the main societal cleavages had already shifted. This mistake was, however, not occasional. The creative class was his most natural supporter, as it strives for an OAO and at the same time, fears any radicals — thereby praising moderate and capable reformers. But to attract this category of voters, Poroshenko should have done much more to effectively implement systemic reforms. In the meantime, relying on conservative slogans such as "Ukrainian [ethnolinguistic] identity", which worked well many times in previous campaigns, along with clericalism and militarism, did not require parting with patronal politics and rent seeking — so the choice was predetermined. However, this strategy could have worked only against an openly pro-Russian challenger, and in reality, repelled many Russian-speaking and purely secular Ukrainian political citizens that have fairly seen these slogans as a substitute for the modernization to which they were aspiring. The positive news from this is that civic identity is thriving in Ukraine more than ever, and the political leadership of the future can build on it and cultivate it, while the gradual but tactful process of spreading the use of the Ukrainian language can and should continue.[107]

---

107 We put aside the very acute question of the specific forms of such proliferation and promotion because our focus is on systemic transformation. At the

All of these and other mistakes were, of course, captured and inflated by the Russian propaganda along with political foes, such as Igor Kolomoisky. But Poroshenko failed to confront this campaign, instead focusing his and his allies' vast media resources on smear campaigns against civil society (mainly anti-corruption) activists, competitors or would-be competitors from the same pro-Western political camp, and those who threatened his or his cronies' business interests, as in the cases of the Donbass blockade or the abolition of protectionism in the automotive industry. Such tactics failed to help him improve his own ratings, but resulted in the political vacuum[108] that Zelensky and his party has filled despite a severe lack of competence.

The very fact that the Ukrainian voters managed to punish these political mistakes by changing the administration in free and fair elections testifies to the Revolution's success. The transition of power was smooth and—admittedly for the first time—the loser congratulated the winner after the exit poll's results were released. Nevertheless, Poroshenko and his party have never stopped their dirty smear campaign against Zelensky and all the other political forces competing with them for the pro-Western electorate. Instead of either trying to broaden his electoral base to the median voters or building a broad Parliament coalition of pro-Western parties (in opposition to the allegedly pro-Russian Zelensky, in the view of many local observers), Poroshenko employed his propaganda machine for building a circle of personally loyal devotees but alienating the rest. For example, his occasionally abusive rhetoric and propaganda messages against Zelensky are well received only by those who already hate the latter, whose hatred they

---

general level, we can suggest that such policies should not hamper this transformation or magnify the ethnolinguistic cleavage in Ukrainian society that undermines its resilience to Russian hybrid aggression.

108 A half year before the Presidential elections, none of the main candidates had a positive net rating (with Poroshenko having the highest negative one), and the combined ratings of all major political parties able to pass the threshold constituted just slightly more than 40%. See: *Press-release of the Rating Group, Autumn 2018*. Available at: http://ratinggroup.ua/en/research/ukraine/ele ktoralnye_nastroeniya_i_problemy_naibolee_volnuyuschih_naselenie_ukrain y_osen_2018.html (author's calculations based on the published data).

magnify to insanity, without adding any new votes for Poroshen-ko. At the same time, they are repulsive even to some of his ad-herents, not to mention the rest of the potential voters. Such tactics look counter-productive for a democratic leader aspiring for victo-ry in free and fair elections, and could have been the fourth factor behind his electoral defeat of 2019.

Some observers describe the result of the 2019 dramatic elec-tion campaign as a defeat of the Revolution of Dignity, or, at least, as a major retreat from its ideas and values. However, in fact the picture is mixed with breakthrough progress in some areas, re-treats in others, and a "Brown movement" of non consecutive back-and-forth steps in the rest. The new president initiated a major elite change (see below) and announced many reforms that should, if implemented, further advance the revolutionary chang-es within the Maidan's agenda. But, as of now, the results are con-tradictory—some of them will play out only as time passes, while in some important areas a retreat in the transition is observed.

In the course of his successful campaign, Volodymyr Zelen-sky pledged to dismantle the System (for instance, stop the nepo-tism and crony appointments), and just like with Yushchenko fifteen years earlier, some voters believed that he would do it be-cause he was not skillful in using the System to his advantage. But so far, the President has preferred to learn the art of operating through informal patronal mechanisms, rather than trying to re-place them with working formal institutions. Particularly, the fact that, unlike his predecessors, Zelensky does not have a direct con-flict of interests concerning the RoL (see Section 2) and institution-building does not mean that he is necessarily willing to implement the reforms that his predecessor obstructed. Instead, at the per-sonal level so far we have seen the continuation of the old-school patronal style of personal rule, often based not on professional credentials but on personal sympathy and loyalty, along with the crony appointments that Zelensky once condemned and pledged to stop. Still, there is a promising chance for genuine judicial re-form, as described in Section 2.

The President's Servant of the People Party's (SoP) landslide victory at the Parliamentary elections has effectively neutralized the institutional checks and balances provided by the Constitution, which is a unique situation for Ukraine that magnifies the risk of fatal mistakes and possible disturbances enormously. Since the independence of the judiciary and the strength of the Parliament are not yet established, an overwhelming victory by one politician leads to an unprecedented concentration of power. These risks were partly manifested during the so-called "turbo-regime" in which the Parliament worked during a few months of the Fall of 2019. "The new team" started with a Bolshevik-style neglect of not only parliamentary, but also constitutional procedures — everything was subordinated to a sort of "revolutionary expediency". The Parliament worked in a "turbo-regime", with draft laws not properly discussed, the opposition's amendments denied blindly, and the MPs having to vote without enough time to even read the bills.

This inevitably resulted in a number of grave mistakes, although it also allowed for a few important and long-awaited changes. In these months a bulk of important legislation was adopted, although many laws were seriously flawed or just lobbied by rent-seeking interest groups. Still, contrary to some expectations, no usurpation of power happened. Rather the opposite: long-awaited laws on impeachment and on proportional elections were adopted, although not without important flaws. Yet another long-demanded law, limiting the immunity of MPs, was adopted too. Fortunately, this law was also flawed and ineffective, as a successful implementation of it would have hurt the system of checks and balances. Finally, when it comes to the land market (lifting the 20-year moratorium on the legal selling and buying of agricultural land) the "turbo-regime" was predictably bogged down by the long — and very much necessary — consultations that eventually led to a reasonable compromise. The habitual Ukrainian inclusive political culture returned, although the lack of political checks and balances still has an effect from time to time, as in the case of the appointment of a controversial Minister of Science and Education accused of plagiarism.

Among other problems, such an approach bears a high risk of abuses and mistakes, as was clearly the case with the Health ministers, and likely in many other cases as well. Overall, the government in most spheres is even less effective than it used to be in previous years. Besides, in most cases the SoP tries to act as if it is taking its name literally — by using the rating as a utility function and running opinion polls biweekly, with policy corrections being made accordingly.

At the same time, in some cases where political interests played out Zelensky turned out to be more resolute and effective — as, for example, with the crusade against the pro-Russian political force led by Putin crony Victor Medvedchuk. While for Poroshenko the latter was a suitable and habitual sparring-partner (not to mention friendly personal relationships), for Zelensky he is a rival in competition for the Russian-speaking Ukrainian voters. So, when Medvedchuk's Opposition Platform for Life (OPfL) party tried to use the natural gas price increase to boost its ratings at the expense of the SoP, the response came immediately in the form of effective, though legally doubtful, sanctions imposed by the President-led National Security and Defense Council of Ukraine (NSDCU) against Medvedchuk and his economic front man Taras Kozak. The important but unpopular land market reform was another positive exception to the above-described rules.

The so-called "de-oligarchization" (see Section 2 for details) can become yet another possible example, with a special law being passed and numerous harsh public claims made against the oligarchs by the President and his subordinates. Note that Zelensky came to power with the help of one of them, Igor Kolomoisky. Poroshenko has even called his rival "Kolomoisky's puppet", and propaganda presented Zelensky and his party as "the servant of Kolomoisky". Predictably, this close partnership did not last for long, because the best strategy for a President in a patronal democracy is to become an arbiter over plural oligarchs — this maximizes his or her power. However, without his own full-fledged political clan[109] and direct access to the media, Zelensky appeared

---

109 To be sure, Zelensky, contrary to his electoral pledges, has brought to power his close friends and colleagues in business that have reputational ties to him and with each other. But they are neither numerous enough, nor organized in a real pyramid.

too dependent on the oligarchs, as described above. Through the aforementioned law, he attempted to alter the balance by authorizing the NSDCU to impose arbitrary sanctions on certain people based on broad and vague criteria.

Even before this law came into force, Zelensky went after Poroshenko using the very same methods of selective law enforcement that his predecessors had used. Regardless of the real legal grounds, this is perceived in Ukraine as political persecution, akin to Tymoshenko's infamous imprisonment arranged by Yanukovich — although many voters hate the fifth President so much that this controversial move may potentially uphold Zelensky's personal rating. The most dangerous consequence, however, is that this undermines the prospects for evolutionary developments, as does any kind of persecution of predecessors who conceded power peacefully.

If effectively implemented, all of this could manifest a "terror phase" of the revolution in the sense of Crane Brinton. However, in practice, given the overall weakness of governance and inclusive political culture that Ukraine features, this would at most be very "mild" terror. It is also possible that it will mostly affect the main political rivals, like Poroshenko and Medvedchuk, rather than the prominent oligarchs. After all, the law stipulates quite symbolic sanctions that can be easily circumvented. Thus, we consider it as primarily a PR action with little, if any, systemic consequences. Still, Zelensky will certainly employ all available institutional leverages in order to subdue the oligarchs and become their arbiter, not servant. Some fears even arise that he can go too far by crashing the oligarchs all together, as Putin did in Russia in the first term of his presidency. This topic is discussed in more detail below. All in all, de-oligarchization will hardly result in any tectonic changes in the political-economic landscape and is even more unlikely to result in a real authoritarian consolidation.

However, another battle seems to be more acute and real. The court and law enforcement mafia seems to be the staunchest enemy of modernization in general, and to the westward orientation in particular — merely because it loses irrevocably if a real RoL is implemented. It comes as no surprise that it is intimately connected to Russian agents of influence, such as Medvedchuk and Portnov. The voice and video records of some prominent members of this mafia, which the NABU published in 2019-20, testify to their overwhelming power and high ambitions, not to mention corruption and abuse of power. Note that the people recorded there are still at their offices, despite the allegations. The Constitutional Court's ruling against the core anti-corruption policies and institutions adopted in November 2020, based on the appeal of a number of MPs representing the OPfL or connected to Kolomoisky, became a moment of truth for Zelensky because this ruling was clearly aimed at undermining Ukraine's relationship with the West.

President Zelensky cannot escape a full-scale battle with this mafia if he has genuine ambitions to exercise real power. The judicial mafia's resistance will certainly be extremely fierce, including the possible involvement of the Kremlin, which perfectly realizes the importance of anti-Western interest groups for its imperial policies. This seems to be the main agenda for the upcoming months or even years. Most probably, Zelensky would like to subordinate the court and law enforcement, as Poroshenko did, but it is hardly possible without his own political clan that could serve as a strong foothold for such subjugation. Therefore, and also given strong and permanent pressure by civil society and the West, there is a good chance that this struggle will result in a more independent and cleaner judiciary. This would be a good foundation for later deliberative action to clean this part of the System, and in this way bring the whole System closer to durable institutional checks and balances. In such an optimistic scenario, this would be the most important step on the way to genuine systemic transition.

Is a new sustainable "single pyramid" possible?

This question deserves special attention because, as described in Theoretical Inference, a patronal democracy is likely to evolve towards a liberal one unless it slides to an autocracy. In the case of

Ukraine, this question can also be existential for the country's independence and unity.

According to Magyar and Madlovics's classification, Ukraine so far fits the definition of a "patronal democracy" almost perfectly. The politics were always competitive throughout the whole period of independence, except the subjects of this competition are not democratic political parties that can from time to time produce strong leaders, but vertically organized "political clans" ("pyramids") created by patronal leaders. Out of three attempts at establishing a patronal autocracy, the first one (in 1996-97 by Leonid Kuchma and Pavlo Lazarenko) failed because of internal conflict within the then-Dnepropetrovsk clan, which resulted in the expulsion of Lazarenko. Kuchma himself built a "single pyramid" successfully, but failed to consolidate a patronal autocracy, or was unwilling to do so until the last months of his tenure in 2004. Then, however, he attempted to transfer power to a designated successor, akin to what Yeltsyn successfully accomplished four years before. This attempt, if successful, would have established patronal autocracy — but the Orange revolution prevented it, in full accordance with Magyar and Madlovics's description of the color revolutions' role in a patronal democracy. The third attempt was made by Yanukovich, who went as far as imprisoning his political opponents and brutally suppressing peaceful protesters. This, predictably, ended with the Revolution of Dignity — again, fully along the lines of a patronal democracy.

Our hypothesis is that the changes brought about by the Revolution of Dignity and subsequent events are sufficient to prevent Ukraine from falling into a patronal autocracy by making these kinds of attempts unlikely. If true, it would mean that the country will be left drifting towards a liberal democracy. Nevertheless, the revolution has so far failed to overcome patronalism in general or change the social consciousness in respect to "strong leadership" in particular. Still, it has added a number of social and institutional factors to the historical and cultural reasons that we listed in the Introduction to explain why Ukraine, unlike many post-Soviet countries, took a non-authoritarian path.

There we mentioned:

- a deep tradition of plurality and no tradition of one-man rule inherent to Ukraine.
- state institutions in Ukraine that remain rather weak and incapable of exercising tight control—and have now become even weaker.
- sources of rents that are plural and of comparable size—and lose their significance over time.
- the east-west division that remained strong enough that a single leader could hardly be sufficiently popular in both parts of the country.

We acknowledge that in the cases of the late Kuchma and Yanukovich periods these factors eventually prevented the consolidation of autocracy, but were not enough to prevent the building of a single pyramid. Is there something that has changed in this respect due to the Revolution of Dignity?

The Revolution of Dignity has clearly shifted the balance from "vertical of power" (or "centralized bureaucracy" in Brian Levy's sense[110]) towards "checks and balances" when compared to the Yanukovich regime, although this shift is not yet complete. Moreover, at least by formal accounts it failed to reach the level of the "Orange era" that was later on successfully reversed under Yanukovich.

The "Voice and Accountability" score of the Worldwide Governance Indicators (WGI), calculated by the World Bank, have returned to positive values since 2016, but only reached their 2008 level (0.09) in 2020. The Polity V indicators,[111] characterizing constraints to the executive (XCONST and EXCONST), are five out of seven, although during the Orange era they were at 6. Overall, these assessments suggest that "checks and balances" are almost at

---

110 See Levy, B. "Governance Reform: Bridging Monitoring and Action." *World Bank*, 2007. Available at: http://documents.worldbank.org/curated/en/27663 1468328173186/Governance-reform-bridging-monitoring-and-action

111 To our unpleasant surprise, the new version of this very useful database, unlike the *Polity IV*, provides counterintuitive assessments of democracy/autocracy and political competition that are higher in the Yanukovich period than now — which is evidently not true.

parity with the "vertical of power", maybe marginally stronger, and the situation is no better than it was ten years ago when it proved to be reversible.[112]

However, these indicators are estimated based mostly on formal rules that do not always correctly represent reality. Besides, the formal indicators may fail to capture some fundamental changes that were brought about by the Revolution.

First of all, the "dual" constitution that had created two centers of power, comparable in strength, was restored as a result of the Euromaidan uprising. Although nobody can be sure about the future, at least until 2019, when Ukraine got a single-party majority, it helped secure checks and balances as described in the previous subsection and prevented building a "single pyramid", despite its inherent vulnerabilities. This is true even though Poroshenko was (unlike Yushchenko) skilled and decisive in employing informal tools for selective reward and punishment and had a fully loyal head of the SBU and head of prosecution.

Another important type of checks and balances that was invigorated in the aftermath of the Revolution is the one between central and local authorities. The main difference from the Orange era, at the level of the polity's organization, is decentralization. Since 2015, about 10% of budget resources were re-allocated to the community level, along with the respective responsibilities and authority. So, as of now, more than half of Ukraine's government spending, and a quarter of its revenue, happens at the local level. This is not necessarily helpful in improving transparency and democracy, since, just as in Italy (as described by Putnam et al.[113]), in modern Ukraine a lot depends on the development of social capital and occasionally on personal factors.

There are numerous success stories of great improvements in communities that managed to really improve their members' lives. At the same time, in many cases decentralization has just en-

112 Similar conclusions were reached in: Matsiyevsky, Y. *Has Ukraine's Regime Changed Since the 2014 Revolution? EU-Eurasian Relations at the Crossroads*. Montreal: The EU Centre of Excellence; PONARS Eurasia, December, 2016.

113 Putnam, R., Leonardi, R., and Nanetti, R. *Making Democracy Work: Civic Traditions in Modern Italy*. Princeton: Princeton University Press, 1993.

hanced the power of local "barons", which has not been balanced by sufficient institutional checks in the form of prefects,[114] whose supervisory role was stipulated by the reform's original design. In this sense, decentralization is now stuck in an "institutional trap", often failing to enhance checks and balances at the local level. However, it has still strengthened them at the level of the whole polity's organization, by empowering the local pyramid networks, which are plural by nature, in their bargaining with central authorities. This makes the possible construction of a single pyramid more costly, and therefore less rational, for a nationwide authoritarian arbiter.[115]

For this reason, it may be tempting for a President, in the pursuit of building a single pyramid, to try to reverse decentralization — and this is indeed what happened with the idea of certain constitutional amendments that would have shifted some power to the central government. Such amendments were put forward by Zelensky's office but faced extremely fierce resistance and eventually failed. A compromise is still to be found, but the story will probably end in the establishment of prefects with limited authority, thereby completing this reform in the right direction.

---

114 There is still some discussion on whether this institution is necessary, for it is not universal across the countries with successful decentralization models. Perhaps, it would be less necessary should the legal culture and civil society at the local level be more mature, and the judiciary act as it should and does in those advanced countries that have no special checks and balances at the local level. Otherwise, the local authorities in many cases adopt unlawful decisions that nobody can oppose and deny, because local civil society activists are intimidated or even repressed (Katheryna Gandzyuk's case is the most notorious because she was assassinated in an especially cruel way, but it is not the only one), while local barons have strong informal ties with judges and law enforcement officers at their level. Under these circumstances, a prefect responsible for oversight of the normative acts produced by local authorities, and endowed with the right to suspend unlawful ones, becomes a necessary countervail, at least partly balancing the arbitrariness of local authorities and serving as a sort of ombudsman for their victims.

115 On the one hand, the presence of a strong local pyramid can reduce the transaction cost because a potential single-pyramid builder should negotiate with just one person — a local baron. But, on the other hand, such a local leader has much stronger bargaining power than dispersed would-be clients competing for the nationwide leader's protection — which means that, as a result, a baron is likely to gain a larger share of the pie, and less will be left for the nationwide level.

We expect that decentralization has its own momentum and will probably continue. At the horizontal level, success stories of neighboring communities are already inspiring citizens to enact "local revolutions" — replacing their long-term "barons" with leaders of the new generation, mostly local civic activists or businesspeople. There is a hope that this process will spread further. At the "vertical" level, the more resources (formal and informal) become allocated to local leaders of both sorts, the more negotiation power they have over central authorities, which potentially leads to a further trickling down of power.[116] Both processes, taken together, can potentially steadily alter the whole polity's nature. The more voters manage to put local authorities under account, thereby establishing real self-governance instead of feudal domains, the more difficult it is to build a national political machine, which is an indispensable part of a "single pyramid". Of course, the process is not linear, and such a pyramid may try to reverse it. However, even at the present stage the cost incurred by the necessity of subduing local leaders (even the ones of the "old" nature) may have become prohibitive for building a single pyramid.

As of now, after their landslide victory at the national elections in 2019, SoP lost the local elections of 2020, which were, for the first time, held on a proportional basis. The "ruling party" failed to win in any large city and had to form coalitions in the local councils with its political rivals at the national level. In fact, the local clans rarely make a bet on a single party; most often they put their eggs in a number of different baskets — so the coalitions that may look unnatural from the ideological perspective are actually often formed by the same clan's representatives. But all in all, this means the absence of a real "vertical of power", even in cases like this.

Last but not least, unlike in the Orange era, the foreign factor now works against a new single pyramid. Previously, the West tried to support checks-and-balances, while Russia favored a sin-

---

116 Of course, this process has its natural limits because the resources are supplemented with responsibilities, and no leader wants to find herself responsible for the things she cannot control.

gle-pyramid arrangement, provided that the President at its top is under the Kremlin's control. This was largely the case with Kuchma after the "tape-gate", when he mostly lost his Western arm and had to employ Victor Yanukovich as PM and Victor Medvedchuk as his chief of staff; and with Yanukovich, who actually outsourced the country's defense and security policies, along with education, to Kremlin agents. At the same time, the Russian leadership feared a strong and patriotic presidency that was wrongly associated with capable governance by Russian tradition. Since Ukraine has become heavily dependent on Western support, the West imposes checks and balances with somewhat larger, although still marginal effect,[117] whereas Russia paradoxically does the same with its informal tools. The problem will occur, however, if the Kremlin analysts eventually recognize that their attempts at undermining the "vertical of power" and sacralization of a president's power only strengthen the Ukrainian state and society.

Some observers expected Zelensky, as an "anti-System" candidate, to further strengthen the checks and balances. Paradoxically, even concentration of power can be conducive for this task, because as long as a President effectively controls all branches of power through purely formal mechanisms, he can safely afford to build real separation of powers and other institutional checks and balances without the risk of a dramatic decrease in his real authority. For instance, unlike his predecessors, he can initiate legislative changes (including even Constitutional ones) necessary for implementing a doable impeachment procedure—because in the current Rada's convocation this procedure will not be used against him. Nor does he necessarily require dependent judges and law enforcement for building and disciplining his team—duly enforced formal norms are sufficient for the execution of his power as President, while intra-party discipline can be imposed in the same way. Hence, the only real matter is maintaining a partnership between the President and his party's leader.

---

117 The EU institutions have an inherently limited effect in this, just as in the case of Hungary and Poland.

However, so far Zelensky has made only a couple of significant moves in this direction (the law on impeachment, the Electoral Code, and some promising initial steps towards real judicial reform), while his modus operandi involves permanently crossing the borders that separate the branches of power "for the peoples' good". Just like his predecessors, he issues decrees with tasks (*doruchennya*) for the Cabinet of Ministries, cancels the appointments of judges to the Constitutional Court, makes informal orders to law enforcement and the courts, and intervenes in the management of SOEs. Unfortunately, this kind of behavior seems to be stubborn because it is supported by the voters.

Still, the public opinion in this regard looks just as ambivalent as it used to be, with no dramatic changes that occurred after Yanukovich's overthrow.

It may turn out that the Euromaidan was a high watermark of enthusiasm for the idea that Ukrainians are not comfortable living under an autocracy, and that the dramatic experience with a "vertical of power" under Yanukovych serves as a lifetime authoritarianism vaccine. However, as the available data suggest, since independence, surveyed Ukrainians in all regions and across all demographic groups, with minor variations, are likely to welcome a charismatic authority. As Max Weber would have put it: an attraction to a strong leader, measured by different surveys, remains eternal (still, its nature is too complex to be taken as a desire to fall under authoritarian rule). It is noticeable that, according to the *Ukrainian Society Survey*, for almost a decade starting from 2010, Belorussian President Alexander Lukashenko remained the most popular foreign leader in Ukraine (and even more popular than any domestic one). However, such favorable attitudes changed after the recent severe mass repressions in Belarus: Ukrainian respondents' support dropped considerably from 7.6 points in 2010 (on a 10-point scale, where 10 is the highest mark) to 4 points in 2021.[118]

---

118 *Українське суспільство: моніторинг соціальних змін. 30 років Незалежності.* Випуск 8(22). Київ: Національна Академія Наук України, Інститут соціології, 2021, с.630. Available here: https://i-soc.com.ua/ua/edition/ukra inske-suspilstvo/issues/

However, it is a thin line between love and hate for domestic leaders, too. A paradoxical characteristic of the local political culture, acutely defined by Evgenii Golovakha as archaic democracy,[119] tends to increase during periods of political turbulence and economic hardships: people seem to prioritize strong leaders over 'laws and talks' (see Table 2). This leads to the personification of political attitudes (when the image of a leader is more important than his party, his ideology, and even his actions). It also partly explains the success of Zelensky among the Ukrainian voters in 2019 (who during his public performances as a candidate and as President-elect continued playing a "good Tsar" type of leader outside his TV series[120]). The thing is that the paradoxical effect of "ambiguous consciousness", which is a characteristic feature of a transitional society,[121] can be misinterpreted by politicians as people's request for a "vertical of power" (obviously, that was Yanukovich's fatal mistake). As Yanukovich's inglorious finale demonstrates, for a political leader to be successful in Ukraine, one should balance strong leadership and a truly democratic type of authority.

Notably, most Ukrainians paid their tribute to democracy and closely watch its development. From 2006 to 2018, nearly 60% of respondents believed that "democracy provides more opportunities for individual political choice, as compared to other political regimes". Moreover, as a remarkable further shift in attitudes, 43% of respondents in 2014 (the year of Euromaidan) reported that the

---

119 The Ukrainian archaic democracy is characterized by a modern vision of the goals but outdated methods of implementation which can be traced back to the Cossack traditions of strong leadership backed by representative participation and a range of individual freedoms. See: Головаха Є. "В українців та росіян різні традиції." *DSNews*, November 28, 2018. Available at: http://www.dsnews.ua/politics/evromaydan---krok-upered-chi-stribok-u-arhayiku−26 112018220000 .

120 See Mashtaler, O. "The 2019 Presidential Election in Ukraine: Populism, the Influence of the Media, and the Victory of the Virtual Candidate" in *The Politics of Authenticity and Populist Discourses*, edited by Christoph Khol et al. Palgrave Macmillan, 2021, 127-160. Available at: https://link.springer.com/book/10.1007/978-3-030-55474-3

121 Also see Фесенко В. "Особливості та тенденції розвитку політичної культури в українському суспільстві". *Українська правда*, March 24, 2018. Available at: https://blogs.pravda.com.ua/authors/fesenko/5ab61e2b1e0ad/

democratic pathway of development is 'very important for them personally' (in 2012 the number was 23%). Overall, democracy was 'very important' and 'rather important' for 79% of respondents in 2018 (however, this dropped to 58% in 2021). According to a recent survey (2021), 54% of respondents reported that "democracy is the best political order for any modern state". At the same time, as mentioned above, a majority (ranging from 53% to 66% across annual waves of the survey) supports the idea that "a few strong leaders could make a better impact on this country than all the laws and discussions" (refer to Table 2). The lack of dynamics itself is a remarkable indicator of the sustainability of the 'strong leader' role in public attitudes over decades. It also highlights its rather mythological nature, independent of the actual political landscape. These seemingly contradictory data provide a clue to understanding the ambivalent public attitudes of Ukrainians towards an ideal "power equilibrium", which is theoretically possible but can hardly be achieved in practice, particularly by political neophytes.

Table 2. A few strong leaders could make a better impact on this country than all the laws and discussions[122]
(*Ukrainian Society Survey*, %)

	1992	2000	2006	2008	2010	2012	2014	2016	2018	2021
I do not agree	30.4	21.4	18.7	20.8	19.6	20.6	20.7	24.4	23.2	23.5
I do not know	17.0	19.9	15.6	16.7	16.9	17.9	16.1	13.1	18.7	19.6
I agree	52.6	58.7	65.7	62.4	63.6	61.4	63.2	62.5	58.2	56.9

Moreover, an attempt to build a new vertical may end much faster and even more disastrously for the country than the one of Yanukovich, because Ukrainians have already proved through their actions that, although some of them support "enlightened autocracy" in theory, they get very agitated when they realize that nor-

---

122 If not indicated otherwise, in this section we refer to the *Ukrainian Society* representative survey conducted by the Institute of Sociology, NAS Ukraine, since 1992 (the sample size is 1800 respondents).

mally autocracy = plutocracy, and for countries like Ukraine this is the only possible scenario due to the already patronal character of power. In short, a hypothetical Ukrainian autocracy would likely be a patronal one. Also, the people do not accept "restoring order" when it comes at the expense of their own interests—the state institutions are simply not trusted enough, as we elaborate in more detail in Section 5. In the meantime, since 2013, when the Maidan started, potentially violent groups became much better-organized, firearms and munitions have spread widely among the population,[123] and tens of thousands of people have received real combat experience.

There are also two controversial developments related to the fourth fundamental cause of Ukrainian non-authoritarianism listed above, the geographical one. On the one hand, the Revolution manifested a dramatic change in the main social cleavage (see Section 5), from East-West to "oligarchic class- creative class", so that now a single leader can be more or less equally popular across the whole country—which was the case with Zelensky when he was elected. This seemingly nullifies the geographical cause, but with the important reservation that such a leader should be supported by the creative class, which may like a democratic leadership but could never accept authoritarianism (a patronal autocracy). On the other hand, Ukraine has, at least temporarily, lost a considerable share of voters in Crimea and Donbas, who were among the most rigid supporters of political forces based on strict hierarchies (support for the Party of the Region was the strongest in these areas). Therefore, the electoral balance has shifted from the southeast, which is more influenced by the industrial culture of hierarchies,[124] towards the rest of Ukraine, which is less supportive of authoritarianism.

---

123 According to official data, there are about 1 million officially registered guns in use, while the total number is estimated at 5 million. See: *UNIAN*, July 25, 2018. Available at: https://www.unian.info/society/10201026-ukrainians-car ry-nearly-1-mln-legal-firearms-official-data.html

124 See Ivashchenko-Stadnik, K. "What's Wrong With the Donbas? The Challenges of Integration Before, During and After the War." in *Ukraine in Transformation,* edited by Veira-Ramos, A. and Liubiva, T. Palgrave Macmillan, 2020.

It may seem that Zelensky and his SoP's victory, with their pledge of de-oligarchization, can be interpreted as a move towards a patronal autocracy—just like it was with Putin in the early 2000s. However, Ukraine is not Russia, especially nowadays, and has little in common with Russia 20 years ago. There are a number of very essential differences making these Russia-like developments hardly possible in Ukraine.

1. Putin did not just have his own strong political clan, he was (and is) backed by the whole KGB-FSB community—an extremely well-organized, motivated, skilled. and powerful network. Nothing comparable was ever present in Ukraine. In sharp contrast to this, Zelensky lacks a political clan and desperately struggles to build one out of a handful of old friends and colleagues—but it takes much longer than the president's tenure, so his chances of success are rather low. As of now, internal cleavages within the SoP party, which was created from scratch in a couple of months just before the elections, have been revealed to the extent that Zelensky struggles to discipline his single-party majority even in the most important votes. The means of persuasion range from blackmailing to the president's personal presence at important Parliament hearings.

2. Putin operates in a country with deep-rooted traditions of personal rule and very weak traditions of pluralist democracy; where the middle class at the time of authoritarian consolidation was weakened by the crisis of 1998-99, and consisted predominantly of white-collar employees that are dependent on their bosses, often in SOEs. His rating rarely fell below 50%. Ukraine has completely different traditions as described above, much stronger and independent oligarchs, and a vibrant civil society. Although largely burned out and split, the latter still can pose a threat to the regime—the risk of a new Maidan remains. Note that Ukraine, unlike Russia, has recent experience with successful revolutions. Their main actor, the middle class, is much stronger than

it was in 1990s Russia, with small entrepreneurs and independent professionals consisting more than 10% of the total labor force.[125]

3. Zelensky's popularity in Ukraine, when compared to the historical popularity of Putin in Russia (as officially measured), is still considerably lower. Moreover, it remains hostage to his relationships with major oligarchs, whose de-facto political power is exercised mostly through their ownership of the media, especially TV. Zelensky is (rationally) obsessed with his rating, which in turn largely depends on the information that layperson voters receive, while TV remains the main source of information for about 70% of respondents. Therefore, as of now, the innumerous owners of the most popular TV channels can manipulate the President through his ratings—and the President has to solve, or at least mitigate, this problem before any crusade against the oligarchs.

4. No external force could prevent Putin from consolidating his authoritarian regime, because Russia at that time was largely self-sufficient economically, and remained a nuclear superpower. Zelensky, by contrast, has to respect at least basic democratic procedures and human rights, otherwise he risks being left alone in the Ukraine-Russia confrontation. Foreign powers (mainly, the West) and multinational organizations, chiefly the IMF, still have leverage over Ukrainian politics.

5. Putin lucked out by assuming power at a very favorable moment, the beginning of the world's price boom, which enriched Russians a lot. This contributed much to his support, as well as to the legitimacy of the autocracy because the public wrongly associated the hardships of the 1990s with democracy, and the rapid growth in their personal wealth with Putin's rule. Nothing like that is in place now in Ukraine. Zelensky's economic policies will hardly bring any sweet fruits, while the coming years seem as though they are going to be hard for the world economy.

6. Last but not least, Putin went through nearly the whole hierarchy within the System, and learned its modus operandi

---

125 According to government statistics, there are nearly 2 million individual entrepreneurs out of a total labor force of 17 million. See: *Економіка українських ФОПів у реальному часі*. Available at: https://opendatabot.ua/ru/open/foponomics

through experience, while Zelensky was elected specifically for being a novice from outside of the System.

Of course, nothing is entirely impossible—who could have thought twenty years ago there would be a patronal autocracy in Hungary?—but, all in all, despite the obvious concentration of power that has resulted from the elections of 2019, preconditions for building a new "vertical or power" are now worse than ever due to systemic long-term changes that occurred over the last eight years. On top of this, at present, Zelensky neither has a strong, premade pyramid besides a handful of former colleagues, nor possesses the skills necessary to build a vertical. It is suggested that he can hire an experienced pyramid-builder, or that such a person is already around. But it seems unlikely that any President would be happy to become a hostage of such a person, as nearly happened with Yushchenko. The demise of strongman Andriy Bohdan as the President's Head of Administration illustrates this point.

Still, Bohdan's successor in this role, Andriy Yermak, so far seems to be doing quite well in building Zelensky's own political clan, at the same remaining the most trusted consigliere of the President and "a person that is comfortable to work with". Thus, the issues of concentration of power and possible attempts of authoritarian consolidation should be watched closely and any move in this direction deserves harsh reaction by civic society and international partners, just like the corruption allegations do.

The change of the elite

A genuine revolution should open social mobility for new people, if not change the whole elite. In the case of Ukraine as a patronal democracy this is especially important, primarily because the disruption of personal ties makes patronal rule less effective and undermines the "stability" that is so needed for a business. Thus, frequent and unavoidable personnel changes increase the payable demand for stable and impersonal "rules of the game"—and this is exactly what is happening in Ukraine now. Such rules, as well as the RoL, are the necessary preconditions for the formation of an impersonal and merit-based "Weberian" bureaucracy. Besides, the latter requires cadres that are very different from the ones that patronal rule selects and nurses — so a major personnel change in all branches of power is necessary but not sufficient. Ukraine has undergone such major changes at least four times: after the Orange Revolution in 2005-08, after Yanukovich's victory in 2010-12, after his ousting by the Euromaidan in 2014-15, and after Zelensky's victory in 2019. We will focus on the last two.

Traditionally, a revolution used to be led by an oppositional political party (or a proto party) representing a contra-elite, and a new class. In Ukraine in 2014, events occurred in an odd way: despite quite significant numbers (see Section 5), only the minor parties "Samopomich" (Self-help) in 2014 and "Holos" (The Voice) in 2019 pretended to represent the "creative class". The former was actually the party of the Lviv Mayor Andriy Sadoviy, and absorbed a number of prominent Maidan leaders, along with some other people respected by the creative class, but it also included several business lobbyists who eventually destroyed its reputation. The latter was created right before the 2019 snap parliamentary elections, under the leadership of the highly popular rock star Svyatoslav Vakarchuk, but he has predictably appeared weak as a politician and party leader and resigned in 2020 — which soon resulted in the internal quarrel that largely damaged Holos's ratings.

Otherwise, the elections held immediately in the aftermath of Yanukovich's ouster brought to power the parties, and President, that had been big in politics since the late 1990s. Still, something has changed.

First of all, civil society, representing mostly the "creative class", has significantly strengthened its positions, as we already described. At the decision-making level, this manifested in the widespread practice of consulting with the expert community, including activists, in commissions that assessed police officers, appointed governors, etc. At the same time, the Civil Council of Integrity was established as a filter for the appointment of judges, the National Council of Reforms discussed the main reform proposals, various working groups appeared in the ministries, and so forth. Zelensky and his team are more self-confident due to their strong voter mandate and continuous popularity, but they still keep listening to civil society and include its representatives in the process of deliberation and appointments, although to a significantly lesser extent than it was in the immediate aftermath of Euromaidan. At the same time, unlike in the Poroshenko era, no nationwide smearing campaigns or adversary legal norms are observed, although individual terror against civil activists (in most cases carried out by local barons) seems to be increasing.[126]

Even more importantly, after the regime change in late February 2014, selected representatives of the creative class and civil society (specifically journalists, NGO activists, entrepreneurs, investment bankers, branch managers of Western corporations, etc.) entered the corridors of power, and for this new political elite Euromaidan represented a watershed moment between a post-Soviet period of development and a new Ukraine. Throughout the previous twenty-three years of independent statehood, members of Ukraine's "neo-bourgeois creative class" would have never even dreamt of entering the government on their own terms, nor would they have been allowed to do so if they had tried. For them, the avenues of social mobility in Ukraine's patronal democracy had been largely closed, so any promotion beyond a certain level was contingent upon accepting the patronalism and the LAO's "rules of the game". In the post-Maidan period, when many representatives of the activist community suddenly entered government, their political program, more often than not, involved the creation of a state that guaranteed a level playing field for entrepreneurs and firms; one in which those with merit (talent, skills, drive, etc.) were able to achieve success; one in which the state was neither partner nor predator with respect to the economy, but whose role in the private sector was limited to that of an impartial arbiter in the case of a dispute. Later on, most of these representatives left

126 Bystrytskyy, Y. et al. *On the Equator of the New Government (the Years of 2019-2021): Achievements, Problems, Prospects,* edited by Yakovlev, M., and Pekar, V. Kyiv: School for Policy Analysis NaUKMA, 2021. Available at: https://spa.ukma.edu.ua/analytics/na-ekvatori-novoi-vlady-2019-2021-dosiahnennia-probl emy-perspektyvy/

the government for various reasons, but many still preserved a strong appetite for reformist activities and will likely re-appear in new political projects in the near future.

This process got new momentum in 2019. Zelensky's team did a good job by providing social opportunities to new people, and the Holos party successfully followed this example—as a result, political novices, predominantly representing the creative class, comprise almost 80% of the Parliament. Particularly, in the new convocation of the Rada elected in 2019, former civil society activists constitute as much as 38%, with several of them heading Parliamentary Committees.[127] Prime Minister Honcharuk, as well as a number of prominent ministers, were also recruited from the creative class. Of course, this does not necessarily mean that these representatives act upon the real interests of this class; nor does it necessarily mean that they are ready to formulate and impose its agenda. But this convocation of the Verkhovna Rada eventually voted for a number of path-breaking reforms, such as the land market one and recently the judicial reform—things that their predecessors failed to accept.

Still, the process is not without its reversals and shortcomings, as with the appointments of incapable novices or "old cadres" with bad reputations on the basis of personal sympathy. No regular, merit-based procedure for promotions and appointments within the SoP has been introduced so far, and it looks like such a procedure would contradict Zelensky's personal management style. Even worse, the transparent and merit-based procedures at public service appointments that had been introduced starting in 2015 have often been emasculated or violated, last time on the pretext of the COVID-19 pandemic. This means that, despite dramatic elite changes, access to political opportunities remains largely limited to those with personal ties and relationships.

Therefore, post-revolutionary developments have probably altered the balance between the "vertical of power" and "checks and balances". However, this balance is still extremely fragile, and

---

127 Sasse, G. "Who Is Who in the Ukrainian Parliament?" *Carnegie Europe*, September, 2019.

not necessarily irreversible. A stable "single pyramid" regime would be difficult to establish now in Ukraine, but an attempt of this sort is still possible and could result in disastrous consequences. It is most necessary and urgent to complete the construction of "checks and balances" throughout the formal institutional platform, to mitigate the impact of informal "street" practices. More institutional checks are needed in order to prevent such developments, including but not limited to:

- closing the opportunities for usurpation that are still present in the Constitution.
- changing the electoral law to open party lists without the single-district model (already done but will only take force in a few years).
- furthering judicial reform with the aim of genuine judicial independence and competence, along with establishing prosecutorial independence.
- completion of decentralization reform with the establishment of sufficient checks to combat possible unconstitutional decisions and other forms of power abuse by local authorities.

Besides, any moves the president makes that undermine the separation of powers and other democratic procedures should be closely watched and immediately condemned, so that they lead to losses and not gains in his popularity.

It is hard to predict how this situation will develop, but given all that we know about Ukraine's society and its political traditions, a bright future under the rule of a politically strong but still democratic leader seems very unlikely. Even less likely is a return to something like Yanukovich's semi-authoritarian regime, not to mention a full-fledged dictatorship comparable to the one established by Lukashenko. There is still an opportunity for a drift toward liberal democracy, but by no means is this direction of evolution guaranteed. The next authoritarian consolidation can be attempted, especially if Zelensky manages to stay for a second tenure (as of now he still outperforms all of his potential competitors), or if he will appear successful in warding off the Russian aggression. But such an attempt is likely doomed to fail and would have disastrous consequences, because a new revolution would open a window of opportunity for the Kremlin to launch a further invasion and may also provide a casus belli. We just hope that both the current President and his political opponents realize this risk well enough. (Editor's note: It remains intriguing to observe the potential impact of the war on the political trajectory of Zelensky.)

5. Sociological perspective
New cleavages, identity shifts, and the rise of the "creative class"

We start from the evidence-based observation that Ukraine's 2014 revolution represented a *social* (bottom-up) appeal for changes that were not, at the time, genuinely supported by any significant faction of the elites. Instead, as the changes unfolded, political and business elites made desperate efforts to align themselves with the shifting landscape, aiming to navigate the transition to the post-revolutionary reality with minimal losses or, if possible, even potential gains. They sought to "invest" in the emerging political order, inadvertently (or intentionally) setting up long-term pitfalls for the overall process. The revolution has not produced a new leader or political movement able to formulate and pursue the respective reform agenda — this was done by civil society, not the elites. With nearly one-fifth of the population[128] involved in the Revolution of Dignity, and more than a third viewing it as a fair protest for people's rights, it has been a powerful expression of mainstream social attitudes and aspirations (yet, not equally supported across all regions and different social strata[129]). Unlike many of the post-communist, partly elite-led[130] transformations in

---

128 According to a survey conducted by the Demographic Initiatives Foundation, up to 20% of the population was directly or indirectly involved in the Revolution of Dignity. 38% of that share did not participate but viewed the protests as a conscious protest for people's rights; 17% viewed it as a spontaneous protest; 31% viewed it as a *coup d'état*, one that was supported either by the West (15%), or by the Ukrainian political opposition (16%). See: Press-release of the Democratic Initiatives Foundation, November 19, 2014. Available at: https://dif.org.ua/article/richnitsya-maydanu-opituvannya-gromadskoi-ta-ekspertnoi-dumki.

129 Ibid.

130 Some of the Central European transformations truly had their origins in broad popular support. Just to mention, the Polish *Solidarność* movement and the Czechoslovak Velvet Revolution produced strong and charismatic political leaders; and in all cases there were political parties pursuing the transformation agenda as opposed to incumbents supporting modification of Com-

the region throughout the 1990s,[131] the institution-building trajectory of the Ukrainian revolution remains open-ended. This process is ongoing: it began with the Euromaidan protests and the ouster of Yanukovych, and its endpoint is (as yet) unknown. It depends on many fundamental factors, in which long-term shifts in the social consciousness or collective self-awareness of Ukrainian citizens will play one of the leading roles. That is why we believe that the analysis of these societal processes is crucial for understanding the nature of recent changes and for predicting, where possible, future developments.

From the perspective of a society, the Ukrainian case is a peculiar example of a transformation that is further complicated by multiple overlapping historical legacies.[132] These include post-colonialism and post-communism,[133] among other phenomena shaping the country's contemporary social and cultural profile. We argue that kaleidoscopic historical settings and diverse contemporary experiences contribute to the fact that post-revolutionary Ukraine cannot be explained or predicted with one typology alone. The Revolution of Dignity certainly stands as a separate case of a transformation, as it took place on the threshold of Ukraine's postponed evolutionary transition from a largely colonial post-Soviet path to an independent pro-European project. This transition, unluckily, was accompanied by the occupation of Crimea and armed conflict in Donbas. This directly affected only a part of Ukraine's territory, but still had a profound impact on the social situations and attitudes of a considerable share of the population.[134]

---

munism. To date, the Ukrainian Revolution of Dignity has not given rise to a similar phenomenon.

131 This refers to the processes that could rightfully be considered "transitions" because they involved democratization and marketization as clear paradigm goals.

132 Todorova, M. *"What is useful about the 'post-' in East European Studies? On post-colonialism, post-socialism, and historical legacies."* Public lecture given at Charles University, Prague, May 2019.

133 In line with the conceptual framework of this study, we suggest that both systems are heavily associated with the logic of the limited access order.

134 According to international humanitarian agencies, prior to the full-scale invasion, approximately 5.5 million people had already been affected by the war in

In this section, we will take a broader theoretical perspective and view the transition from LAO to OAO in the context of nation-building in the post-Soviet era,[135] societal change (e.g., the emergence of the creative class), and other phenomena that impact this transition. In this regard, it is instrumental to define a social stratum that is potentially more susceptible to the transformation processes ('agents of change') and understand the roles this stratum can play in developing a state.

We suggest that it is precisely because of the vague role of political elites or "clans",[136] and other actors driving Ukraine's

---

eastern Ukraine (this figure accounts for roughly 13% of the total population) and nearly a third (according to a survey conducted by the Institute of Sociology of the National Academy of Sciences of Ukraine) have relatives and friends who either live in the war zone or are currently displaced from their homes. According to the *Ukrainian Society Survey* conducted in 2015, 1.8% of the respondents interviewed in government-controlled territory had lost their businesses due to the war in the Donbas; 1.9% had been forced to abandon their houses or other property; 0.7% had been wounded; and 1.4% had lost relatives during the armed conflict. Here, we should also add lots of seemingly unaffected people that nevertheless were touched by the war emotionally and who voluntarily sacrificed their time, money, and efforts to support the Ukrainian forces or help the displaced people. It should be also kept in mind that the consequences of the war — as an emergency affecting different spheres of human life, destroying infrastructure networks, and creating a complex set of political, economic, and humanitarian challenges — remain to be observed during the following decades.

135 Beyond the "end of history", described by Francis Fukuyama in 1989 in a now widely criticized article (see Fukuyama F. "The End of History?". *The National Interest*, no. 16 (Summer 1989), 3-18), the Russian imperial doctrine of intervening in the affairs of its satellites survived the end of the Cold War and the collapse of the Soviet Union. Almost thirty years after Gorbachev's historic speech to the United Nations in December 1988, democratic developments in the Russian neighborhood have triggered a range of interventionist policies on the side of the Russian state, as has been observed most prominently in Georgia, Moldova, and Ukraine. In this respect, the end of the Soviet empire did not mean the end of the imperial project stemming from its legacy. In November 2016, during an award ceremony for geography students, Putin claimed that "Russia doesn't end anywhere", and this has been taken as a new doctrine for taking care of Russian interests beyond the boundaries of Russia. Throughout the eight years after the Revolution of Dignity Ukraine has been facing the ever-increasing escalation of the Russian aggression, threatening its independence.

136 Hale, H. "Patronal Politics: Eurasian Regime Dynamics" in *Comparative Perspective (Problems of International Politics)*. Cambridge: Cambridge University Press, 2014.

bottom-up revolution, that the whole scenario of events remains fragmented and undone. As argued further below, as of 2022 it remains an open question whether the trajectory of society-driven revolutionary change has proceeded sufficiently for the transformations to be sustainable, and if a return to a basic LAO is now impossible. What is clear, however, is that the balance of pro-imperial and anti-imperial inclinations has shifted toward the latter, and it is not likely to be reversible since a part of the Ukrainian population changed their fundamental attitudes and values due to fierce distress caused by the war. Usually, the reversal of such changes takes a shock of equal magnitude but in the opposite direction.

In our view, altering the main societal cleavages can become yet another irreversible result of the revolution. In their seminal article from 1967, political scientists Seymour Martin Lipset and Stein Rokkan[137] drew a link between the development of European political parties (i.e., in terms of national voting patterns) and their respective societies' historical experiences of revolution. Their claim was that three waves of revolution—involving the Church (the Reformation), the Nation (the dissolution of empires), and the Economy (the industrial revolution)—were experienced by European societies differently, and so left different legacies in the form of lasting electoral cleavages. In Ukraine in 2014, Yanukovych's ouster and Russia's aggression seemed to unite a majority of the country's regions and partly diminish previous cleavages of an ethno-linguistic nature. Still, this was only part of the story of Ukraine's revolution. Socioeconomic tensions between proponents of a closed, broadly termed "oligarchic" vision of development (LAO) and advocates of an OAO—tensions that had previously remained hidden—became explicit.

Two fundamental processes of change can be identified as having transformed the Ukrainian society considerably in the eight years following the ouster of Yanukovych:

---

137 See *Party Systems and Voter Alignments: Cross-National Perspectives*, edited by Lipset, S. and Rokkan, S. New York: The Free Press, 1967.

(a) an unprecedented identity change during the Euro-maidan protests in Kyiv and other Ukrainian cities, (largely) in the wake of Russian aggression, resulted in the consolidation of an active part of society into a newly fledged entity. This negated previous ethnolinguistic regional cleavages and established the foundations of a Ukrainian political nation which is pursuing a new geopolitical pathway.

(b) the acceleration of the ongoing recalibration of Ukraine's economic structure, which by 2013 led to the emergence of both new political constituencies and new cleavages (though it has not yet contributed to the consolidation of an ideology-based political force). One of the identified post-Maidan constituencies (the so-called "urban creative class"—see below) openly supports an OAO, whereas other socioeconomic groups were ambivalent, if not hostile, to such a system. Specifically, a stratum that we can call the "oligarchic class" remains the LAO's main beneficiary. It openly and fiercely obstructs transformations at all levels of social hierarchy.

We suggest that, taken together, the two mentioned trends may be capable of altering the main societal cleavages that represent yet another component of a genuine revolution. Namely, instead of the cleavage that has been partly mitigated, the new, value-based identity has emerged as no less important of a phenomenon.

In this section, we will use available data-based evidence to discuss a part of the interactive dynamics that offer clear and stable trends in social attitudes. Specifically, using the available sociological data,[138] we try to trace the most remarkable societal changes that have been observed since 2014 as compared to the preceding period. Still, the hypothesis of their long-term sustainability, in most cases, remains to be tested by follow-up research

---

138 If not indicated otherwise, in this section we refer to the *Ukrainian Society* representative survey conducted by the Institute of Sociology, NAS Ukraine, since 1992 (the sample size is 1800 respondents). Until 2014, the survey was conducted in all administrative regions of Ukraine, including Donetsk and Luhansk oblasts and Crimea.

and verified by observing the course of Ukraine's trajectory as it unfolds.

Reviewing the processes from the sociological perspective suggests that "learning from history" cannot give us a "program for the future, but it can enable a fuller understanding of ourselves to better face the future".[139] We believe that for the significant social changes in the aftermath of the Revolution of Dignity to become irreversible, further coordinated efforts and the instrumental coherence[140] of many actors — both regional and national, local and international — are needed to implement long-term and nation-wide reforms. We don't know yet if this will be accomplished. Still, we are positive that the Euromaidan created momentum for, as Gellner might have put it, "a shared high culture which defines a nation".[141] And this nation, as a "natural social unit", although heterogeneous and diverse, is capable of uniting under the universal banners of human dignity, freedoms, and eventually transformations, growth, and success.

Where does Ukraine stand in the transition from LAO to OAO?

According to North et al.,[142] open access is sustainable when a society is able to produce three outcomes: (1) when entry into economic, political, religious,[143] and educational activities is open

---

139   Warren, R., an American poet and novelist.
140   Jean-Paul Faguet's concept of "instrumental incoherence" refers to cases where politicians pursue discrete, short-term objectives via deep institutional changes whose effects are long-term, multidimensional, and highly unpredictable. Faguet J., Shami M. "Instrumental Incoherence in Institutional Reform." London: LSE Working Paper Series, 2015.
141   Gellner, E. Nations and Nationalism. Second edition. Blackwell Publishing, 2008, 136.
142   North, D., Wallis, J. et al. "Limited Access Order in the Developing World: A New Approach to the Problem of Development." Policy Research Working Paper 4359. The World Bank, Independent Evaluation Group, 2007, 17-18.
143   Although religious issues are not discussed in this section, it is worth mentioning that this aspect of OAO requires attention regarding recent developments over the tomos of autocephaly of the Ukrainian Orthodox Church, and discussion on the activities and status of the Moscow Patriarchy in Ukraine.

to all citizens without restraint; (2) when there exists support for organizational forms in each of those activities that are open to all citizens; and (3) when the rule of law is enforced impartially for all citizens. North et al. discuss how big a portion of the population enjoying open access needs to be to sustain open entry into economic and political systems, and point to the importance of defining citizens as "individuals who possess the right to engage fully in political and economic activities and organizations". He argues that a society where 5% of the population enjoys the rights of citizens is likely to be a limited access order; a society where a third or more of the population enjoys the rights of citizens is likely to be an open-access order that can sustain itself through intra-elite (intra-citizen) competition.

Stemming from the theoretical model of our analysis, we are keen to find answers to the following questions: "Where can Ukraine be placed on the path to an OAO?" and "Has it reached the 'sustainability mark?'". Although the data gathered from the *Ukrainian Society Survey* do not directly correspond to North's indicators, they show the dynamics in the perceived availability of different activities or resources since the 2000s. In further stages of research these dynamics can be used to develop indicators measuring distance from OAO by combining evidence from different data sources[144] (see Table 3 below).

Education, as well as information, are not discussed here, either: these are research questions that require future detailed analysis.

144   Among different sources to consider are the Human Development Index, where Ukraine was ranked 88th among 189 countries in 2018 and 75th among 184 countries in 2020; or the Democracy Index, where Ukraine was ranked 84th in 2018 and 79th among 167 countries in 2020 (of note, Ukraine is defined there as a hybrid regime, above authoritarian, but below flawed or full democracies). Just to mention, the Democracy Index is published by the Economist Intelligence Unit and measures the state of democracy in a given country by rating electoral processes and pluralism, the state of civil liberties, the functioning of government, political participation, and political culture. The Democracy Index for 2018 states that "democracy is in decline" everywhere. Another valuable source of information on the retrospective changes is the World Value Survey (WVS). Ukraine joined the WVS in 1999 and participated in several waves, specifically in 2006, 2011, and 2020; *Ukraine in World Values Survey*. World Values Survey, NGO Ukrainian Centre for European Policy, 2020, 79. Available at: http://ucep.org.ua/wp-content/uploads/2020/11/WVS_UA_2020_report_ENG_WEB.pdf

Table 3. Perceived social well-being in 2000-2021
(Ukrainian Society Survey, %)

What of the following are you lacking? (% of those who answered "I have enough")	2000	2004	2008	2012	2014	2018	2021
1 Ability to live under new social conditions	14.2	24.6	28.4	27.2	30.6	37.6	35.4
2 Health	28.8	36	34.9	31.2	36.9	43.6	42.4
3 Good job	19	25.3	32	22.6	28.8	36.1	31.9
4 Necessary clothing	31.2	45.5	57.6	50.3	60.4	59.3	60.9
5 Good housing	41.9	43.4	46.3	39.1	45	49.8	51.9
6 Contemporary economic knowledge	11.4	15.4	21.2	18.1	19.8	27.9	22.1
7 Confidence in your own abilities	29.5	37.6	40.4	34.1	40.9	44.7	41.8
8 Necessary medical care	13.6	18.8	25.4	18.5	21.8	29.4	23.8
9 Fashionable and beautiful clothing	10.2	14.9	23.4	20.6	25.9	32.4	32.8
10 Basic furniture	35.4	38.7	45.9	42.9	49.2	48.6	52.1
11 Contemporary political knowledge	15.4	15.4	24.4	20.2	25	25.6	21.4
12 Courage in pursuing your goals	25.4	31.5	37.5	31.2	35.5	38.4	38.1
13 Legal protection for defending your rights and interests	8.8	9.4	14.8	10.8	13.4	20.1	15.3
14 Possibility of having a quality vacation	8.1	13.9	16.8	14.1	16.9	20.2	21.3
15 Possibilities to have subsidiary earnings	11.7	21.3	23.8	15.9	19.9	28	24.5
16 Possibility to buy the most necessary food (subsistence)	22.8	41.6	47.5	44.3	50	53.2	51.1
17 Initiative and independence in solving daily problems	33.6	40	45.2	36	41.7	47.4	41.8
18 Adequate leisure time	18.3	22.6	26.3	23.1	26.4	29.3	29.3
19 Opportunity to work to full potential	23	33.5	39.3	28.7	36.4	41.3	38.3
20 Opportunity to be fed according to your tastes	11.4	18.8	29.5	23.8	27.9	34.9	38.5

Although not all 20 material and non-material indicators of subjective social well-being directly refer to an OAO, we present them here for the sake of the methodology used during the survey. It is worth noting, however, that the estimation of such indicators as "health" and "adequate leisure time" are not necessarily order-dependent (in contrast to "necessary medical care" or options related to work and lifestyle). All indicators directly related to OAO are marked in bold.

Overall, perceived social well-being, measured as an integral indicator (based on the assessed availability of twenty material and non-material "social goods"), has tended to increase over the last two decades, including the post-Maidan period.[145] The aggregated score from 20 to 60 points, where 40 points indicate a conditional "zero" level (all scores below 40 indicate lack of access to social goods, and all scores above mean enough access), has changed from 34.8 points in 2000 to 40.8 points in 2021.[146] For all years of the survey, starting from 1996, the score was below 40 until 2018 and has grown ever since then. Ukrainians increasingly perceive themselves as being better-off: basic nutrition needs, housing, and necessary clothing is no longer an urgent problem for a relative majority of respondents (which was not the case during the first two decades of Independence). This observation is important as positive dynamics in the perceived well-being lead to the revision of demands (we will focus on this in the further sections[147]). As the data demonstrate (see Table 3), indirect assessment confirms that Ukraine is steadily evolving toward an OAO, and in many dimensions even meets the "30%" criteria (see the aforementioned study by North et al). As Evgenii Golovakha argued, Ukraine is a perfect illustration of the James Davies theory explaining social unrest after a long period of economic growth as an effect of rising individual expectations.[148] However, an alarming observation is that the rule of law remains the weakest point

---

145 Golovakha, E. "The Changes of the Integral Indicator of Social and Psychological Well-being of the Ukrainian Population During the Years of Independence." In *Ukrainian Society: the Dynamics of Change*, edited by Vorona V. et al. Kyiv: Institute of Sociology NAS Ukraine, 2019, 300-308.

146 Index of Social Well-Being is a scale where below 37 points refers to low social well-being, 37-43 indicates an average level of well-being, and 43 points or more characterizes high social well-being. For more on the method, see: Golovakha, E., Panina, N., Gorbachyk, A. "Measuring Index of Social Well-Being." *Sociology: Methodology, Methods, Marketing*, 1998. No.10, 47-71.

147 Hrytsak, Y. Overcoming the Past. The Global History of Ukraine. Kyiv: Portal, 2021, 412.

148 Davies, J. "Towards a Theory of Revolution." *American Sociological Review*, No 27, 1962, 5-19.

and the suggested bottleneck in this evolution. Apparently Ukraine, while showing progress on its way to an OAO, might become a place of civil unrest if people "subjectively fear that ground gained with great efforts will be quite lost".[149] This is particularly true if they feel that their rights are not protected and when they have low trust in institutions (we will further briefly discuss the data on the correlation between subjective social well-being and trust in Ukraine). As Davies continued in his work, "their mood [then] becomes revolutionary".

Ukraine's identity shifts: changes in geo-political attitudes and hierarchy of self-identifications

According to a commonly accepted narrative, prior to 2014 Ukraine was a deeply divided country split along ethnolinguistic lines. Ostensibly (and according to most experts),[150] residents of the predominantly Russian-speaking east and south preferred closer integration with Russia, whereas the predominantly Ukrainian-speaking West was pro-European. Electoral maps showing the country's west and center voting for "orange" candidates (broadly termed), and the south and east voting overwhelmingly for Communists and the pro-Russian Party of Regions were repeatedly seen as demonstrative of the pervasive ethnolinguistic cleavage that was said to define Ukraine's political geography. During the crucial months of 2014, however, when the Russian-

---

149 Ibid.
150 This argument has been repeated extensively. For examples, see Arel, D. "Language and Group Boundaries in the Two Ukraines." Paper presentation at the conference "National Minorities, Nationalizing States, and External National Homelands in the New Europe", Bellagio Study and Conference Center, August 1994; Zimmerman, W. "Is Ukraine a Political Community?" *Communist and Post-Communist Studies*, no. 1 (1998); D'Anieri, P. "Introduction: Debating the Assumptions of State-led Nation Building in Ukraine." In *Dilemmas of State-Led Nation Building in Ukraine*, edited by T. Kuzio and P. D'Anieri, 1-17. Westport, CT: Praeger, 2002; Hrycak, A. "Institutional Legacies and Language Revival in Ukraine." In *Rebounding Identities: The Politics of Identity in Ukraine and Russia*, edited by Arel, D. and Ruble, B. Baltimore: The Johns Hopkins University Press, 2006; D'Anieri, P. "Societal Divisions and the Challenge of Liberal Democracy in Ukraine." Chap. 5 in *Understanding Ukrainian Politics: Power, Politics, and Institutional Design*. Armonk, NY: M.E. Sharpe, 2007.

speaking ethnic Ukrainians of the south and east became a key constituency that led to the failure of Putin's *Novorossiya* project, choosing loyalty to the Ukrainian state over the "Russian world" (*russkiy mir*), the "cleft-country" stereotype proved patently incorrect.

Supporting numerous research-based observations on the widespread pro-Russian vs pro-West orientations, mainly across the right and left banks Ukraine, the *Ukrainian Society Survey*'s empirical data, during all historical periods of Ukrainian independence, show a great degree of ambivalence, uncertainty, and volatility in geopolitical attitudes across all regions, including the Donbas. Still, three main national trends are worth underlining here (see Table 4).[151]

---

151 This is also discussed in Ivashchenko-Stadnik, K. "What's Wrong With the Donbas? The Challenges of Integration Before, During and After the War." in *Ukraine in Transformation,* edited by Veira-Ramos, A., Liubiva, T., and Golovakha, E. London: Routledge, McMillan, 2020, 236-242.

Table 4. Geopolitical attitudes in 2000-2021
(Ukrainian Society Survey, % in the macroregions)

	Donbas				South			
	2000	2012	2017	2021	2000	2012	2017	2021
Positive attitudes towards joining the union with Russia and Belarus	70.7	74.8	28.9	44.4	50.3	65.6	37.7	26.4
Positive attitudes toward Ukraine joining the European Union	49	27	25.6	28.5	51.1	45.3	50.5	27.1
Positive attitudes toward Ukraine joining NATO	12.8	4.6	18.7	17.5	14.4	12.3	29.7	17.7
	Center				Kyiv city			
	2000	2000	2000	2000	2000	2012	2017	2021
Positive attitudes towards joining the union with Russia and Belarus	34.4	16	16	16	16	60.4	13.5	13.6
Positive attitudes toward Ukraine joining the European Union	54.2	73	73	73	73	50.4	62.8	51.5
Positive attitudes toward Ukraine joining NATO	24.1	42	42	42	42	12.8	46.2	43.6
	West				East			
	2000	2012	2017	2021	2000	2012	2017	2021
Positive attitudes towards joining the union with Russia and Belarus	6.7	14.3	4.3	5.4	49.7	74.2	32.8	31.7
Positive attitudes toward Ukraine joining the European Union	67.5	66.7	75.3	69.6	53.4	29.8	40.1	33.7
Positive attitudes toward Ukraine joining NATO	43.9	37.2	60.3	65.8	21.6	6.7	30.8	26.7

	All regions			
	2000	2012	2017	2021
Positive attitudes towards joining the union with Russia and Belarus	40.8	56.3	20.3	18.8
Positive attitudes toward Ukraine joining the European Union	56	45.9	55.1	48.5
Positive attitudes toward Ukraine joining NATO	24.9	15.3	40.7	41.5

First, from the late 1990s, when geopolitical questions were introduced into the survey, to 2012, the idea of Ukraine joining a union of Russia and Belarus remained a popular geopolitical plan with a relative majority of supporters countrywide. This changed just before Yanukovych's rejection of the EU Association Agreement: since then, pro-Russian (as a union with Russia and Belarus) attitudes as a geopolitical goal decreased from 56% in 2012 to 19% in 2021. Although pro-Slavic attitudes have remained an important mindset reference on the individual level (45% of respondents in 2017 agreed that they felt closest to the traditions, norms, and values of Eastern Slavic countries), public views on the geopolitical vector become less stable and straightforward, as we will see in the data.

Second, parallel to the "Slavic-partnership" project, pro-EU attitudes have been steadily strong since the early 2000s (with 56% of respondents in favor of Ukraine joining the EU in 2000 and 55% in 2017, the year when a visa-free regime with the EU was introduced).[152] The shares of EU-supporters remained robust in most regions, except for the east and south, although varying in extent

---

152 An intergenerational shift also slowly but irreversibly works towards the European choice away from the Eurasian one. To give an example, in 2018, the midpoint between the Revolution of Dignity and now, 37% of respondents above 60 were in favor of Ukraine joining the EU; while among the younger group (under 29) this share was 55%. The regional distribution among the young people (18-29) supporting Ukraine joining the EU is the strongest in Western Ukraine (77%) and weakest in the government-controlled part of Donbas (44%), but the tendency is clear that the European direction dominates everywhere (compare these 44% of young respondents supporting the EU in the Donbas with 22% supporting possible union with Russia and Belarus).

(particularly higher in the west and Kyiv city).[153] Yet, the recent data showcased some changing dynamics in 2021: a drop of pro-EU support should be the subject of thoughtful analysis linked to both internal and external factors (including the growing threat of Russian invasion amid a lack of clear and unanimous response from the EU).

Third, a share of "geopolitically uncertain" respondents remained substantial until the threshold of 2014, reflecting the problem of low public awareness when it comes to strategic political issues. This share gradually decreased until 2017 and shifted in favor of the EU (until the later-mentioned drop). Since 2018, the number of uncertain respondents has started to increase again. This also refers to pro-NATO attitudes: while the number of those considered geopolitically uncertain dropped from 42% in 2000 to 23% in 2017 and 31% in 2021, the share of those who support Ukraine joining NATO increased from 25% in 2000 to 41% in 2017 and 42% in 2021.

Observers of post-Euromaidan Ukraine noted a significant decline in previously manifested regional divisions and an upsurge of *national* self-identification, which remain dominant in the hierarchy of other identities. This tendency has still been observed eight years after the Revolution of Dignity: besides the remaining significant role of local identities, Ukrainian political identity (e.g., "I am a citizen of Ukraine first") has increased in all regions over time, including the east. Although it remains the lowest there as compared to other regions, the progress over the decades is impressive (see Tables 5 and 6). Significantly, the proportion of respondents expressing pride in their Ukrainian citizenship exhibit-

---

153 Certainly, we should bear in mind that identifying attitudes toward the EU with a pro-Western orientation or "European values" is not fully correct. Apparently, most of the "euro-optimists" are Western-oriented. However, the opposite is not always true: just as in other European countries, not every pro-Western person wants their country to be a member of the EU for various reasons. Thus, we can cautiously assume that the actual share of Ukrainians sharing pro-Western values might be somewhat larger than what is indicated in the data on geopolitical orientations. This does not necessarily mean that all citizens who show positive attitudes toward Ukraine joining the European Union share European values. However, it is quite likely that most of them see such values as, at least, attractive.

ed an upward trend across all regions, albeit at varying rates. The figures rose from 41% in 2002 to 70% in 2019[154] (although there was a slight decrease to 63% in 2021 — see Table 5 — it will increase further after 2022[155]).

Table 5. Whom do you most consider yourself?
(2000-2021, Ukrainian Society Survey, %)

	2000	2012	2021
Village / city inhabitant	31.3	29.8	20.8
Resident of a region	6.9	7.6	5.6
Ukrainian citizen	41.1	48.5	62.6
Representative of an ethnic group or a nation	n/a	1.8	2.7
Former Soviet Union citizen	12.2	8.4	2.8
European citizen	2.8	1.2	0.9
World citizen	5.6	2.4	3.1

Table 6. Ukrainian citizen self-identification *(2000-2021, Ukrainian Society Survey, % in the selected regions)*

Regions	2000	2012	2021
Center	47.1	47.8	63.3
West	43.9	54.4	69.0
East	37.7	55.2	53.8
South	36.1	39.8	63.3
Donbas	31.8	37.4	56.8
Kyiv city	63.6	71.0	67.4
All regions	41.1	48.5	62.6

---

154 This is also confirmed by the findings of the World Value Survey in Ukraine. In 2011, 67% of respondents were proud of Ukrainian citizenship (26% were very proud, and 41% were rather proud). In 2020 82.2% were proud (34.7% were very proud and 47.5% were rather proud). See: "Ukraine in World Values Survey." *World Values Survey,* 2020, 79. Available at: http://ucep.org.ua/wp-content/uploads/2020/11/WVS_UA_2020_report_ENG_WEB.pdf

155 See Golovakha, E., Ivashchenko-Stadnik, K., Mikheieva, O., and Sereda, V. "From Patronalism to Civic Belonging: The Changing Dynamics of the National-Civic Identity in Ukraine." In *Ukraine: Patronal Democracy and the Russian Invasion: The Russia-Ukraine War, Volume One,* edited by Madlovics, B. and Magyar, B. Budapest–Vienna–New York: CEU Press, 2023.

To conclude, the Euromaidan protests and their immediate after-math (i.e., Russia's annexation of Crimea and the first months of conflict in the Donbas) produced a new conceptualization of geo-political attitudes and self-identification for many Ukrainian citi-zens throughout the country. Aside from the obvious and striking increase throughout Ukraine in the number of respondents identi-fying themselves as citizens of Ukraine first and foremost, this shift has reflected a deeply personal process, reported by many as involving introspective participation in collective actions. Albeit with some variations across the regions, the pro-Russian or, wide-ly, pro-Slavic geopolitical orientation is diminishing in Ukraine, while pro-EU and pro-NATO attitudes increase; after the Revolu-tion of Dignity, for the first time since Ukrainian Independence, the Ukrainian civic identity dominates over all other identities in all regions of Ukraine. Rather than being taught or implanted by elites (as had been recommended by policy analysts throughout the post-Soviet period), nation-building seems to have occurred organically from the bottom-up. However, for these fundamental identity shifts to become mainstream and irreversible, similar to what was said in the previous section, it is imperative to foster a cohesive national development plan that emphasizes cultural ad-vancement and the growing significance of education in all re-gions of Ukraine.

The changes in social stratification and main cleavages on the way to an OAO: the emergence of the urban creative class

The central question often asked about the results of the Euro-maidan protests refers to the nature of social changes it has pro-duced. In the view of Yaroslav Hrytsak, who reviewed various versions of this text, Euromaidan has not triggered social trans-formations; instead, Euromaidan was itself a result of them. The dramatic events of late 2013-early 2015 "enhanced and multiplied" what was already in the air for years, if not decades. What was that, and is it confirmed by the data we have?

We support the view that the Euromaidan protests were a symbolic catharsis that gave voice to the new class, understood in its metaphoric sense. Here we mean that we do not dive deep into class analysis based on socio-economic indicators such as income, employment, consumption, etc. but rather the subjective (self) perception of different social strata and their roles in society.[156] While the middle class was traditionally seen as a social foundation for stability, adhering to traditional values (which is an essential predicament for growth in industrial societies), the new creative class is understood as a "clustering force of young creatives and tech workers in metropolitan areas leading to greater economic prosperity", in the words of Richard Florida.[157] Being aware of the conditionality of the approach, we still find it useful for depicting the changes that we saw in Ukraine, which occurred later than in the West but brought about far more remarkable results in terms of rapid value evolution. Certainly, it took a long time for this class to crystallize in the changing socioeconomic environment of Independent Ukraine. As we saw in the previous section, the rise of non-material demands was a result of economic growth since the early 2000s. Still, the Euromaidan became the first historical manifestation of the cleavage between the new OAO-oriented stratum—the "creative class" described below—and its enemies (notably the LAO beneficiaries that can be broadly called the "oligarchic class"). Euromaidan was a trigger for this new class to speak up and call for an alternative path to prosperity.

Before we proceed, it is important to emphasize that the events prior to the revolution in November 2013 began as the Student's Euromaidan in Kyiv. In response to the brutality faced by the young people, it expanded in December to become a broader

---

156 Discussions of social stratifications both in Ukraine and abroad is a big topic to discover. See for example: *Середній клас в Україні. Критерії ідентифікації.* Razumkov Centre & Friedrich Naumann Stiftung, Kyiv, 2014. Available at: https://razumkov.org.ua/uploads/article/2014_ser_klass_kryterii_ident.pdf Specifically, see comments by Vladimir Paniotto and Sergii Makeev, 9-14.

157 See Florida, R. "'Everything is gentrification now': but Richard Florida isn't sorry". Interview conducted by Oliver Wainwright. *The Guardian*, October 26, 2017. Available at: https://www.theguardian.com/cities/2017/oct/26/gentryfication-richard-florida-interview-creative-class-new-urban-crisis

"Maidan-camp", and as the oppression by Yanukovych's authorities intensified from January to February 2014, it transformed into the "Maidan-Sich". However, it is crucial to note that the demographics of the Revolution of Dignity cannot be solely attributed to generational factors or geography, such as being "central" or "western" (or Ukrainian-speaking). It is true that, as Shveda and Ho Park argue in their article cited here, "this new generation, who has not smelled the gunpowder and has not participated in the previous revolutionary events, were the most active protesters this time around".[158] It is also likely that, among regional protesters, people from the western oblasts prevailed. At the same time, the heroes of the "Heavenly Hundred" were of ages ranging from 17 to 82 and represented the whole of Ukraine as well as other countries.

With a certain degree of generalization, one goal of the protagonists of Ukraine's Revolution of Dignity has been the creation of social pressure to transition the country from an LAO to an OAO: (1) the notion of "Europe" referenced during the revolution was associated with perceived European values (which can be seen as the basis for an OAO); there was (2) a strive for "equal opportunities", which belongs to the vocabulary of the OAO; (3) the protest against corruption has been targeted against the LAO; and (4) the very word "dignity" signifies a transition from LAO-bound personal dependency to one's right to be valued and respected for who you are and what you do.

The values that the Euromaidan (as a collective actor which acted horizontally, for a long time, with no pronounced top-down hierarchy) stood for, and the economic and political reforms that its activists lobbied for in the wake of the collapse of the Yanukovych regime, approximated those generally associated with an OAO: self-reliance, innovation, limited government, entrepreneurial freedom, and meritocracy. These values represented the core beliefs of Ukraine's entrepreneurs, managers, artists, young aca-

---

158 Shveda, Y., and Ho Park, J. "Ukraine's Revolution of Dignity: The Dynamics of Euromaidan." *Journal of Eurasian Studies*, November 2015, 86. Available at: http s://doi.org/http://dx.doi.org/10.1016/j.euras.2015.10.007.

demics, journalists, etc., who made up a majority of early Maidan protesters. Paradoxically, they differed significantly from those of the Ukrainian majority. In the words of Kyiv-Mohyla Academy researchers Svyatoslav Sviatnenko and Oleksandr Vinogradov, who compared the results of a survey of Maidan activists, taken in early December 2013, with representative values survey data from Ukraine and several EU countries:

> The average Ukrainian and average protester on Maidan are situated on different ends of a trend line. That is why we are speaking about some sort of value or paradigm shift: compared to (the rest of) Ukraine, the Euromaidan (survey data) shows a "value shift", where instead of conservatism and dependence on state, the dominant value orientations are Universalism and Benevolence... a Euromaidaner, similar to a typical resident of Denmark, Finland, Germany, Sweden, Netherlands, and Belgium, can be characterized with high demand for openness to changes...The protester on Maidan is also characterized by a high degree of independence and non-conformism, courage to take responsibility, appetite for risk; (s)he is not in need of defense by the state, strongly expresses the need for novelty, creativity, freedom...[159]

The above observation was based on survey data from December 2013. As the protests dragged on, carriers of these OAO values (the capital's self-employed, entrepreneurs, and company managers) encouraged their subordinates to take leave of their jobs to demonstrate on Independence Square during working hours, and it was this "bourgeoisie" that financed much of the supply effort for the Maidan camp. This same bourgeoisie formed the heart of the Automaidan as well—a very effective "cavalry" force of protesters who would drive their midrange and upscale passenger vehicles to picket the homes of regime representatives. After Yanukovych's flight, it was this bourgeoisie that financed the volunteer battalions and rejuvenated the Armed Forces whose (often rural and/or working-class) soldiers defended Ukraine in the face of Russian aggression. And it was members of this bourgeoisie who triumphantly, although temporally, entered the corridors of power after the culmination of the Maidan protests.

---

159 Sviatnenko, S., Vynogradov, O. "Euromaidan Values from a Comparative Perspective." *Social, Health, and Communication Studies*, 2014, No. 1(1), 41-61.

Therefore, it was mostly the urban creative class that eventually ousted the incumbent regime in 2014—because by that time, it was strong enough. British scholar Andrew Wilson noted that one of the reasons for the failure of the Orange protests to develop into a full-fledged socioeconomic revolution in 2004 (i.e., resulting in structural change) was the weakness, at the time, of Ukraine's "middle class".[160] But by 2013-2014, entrepreneurs and managers of firms operating in Ukraine's services sector, together with journalists, academics, programmers, and other representatives of the country's "creative class", were able to form a critical mass of vocal and mobilized protest against the material excesses of the Yanukovych regime.

Getting back to an uneasy issue of classification, according to the 2016 comprehensive study of Ukraine's "middle class" by the Razumkov Center, 27% of respondents (the sample size was 10,054) identified themselves as belonging to this "socioeconomic stratum" or "class".[161] Interestingly, a more significant number self-identified as belonging to the "middle class" (almost 50%, just about the numbers that the other polls yield), but when investigators controlled for other factors (e.g., education level, consumption capacity, friends and acquaintances from the relevant class/stratum, etc.) the proportion of respondents who actually adhered to a "middle class" lifestyle declined significantly. The authors concluded that Ukraine's "middle class" consisted of a "core" (amounting to 14% of respondents) and a "periphery" (numbering an additional 35%). The "core" included entrepreneurs, qualified professionals, managers, specialists, and others employed in creative service sector jobs.

Applying the categorization of occupations developed by Richard Florida to the Razumkov dataset, we find that 26% of the

---

160 Wilson, A. *Ukraine Crisis: What It Means for the West*. New Haven: Yale University Press, 2014, 39.
161 The term "middle class" is problematic in the Ukrainian case because it does not necessarily reflect income or spending power. However, as a term designating a values category it is valid. See: Rachok, A. et. al. *Middle Class in Ukraine: Prevalence and Relevance of the Notion*. Kyiv: Razumkov Center, 2016. Available at: http://razumkov.org.ua/uploads/article/2016_Seredn_klas.pdf

mentioned study's respondents were employed in jobs classified as a part of the "creative class" (a term that more accurately reflects the socioeconomic status of the Euromaidan activists and ATO volunteers than the "middle class").[162] Applying the same occupational categories to *World Values Survey* (WVS) and *European Social Survey* (ESS) datasets from Ukraine, we find 30% and 22% of the respective samples represent the "middle class". In each case, the "creative core" (as defined by Florida) represents roughly 13% nationally, with slightly higher numbers in Ukraine's West and Center (17% and 16%, respectively) than in the east (12%) and south (10%). Still, reliable, up-to-date statistics are scarce and should be the subject of thoughtful studies based on state statistical service records and expert estimations.

Functionally, we try to localize the notion of "creative class" and place it in the post-Soviet transformational context. We reconfirm that, in Ukraine, it is a group of mostly "post-industrial" sector professionals and/or entrepreneurs, residing mainly in the urban areas, sharing liberal attitudes, and (here comes something which makes their role civilizationally important) being a "medium" to uphold the OAO values essential for its inclusion of wider groups of society. It is important to bear in mind that the allies of the OAO might be scattered among different strata, and that belonging to the "middle class" in its purely economic definition might easily coincide with an LAO mindset, and even with being an LAO beneficiary. It is a combination of status, values, and pro-activity that matters.

Within this study, we could not capture the "urban creative class" in the available data (as the questionnaire was not designed to filter for the appropriate characteristics). What we are able to discover, though, is the changing dynamics of self-perception in the hierarchy of classes and, importantly, changes in value orientations.

---

162 Lavryk, D. "*The Creative Class in Ukraine in the Context of Revised Modernization Theory.*" Dissertation prepared in fulfillment of the requirements of the Masters of Sociology degree, National University "Kyiv-Mohyla Academy", June 2017.

The dynamics here are modestly promising: since the early 1990s, data from the *Ukrainian Society Survey* show a steady but rather slow and uneasy growth of proactive people who believe that their life entirely depends on their own efforts: from 6.6% in 1992 to 12.4% in 2018[163] (however, this dropped to 8% in 2021). Overall, the number of those who believe that their life fully or mainly depends on their own efforts increased from 19.1% in 1992 to 29.5% in 2018, falling to 22.5% in 2021—which almost exactly corresponds to the above-provided numbers on "proactive strata" from other studies. The data also demonstrate some stable share of respondents who consider themselves "middle-class" (nearly 40% between 2006 and 2018, rather equally distributed across all regions) and a leap for those who support radical market liberalization (from 6.2% in 2012 to 14.3% in 2017). We suggest that with the observed subjective basic needs fulfillment (such as necessary clothing, housing, and food—as shown in Table 3.), a promising social environment for economic growth can be provided. The rise in indicators which refer to access to contemporary economic and political knowledge, confidence in own abilities, courage in pursuing own goals, as well as initiative and independence in solving daily problems, also seems to be a promising development toward increasing non-material demands (see Table 3). Notably, the share of those who are satisfied by their social status has steadily increased from 15% in 2004 to 18% in 2013, 23% in 2014, 24% in 2017, and 27% in 2018 (see Table 7, and the *Proactive democrats* section below).

**Table 7. Would you refer to yourself as middle class in Ukraine?
(2006-2018, *Ukrainian Society Survey* %)[164]**

	2006	2010	2013	2014	2016	2018
Rather yes	38.9	38	33.5	37.9	38.5	42.9
Rather no	45.6	49.3	55.8	49.7	51.6	45.6
Difficult to answer	15.4	12.6	10.6	12.2	9.6	11.6

163 *Ukrainian Society: The Dynamics of Social Change.* Kyiv: Institute for Sociology, NAS Ukraine, 2018, 465.

164 The question was not included in the *Ukrainian Society Survey* QNR since 2018.

Our main finding remains rather intuitive, but would need to be confirmed in future studies that are more granularly designed to calibrate for ongoing changes and their long-term effects. We argue that, as far as the available evidence shows, the urban creative class, proactive and inclined toward OAO values, has been one of the most sustainable and fundamental phenomena created during the years of Ukrainian Independence and shaped as a "medium" of changes during the Revolution of Dignity. As the data show, a slow and gradual improvement of well-being throughout the previous decades created prerequisites for change. However, it is the Revolution of Dignity that created a moment for its collective voice to erupt, unlike the Orange Revolution, which established a scene for political leaders, not groups. Shaped as a class or a stratum, these groups are now supposed to drive further changes: they have both the motivation and potential to do so. Further economic reforms, together with pro-European developments and globalization processes in different sectors, will enhance the status stability of the most proactive segments of population, and facilitate growing demand for Ukraine's systemic transition to an OAO. As the urban creative class is highly mobile and globalized, it can be eroded by outward migration unless socioeconomic conditions (e.g., security, availability of basic services, opportunities, etc.) dramatically improve. To sustain the changes it promises, broader social support for OAO needs to grow.

Proactive democrats: who are they?

The zoom-in exercise below is an attempt to use the available retrospective survey data to get a better understanding of the group which we call "proactive democrats". We define this group as those who believe that their life mostly or entirely depends on their own efforts, who consider a democratic path of development to be essential for them, and who can become the leading actors of change in the next decade. In our opinion, this experimental, value-based group is formed around pillars other than the broad "middle class" or narrower "urban creative class". This is more a value-based and mindset-drawn category (which might not necessarily overlap with status-based class categories) leading us to the discussion about culture, values, and behaviors: specifically, we are keen to know if the Revolution of Dignity brought about any transformations to the group that can be called "agents of change".[165]

The WVS results showed an interesting dynamic in the dimension of values and culture: an increase in the share of those who believe that it is important to live in a democratic country, respect human rights, be equal before the law, be self-fulfilled, tolerant, and open to changes, bear responsibilities, and assist each other. At the same time, civic participation indicators remain low. Although the share of respondents who believe that votes are counted fairly during the elections rose from 30% in 2011 to 54.4% in 2020,[166] turnout remains lower than in developed democracies. Notably, 2020 data showed a decrease in the perceived readiness to vote both during the elections to the Verkhovna Rada (from 62% of those who always voted, to 55%) and in local elections (from 61% to 50.8%, respectively).[167] The authors of the WVS Report made a critical conclusion worthy of attention: "When comparing Ukraine with other countries, it remains closest to the group of European Orthodox countries such as Bulgaria and Romania. At the same time, Ukraine outranks these countries in many indicators of secular and rational values, and values of self-expression".

Both *WVS* and *Ukrainian Society Survey* data proved that Ukrainians overall became wealthier and happier as compared to

---

165 It should be emphasized that groups based on status, income, or occupation ("middle class," "urban creative class") and groups based on values and behavior ("proactive democrats") are not categories from the same taxonomy. It is quite likely that some representatives of the "urban creative class" can be found among proactive democrats in the data, but proactive democrats is a broader category that does not adhere to "class," "age," or type of settlements. Thus, we can presume that the social basis for reforms can be wider than the "urban creative class," which, according to our theory, remains the main engine/generator of changes because they create a new demand for reforms and transformations.

166 *World Values Survey Report,* 2020, 78-79. Available at: http://ucep.org.ua/wp-content/uploads/2020/11/WVS_UA_2020_report_ENG_WEB.pdf

167 Ibid, 79.

the previous decade. They have been through dramatic events since 2014, and now (as of January 2022, amid escalation of aggression by the Russian Federation) are facing a danger of full-fledged war on a wider part of Ukraine's territory. They now know the high costs of independence and democracy and, as current social media and public discussions show, feel more committed to fighting for them (a flash mob with Ukrainian flags showing solidarity and resistance became viral during the last week of January 2022, a month marked by anticipation of hot war). We assume that revolutionary changes are usually triggered by individuals, while evolutionary transformations are made by groups (or a mass of collective selves, sharing the same values and aspirations). Do we see such groups acting as agents of change, or able to become such agents?

The data from 2012-2021 indicate an uneasy dynamic of a group of proactive democrats: although it has not grown considerably from pre-Euromaidan times, it has seen peaks in the revolutionary year of 2014 and in 2018-2020. This followed visa-free travel, changes in the political landscape, and growing uncertainties about Ukraine's future. These fluctuations, usually caused by challenges, are very suggestive of the potential scope of this group during hard times: up to a quarter of the adult population (see Figure 2).

Figure 2. Proactive democrats: growth and drops dynamics (2012-2021,%)

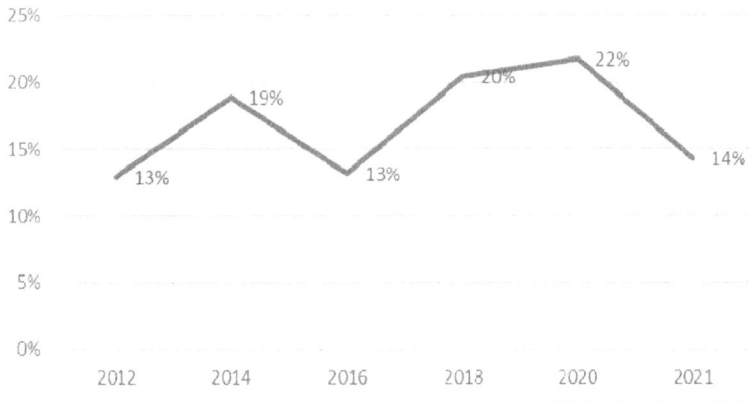

Source: data selection from the Ukrainian Society Survey, Institute of Sociology, NAS Ukraine.

They are increasingly pro-EU (from 54% in 2012 to 66% in 2021; for comparison, the share of pro-EU attitudes in the remaining respondents stays at the level of 45-48%). They are more optimistic about Ukraine joining NATO over time (from 24% to 57%; this is also true of the remaining group, growing from 15% to 42%). Proactive democrats do not necessarily need to live in a big city to support this mindset (they are scattered among different types of urban settlements, with a large share living in rural areas). It's also a non-geographic category: support in the center and east showed some growth over time, while the south and west dropped considerably, and Donbas and Kyiv remained relatively stable (see Figure 3). They are relatively better-off: in 2018, nearly 60% would refer to themselves as middle class (this indicator is 20% lower in the other group). Although the share of proactive democrats in older groups is half that of the youth, the distribution looks rather promising: the allies of the OAO are not limited to the young generation only (in 2021, there proactive democrats were 19% of the 18-29 group, 16% of 30-55, and 9% of the 56+ group).

Figure 3. Proactive democrats in the regions *(2012, 2014, 2021,%)*

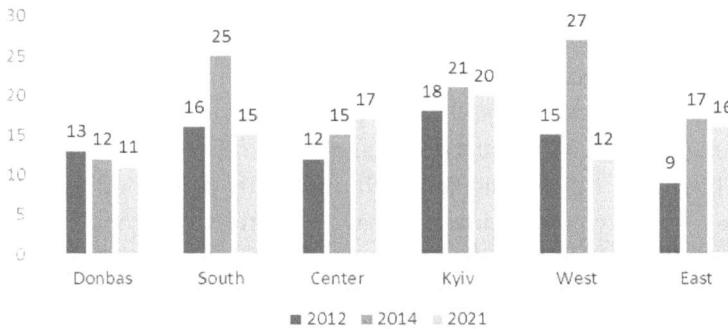

Source: data selection from the Ukrainian Society Survey, Institute of Sociology, NAS Ukraine.

They have a similar level of distrust of central authorities to the remaining group but show relatively more trust of local authorities (in 2021, 28% compared to 18% in the remaining group). This observation suggests that possible interventions can develop a constructive dialogue between local authorities and citizens, prioritize local civic engagement, and increase local ownership of reforms.

Post-revolutionary cleavages in attitudes: is Ukrainian society increasingly polarized, and is that a risk for OAO?

During the two 2014 national elections (the Presidential in April and the Parliamentary in October), the regional cleavages that had defined geographic voting patterns for over two decades seemed to vanish. This political unity may well have been temporary — prompted by a patriotic reaction to the Russian military aggression in the name of "protecting" the interests of Russian speakers who needed no protection, and by the complete discrediting of the once-dominant Party of Regions (a result of the unmasking of Yanukovych's corruption and his lack of leadership during the Euromaidan protests). It also may have been indicative of more fundamental structural transformations.

The 2019 Presidential and Parliamentary elections have been a new test of whether the regional electoral cleavages that plagued Ukraine for decades would return, or whether other cleavages will replace them. Although their results mostly reinforce the hypothesis of shifting cleavages (the new president won in all major macro-regions and all regions (oblasts) of Ukraine, with the exception of Lviv), we still assume that such uniformity does not mean that the regional electoral cleavages have been fully overcome during these elections, although they certainly do not prevail anymore. We suggest that this was partly the result of protest voting against Poroshenko, who apparently did not succeed in meeting post-Euromaidan public expectations (this message also prevailed in the top-rated media channels, giving more chances to a new alternative candidate) and because of the aforementioned protest against too strong a push for ethnolinguistic identity politics (see Section 4).[168]

Dramatic events in Crimea and Donbas from 2014 onward created yet another alarming agenda in the social consciousness that could potentially lead to a split: the Revolution of Dignity started in a hard year, when war, occupation, destruction of infrastructure, and war-driven mass displacement occurred for the first time since Ukraine's independence. As recent studies argue, not only Donbas but other regions in Ukraine also appear to be increasingly polarized and fragmented by the conflict.[169] As the results of the 2019 Presidential elections show, people are united by a growing demand for positive changes on both national and

---

168 "Ze' Support. What Do the Final Presidential Election Results in Ukraine Reveal?". *New Eastern Europe*, April 29, 2019. Available at: http://neweasterne urope.eu/2019/04/29/ze-support-what-do-the-final-presidential-election-res ults-in-ukraine-reveal/; Бекешкіна I. "Непрогнозований і непередбачуваний: чому і що далі?". *Українська правда,* May 19, 2019. Available at: h ttps://www.pravda.com.ua/articles/2019/05/19/7215427/.

169 Dunavova, D. et al. "Violent Conflict and Online Segregation: An Analysis of Social Network Communication Across Ukraine's Regions." *Journal of Comparative Economics*, No. 1, 2016, 177.

local levels, but divided by divergent solutions to reach their goals.[170]

Despite sharp, conflict-related concerns, economic "worries" prevail in the hierarchy of subjective problems that "people fear most of all". However, as it stands in the recent data, new cleavages over ethnic and religious issues are unlikely (see Table 8).

Table 8. In your opinion, what do people currently fear most?
   (Ukrainian Society Survey, %)

	2004	2014	2018	2021
An increase in crime	54.9	42.5	43.4	32.4
Unemployment	67.9	60.2	57.8	61.3
Attack of a foreign enemy on Ukraine	10.5	59.6	36.9	34.2[171]
Interethnic conflicts	12.8	35	20.1	11.6
Religious conflicts	6.4	12.3	14.7	7.9
Influx of refugees, immigrants and visitors	7.4	13.9	12.3	13.8
Shutdown	35.3	36	27.4	24.7
Hunger	45.5	33.4	27.3	33.0
Mass street violence	16.1	32.8	21.4	12.8
Not getting paid or receiving pensions	56.5	60.8	57	53.1
Unregulated inflation	75.2	63	74.3	70.2
Dictatorship in country	10.2	16.8	19.1	13.4
Dissolution of Ukraine into separate states	10.8	45.9	25.6	20.8
Consequences of the Chernobyl NPS disaster	24.9	9.2	12.2	4.7
Contagious disease which is life threatening (TB, AIDS or other)	43	17.4	23.2	19.2[172]
Unheated homes	30.7	23.7	31.3	26.9

We conclude that, as it stands now, public concern over possible internal ethnic-religious conflicts is low across all regions. These have given way, to a large extent, to more "secular" and "civic level" cleavages, such as region vs. center, LAO vs. OAO, and national and supranational concerns (such as a risk of external

---

170 Гіць А. Боротьба за дійсність в підміненій реальності. *Українська правда*, April 5, 2019. Available at: https://www.pravda.com.ua/columns/2019/04/5/7211378/.

171 In 2021, "war in the east" was included as a new item in the scale, and 46.6% of respondents chose it.

172 In 2021, "COVID-19 pandemic" was included as a new item in the scale, and 41.7% of respondents chose it.

aggression and pandemic). The data demonstrate growing public anxieties over a set of divergent problems across Ukraine, such as unemployment (high everywhere outside Kyiv), war in the east (highest in Donbas, Kyiv, and the west), shutdown (highest in Donbas), unheated homes, mass street violence, and increase in crime (highest in Donbas and the south), foreign attack (highest in Kyiv and the west), and the COVID-pandemic (highest in the south). Apparently, the violation of people's rights in Ukraine (human rights, labor rights, other rights related to individual freedoms) is more likely to cause protests than ethnolinguistic issues.

We suggest that yet another risk is attributable to uneven development and postponed modernization in Ukraine and, consequently, different types of life strategies and practices that involve communication problems between the different "centuries" within one country. Ukraine is in a cross-civilizational trap, with heavy post-Soviet legacies, a lack of critical thinking, old feudal-type hierarchies, outdated technologies, and an underpaid labor force. On the other hand, it has an urban creative class, Western high school graduates, and segments of highly organized civil society, activists, volunteers, etc. This is yet another challenge for the transmission of OAO values, reaching consensus, and ensuring the sustainability of changes.

Further polarization and cleavage are provoked by external hybrid aggression by the Russian Federation, showing sharp escalation during 2021, and dramatic war-time experiences gained by a part of Ukraine's population (either through direct participation in combat or through family members directly affected by the conflict). Unparalleled skills gained by the army, volunteers, civilians, and institutions is a new phenomenon for Ukraine. Yet, overcoming the severe consequences of the war and creating conditions for reconciliation remain among the most pivotal future tasks.

Potential for evolutionary development

The already quite powerful and growing creative class provides the engine for further evolution, but the next question is whether these changes can be smooth. Of course, this mostly depends on the political system, but only to the extent it is trusted. Besides, society's readiness to protest plays an important role.

Predictably, the most alarming sphere of post-revolutionary Ukrainian society, where the share of respondents who "have enough / full access" is the lowest, was the rule of law (although the recent developments after the Revolution of Dignity have demonstrated a moderate positive dynamic, as we saw in the data). The lack of legal protection for defending rights and interests involves high pessimism in estimating one's personal future and the future of Ukraine (notably, the level of pessimism and despair increases in pre-revolutionary years and drops shortly afterward).

This confirms our conclusion that RoL remains the most problematic issue in the transition. Particularly, Poroshenko's election defeat is largely related to his inability or unwillingness to provide full-fledged RoL.[173] Yet, on the positive side we should admit that the existence of high demand for RoL seems to presage its conversion into tangible progress. However, given the importance of personal rule to the functioning of the LAO in general and patronal politics in particular, the battle is already fierce and is expected to become exacerbated. Then, the next question is whether it will result in further violent episodes, or whether democratic institutions are already able to conduct further changes smoothly. As long as these institutions are still immature, a lot depends on the attitudes of the population toward violent actions as opposed to using democratic mechanisms and amending them, when necessary, with non-violent protests.

According to 28% of the respondents in 2021, mass protests against the violation of people's rights are possible (these include mostly legal forms of protests, although up to 5% anticipate unau-

---

173 We assume that the sharp decrease of Poroshenko's mass popularity was directly connected to his image of an "LAO-keeper", particularly in the sphere of RoL. This was widely promoted by the top-rated media channels, particularly before and during the election campaign. However, the very fact that there was such open criticism of him as acting President provides evidence in favor of freedom of speech under Poroshenko, something which refers to an OAO.

thorized meetings and picketing, 2% expect the seizure of public buildings, and 1% expect the formation of paramilitary forces beyond the government's control). It is noteworthy that in 2014 the estimated likelihood of protests (for example, in the form of picketing of public buildings) was twice as high (10%, compared to 5% in 2021). Only a third of respondents in 2021 were skeptical about protests and would not have participated personally in any manifestation, and about 11% were uncertain.

The data show that people in Ukraine traditionally have a low level of trust in state institutions, including the president, parliament, central government, courts, prosecutor's office, police, and local authorities.[174] Such a trend was widely observed in most post-communist societies that experienced "unsatisfactory financial status", which then created "pessimism about political institutions".[175] This was in turn openly manifested after a long period of forceful public legitimization of the political regime under communist rule. However, the developments in the post-revolutionary years went in a different direction. Comparative survey data suggest (see Table 9) that the levels of trust directed toward state institutions have always been low in Ukraine. Also, there is a tendency toward reducing poverty and an increase in perceived well-being parallel to a growing distrust in authorities. This creates an interesting phenomenon that can be called "Fata Morgana claims": as well-being increases, expectations grow, and people become less satisfied with what they get from the state.

---

174 Since the Revolution of Dignity, it is only the army, church, volunteers, and scholars who enjoy relative trust (3.1–3.5 on a five-point scale, where 1 is full distrust and 5 is full trust).

175 Pehlivanova P. "The Decline in Trust in Post-Communist Societies: The Case of Bulgaria and Russia." *Contemporary Issues*, No.1, 2019, 32–47.

Table 9. Trust in state institutions ("Central trust") (*2004-2018,*
balance of trust vs distrust, Ukrainian Society Survey,
*%)**

	2004	2008	2013	2018	2021
President	-43.1	-26.5	-56	-65.1	-40.9
Parliament	-54	-46.7	-71.8	-72.4	-62.3
Cabinet of Ministries	-46.5	-35.2	-61.9	-72.4	-62.4
Prosecutor's Office	-37.6	-41.6	-63	-58.9	-49.8
Courts	-35.9	-42.2	-66.6	-63.4	-53.2
Police	-43.8	-42	-57.7	-46.7	-36.3
Local authorities	-34.1	-29.8	-46.1	-37.2	-28.6

*Either the last or second to last year of the Kuchma, Yanukovych, Yushchenko,
Poroshenko, and Zelensky presidency is taken for analysis.
**The data on the attitudes toward police is for 2012 (as it was not available for
2013).[176]

Here, the nature and functioning of political institutions is primarily important. We suggest that the high degree of distrust in state institutions at all levels that was reported in all regions in the pre- and post-Euromaidan periods is a sign of Ukraine's belonging to the post-authoritarian stage, which is good news (as cautious attitudes are characteristic of aware citizens watching their authorities rather than praising them).

However, supporting Patti Tamara Lenard's argument that "distrust is inimical to democracy and trust is central to its flourishing,"[177] we argue that the further development of Ukraine as a democratic country requires more trust on top of critical attitudes. It is trust that makes people ready to abide by shared regulations and encourages them to participate in the process of reform.

Taking this perspective into account, and analyzing the potential revolutionary path involving a divergence in development

176 To compare, in 2021 the balance of trust and distrust towards the Ukrainian army was +29.7, towards volunteers +30.5, and towards the church +22.3 (in line with the data, these are currently the most trusted agents for Ukrainians). Notably, volunteers are the only trusted agent which was formed during and shaped in the aftermath of the Revolution of Dignity.
177 Lenard, P. "Trust Your Compatriots, but Count Your Change: The Roles of Trust, Mistrust, and Distrust in Democracy." *Political Studies*, Vol. 56 issue 2 2008, 312. Available at: https://onlinelibrary.wiley.com/doi/abs/10.1111/j.14 67-9248.2007.00693.x

between "protests, violence, and terror" and "developing institutions", and drawing upon the available data, we propose that the decline in trust towards state authorities and public institutions in Ukraine does not inevitably result in widespread protests and grassroots violence.[178] However, discontent is possible over a range of pivotal issues, such as human rights, the RoL, and security problems caused by Russian aggression.

Summing up, the sociological data and evidence-based observations support the hypothesis that Ukraine has undergone fundamental changes in social attitudes that have made the Revolution of Dignity possible; and the Revolution (along with ensuing dramatic events) has further accelerated these changes. The most important of them—the identity shift, the emergence of the creative class, and of the shift the main societal cleavages—are difficult, if possible, to reverse within the near future. At the same time, social problems related to well-being are not likely to cause violent protests. The most likely issue that may cause an uprising in the future is a possible clash with authorities over the RoL, human rights violations, lack of public consensus, transparency, and proper communication by the authorities on reforms and defense/peacemaking initiatives (or lack of them).

In the aftermath of the Euromaidan, post-revolutionary Ukraine, as a society, seems to have gained the muscles to move ahead. It's not unanimous in its views about the future, but not critically divided. It is neither too unwillful to protest against the vested interests of the authorities, nor too romantic to tolerate them for too long. The new creative class, although not rooted enough to become an eternal vessel of passion, serves as a power-

---

178   The course of events from 2016 to 2019 also confirms this conclusion: despite the extremely low popularity of the political class and its institutions, even hatred directed toward President Poroshenko and many other people in power (largely inflated by the media), all attempts to organize violent and massive non-violent rallies failed. However, even those who were opposed to Poroshenko eventually tolerated his leadership until he was democratically voted out. We suggest that in Ukraine, democracy is an established asset for a wide public. A promising sign is that the share of respondents who think that democratic development is important for them remains rather stable (from 64.1% in 2002 to 66.8% in 2017). Freedom of speech remains important as well (from 69.1% in 2002 to 73.1% in 2017).

ful promoter of OAO values as a path to prosperity among a wider circle of potential supporters. And there can be little doubt that (let us cite Gellner here again) the multiplication of efforts and the unity of many individualized selves "succeeds only in those cases where the external disadvantages of fragmentation are very great and visible".[179] As of today, Ukraine finds itself in a situation where "unity" in the form of a political nation is the only possible way to sustain itself.

---

179 Gellner, E. *Nations and Nationalism.* Second edition. Blackwell Publishing, 2008, 130. In his writings originally published in 1983, Gellner used the word "unification", which refers to nation-state formation through bringing together a number of states into a single national state. In our context, we refer to "unity" as integration that involves all citizens sharing common goals and cooperating for the collective good.

Conclusions and discussions

Overall, the collected evidence supports most of our hypotheses presented in the Introduction (at least, as of February 2022, when the book was finished). This means that Ukraine is still an LAO, rather than an OAO, but is steadily moving forward and has better prospects than ever for transformation due to much stronger driving forces, and sufficiently mature political institutions able to conduct the necessary changes and corrections in a democratic way.

However, the *doorstep conditions* for this transformation (according to North et al). have not yet been met, with the lack of RoL remaining the key problem. The balance has shifted in a positive direction but is still in the red, and the achievements can be reversed at any moment. There is some hope that the High Anti-Corruption Court will eventually become a critical tool for cleaning up the court system, but so far it is too early to predict. The establishment of RoL is also the most complex institutional challenge that cannot be resolved within "patronal politics". Substitution of informal personal rule with modern institutions takes lots of time and concentrated effort; moreover, such a change cannot occur within the system of patronal politics and thus requires an external foothold due to the lack of reliable leverage over old institutions and practices. Civil society and Western/multinational donors — or ideally an alliance between the two — can serve as such a foothold. This could only happen under the pressure of some irresistible circumstances: however, such circumstances already exist.

Rent-seeking has partly succumbed to the joint forces of civil society, donors, and the fiscal crisis. Nevertheless, it remains dominant, especially in the energy sector, natural monopolies, agriculture, and other large industries. The share of such predominantly rent-seeking sectors in the overall economy has decreased, but they still dominate in the industrial mix by value-added. New sectors and "de novo" firms have emerged and strengthened rapidly. The shifting of exports from Russia towards other markets, primarily the EU, has also contributed to systemic change. The overall trend is therefore positive, but its sustainability will depend on exogenous pressure, because so far the profit-seeking macro sector by itself, though strengthened politically, still cannot overcome the rent-seeking macro sector alone.

The significant transition in foreign trade from the CIS to the EU, coupled with new prospects for labor migration facilitated by the visa-free regime and profound structural shifts in the production mix and economic geography, including the emergence of new post-industrial sectors, are expected to serve as long-term and nearly irreversible drivers for socioeconomic transformations. These changes are likely to primarily uplift the creative class and shift Ukraine's economic center of gravity westward. Therefore, the economy also anchors Ukraine's geopolitical choice to a significant extent. Besides, with time the new sectors will play an increasing political role, driving not only economic, but also social and political development. Still, permanent outmigration of active people, especially from the creative class, can erode the basis for these changes.

Political checks and balances have significantly strengthened, primarily due to the return to the "dual" constitution of 2004 and decentralization. We consider both achievements irreversible, because any attempt to cancel either of them will meet very harsh and strong opposition. However, in their present form, the political institutions can still fail to secure smooth change, primarily due to the incompleteness of both reforms. The president still holds ample informal power through his influence on the SBU and PGO, now along with the SBI and the ESBU, with the "economic departments" of the former still functioning and supplying their boss with *kompromat* on his friends and foes. This can be used as a powerful weapon, either directly (through the PGO/SBI/ESBU), or indirectly through the media. Last but not least, although the law on impeachment was eventually adopted after 23 years, which is an unquestionable achievement, the constitutional procedure remains impractical, thus unfeasible and in need of correction. Furthermore, decentralization is still to be completed by establishing the institution of prefects that was, according to the reform's original design, to balance the power of elected local leaders — but without emasculating the already achieved degree of responsibility and independence of local governments.

The good news is that as soon as all of the above is accomplished, and given that the crucial 2019 election season has passed without any violence and major mass protests, there is a good chance that Ukraine will eventually get a political system able to conduct even radical changes of power in a peaceful, democratic manner. However dissatisfied the majority of voters were during President Poroshenko's rule, none of the attempts at organizing a protest movement to prematurely oust him from office turned out to be successful. On the other hand, even if he indeed wished to establish a "single pyramid" rule, as some observers suggested,[180] this attempt has also failed. Ultimately, he has lost in free and fair elections, and now Ukrainian democracy faces a new test: whether the winner will not eventually "take it all", and the loser will not, respectively, lose it all. If this is the case, then we could conclude that the country's democracy is mature enough that there is a chance for further evolutionary development. Of course, it does not mean that this path would never entail further complications and even reversals, such as the ongoing persecution of Poroshenko that, if it goes too far, may jeopardize further democratic development.

This test is also important because it would ultimately answer the question of whether Ukraine's revolution is taking a "French" path (where the moderate reformers are followed by radicals, and then a "thermidor" that eventually paves the way for further revolution), or a smoother and more evolutionary "American" one. So far both trends are present: on the one hand, the leftist, material, radical discourse that is considered part of the "French" way[30] is on the agenda (lowering of utility tariffs, increases in pensions and wages, expropriation of "oligarchs", etc.);

---

180 Minakov, M. "Reconstructing the Power Vertical: the Authoritarian Threat in Ukraine." *Open Democracy*, June, 2017. Available at: https://www.opendemoc racy.net/en/odr/reconstructing-power-vertical-authoritarian-threat-in-ukrai ne/

but on the other hand, its main proponents, the OPfL and the Bat-kivshchyna, lost the elections in 2019.

The winner has not, as a rule, clearly articulated any concrete slogans or pledges, but rather a few that can be (cautiously) considered as more "idealistic" than "materialistic" — which, if true, would suggest an "American" path. His campaign was focused on anti-elitist, anti-corruption messages, and the main, if not only, clear promise was "change". To some extent, this can be interpreted as an appeal to the aspirations of those who want more social mobility, various opportunities, etc. However, this does not necessarily mean that about half of all Ukrainian voters (and 73% of those who voted in the run-off) indeed support "openness". In fact, the extremely opaque and vague communication of Zelensky's campaign, along with the extensive use of modern psychological influence tools by both sides, resulted in predominantly irrational voting that had little to do with real messages. And the subsequent record of Zelensky's policies was also mixed.

Therefore, although the demand for change is clear, the sense of the changes desired by different strata of voters varies tremendously and requires further inquiry. Preliminarily, we can hypothesize that "anti-corruption" functions as a proxy for "anti-LAO", because the kinds of corruption that are most irritating are those associated with the inherent features of an LAO, like the fusion of business and power, and the lack of RoL, as manifested in the court system. In this sense, voting for "change" and "against corruption" may be cautiously associated with aspirations of modernization. Still, many voted for Zelensky because he looks like the average guy next door, because he is a Russian speaker, because they can easily imagine him as president due to his show "The Servant of the People", or even because they were dissatisfied with Poroshenko's reforms themselves or the way they were implemented.

After the early Parliamentary elections, Ukraine, for the first time, has seen a political leadership able to attract a unilateral majority in the Parliament. Zelensky and his team now have all the requisite means to conduct their policies, and all the accompanying responsibility. At the same time, for all of his time in the office he has faced fierce opposition, even hatred, among an important and well-organized minority, alongside skepticism from many of the creative class, even those supporting him. Despite a shocking (by Ukrainian standards) electoral harvest, his and his party's ratings as of now are down to about 20%. This is still a minority, although a record high by the standards of a Ukrainian president in his third year in office, and still a bit larger than any other politician and political forces have.

And here the aforementioned "fork" of the revolution's path appears again: if the winners use their incredible power predominantly for individual terror against the losers (as well as, most probably, former allies and some disloyal members), then the French-Russian path will soon lead to a thermidor in some form, however popular such terror may currently look. If, however, the winners' zeal for radical changes materializes in inclusive institution-building with the aim of an OAO, and personal repressions, are limited to the staunchest opponents of such changes, then Ukraine has a good chance to find itself on an "American" path. Unfortunately, as of now we observe more or less random persecution of various members of the old elite, with a suspected emphasis on predecessors and an announced crusade against the vaguely defined "oligarchs", which looks more like an admittedly mild "terror" phase characteristic of the "French" path.

What is sure, however, is that the "nation-building" agenda in a strictly ethnolinguistic sense, as offered by Poroshenko, has lost to a conditional "modernization" one. This is in line with our observation, also supported by the Nestor Group, that the Ukrainian political nation has already emerged, and consequently, the need for a nation-building agenda has become less acute than it was before 2014. For most of the country except the Eastern borders and part of Western Ukraine, the most acute issues and corresponding cleavages have altered; this, in turn, means change in the forces driving further the development of the country. As the Nestor Group noted in its 2015 Manifesto,[181] the political nation has emerged, but now it is time to modernize it.

---

181 *Vision of Ukraine – 2025: Contract of Dignity for Sustainable Development.* Nestor Group, February 25, 2015. Available at: https://zbruc.eu/node/33017.

Of course, nation-building should not drop out of the agenda—it still deserves attention and poses challenges—but modernization has become the priority. Among other important things, even many Ukrainian ethno-nationalists admit that Ukraine can hardly sustain its independence and unity without offering its citizens a lucrative and feasible modernization project, not to mention economic viability. After all, the Ukrainian political nation has emerged on anti-Empire, anti-Eurasian, and pro-European ground, and moving along the "European way" (not necessarily towards the current EU, but as a general civilizational vector) is synonymous with modernization.

It is still debatable whether these changes are indeed irreversible, given that about twenty years ago there was also a pro-Western majority in Ukraine that soon disappeared. However, this time the situation is different.

First, at that time the pro-Western mood was "immature", based mostly on some ideas about the West seen on TV that did not necessarily correspond to reality. When the TV started broadcasting other messages, these myths partly disappeared. Now more Ukrainians have personal insights: in 2021, 45% of survey respondents had visited EU countries at least once,[182] among them one-third visited more than once, and a quarter have personal experience of working and living in the EU. Those people shared their observations with friends, relatives, and neighbors, so that many more compatriots can now make a conscious choice. The problem, however, is that active travelers are not equally distributed among the regions (Western Ukraine, closest to the EU border, traditionally sees higher population mobility).

Second, as we demonstrated in Section 5, Ukrainians across different regions and generations are becoming increasingly pro-European (although we saw some slowdown of the process in recent years, the progress through decades is pervasive). Parallel

---

182 Іващенко К. Динаміка міграційних настроїв населення України: що змінилось за 30 років? *Українське суспільство: моніторинг соціальних змін. 30 років незалежності.* Київ: Інститут соціології НАН України, 2021, Випуск 8 (22), с. 169–184. Available at: https://i-soc.com.ua/assets/files/monitoring/monitoring-2021-bez-dodatkov.pdf .

to this, pro-Russian attitudes and pro-Slavic geopolitical orientations are fading away. Since its Independence, Ukraine has seen a
dramatic evolution of demands: while the socio-economic status
of the people improved, non-material aspirations took over. With
a growing share of conscious Ukrainian citizens and a more pronounced pro-democratic and proactive worldview, Ukrainians are
paving their way towards a more considerate "sense of country"
and its essential pathways.

Finally, the most important point is that unlike at the beginning of the 2000s, this time both the nation's unity and its westward turn come as a result of shocking events that dramatically
changed the public consciousness within just half a year. This may
be reversed with the same kind of shock, but it remains highly
unlikely otherwise. Of course, we cannot completely rule out the
possibility of such a shock in the future, but it is hard to imagine
where it would come from. The most likely kind of dramatic
events in the foreseeable future are related to Russia's aggression,
but they would likely just further amplify the impact previously
made on Ukrainian nation-building in 2014.

Therefore, we conclude that unless some extreme events occur, the Ukrainian political nation will sustain and develop further. This could become one of the main drivers for systemic
transformation, as described in the Introduction.

The dramatic events of 2014 have made abundantly clear that
Russia is not going to tolerate any true independence of Ukraine,
while continually insisting that "we are the same people", and
therefore ought to re-merge sooner or later. And it is ready to
prove this by brute force. Ukraine's economic and military capacity is not comparable to Russia's, nor does it have nuclear weap-
ons, hence it cannot win any war of independence without external support. Besides, the desperate economic situation in 2014–15
also required massive help that could be provided only by the
West, and Ukraine still needs more loans to manage its huge debt.

While previous governments could, at least in theory, try to
sit on two chairs, trading their loyalty to Russia and the West simultaneously, after the Revolution of Dignity Russian aggression
and the beginning of the new Cold War rendered this impossible.

At the same time, Ukraine is not strong enough to sustain a fully independent "neutral" status. It therefore has no choice but to lean towards the West. However, this option entails forced systemic transition, because Western leaders cannot persuade their voters that an LAO patronal regime perceived as repressive, unlawful, and corrupt from the OAO perspective is worthy of their support: the concept of "our son-of-a-bitch" is left back in the mid-twentieth century.

Thus, the logic of sustaining the new Ukrainian political nation's unity and independence will drive the country westward (including in terms of values and beliefs), and, at the same time, provide the West with critically important leverages over its development. This, in turn, may help to solve other problems, like the aforementioned reform of political institutions. But a full-fledged transformation to an OAO requires a dramatic personnel change at the elite level, along with a change in the rules, which normally takes a few generations or a revolution—and Ukraine cannot afford either of those. As such, the Western powers, along with Ukrainian civil society and their allies in the incumbent elites, should carefully implement a sort of "soft revolution" in order to achieve systemic transition within a couple of decades.

This is probably not impossible, but requires cautious treatment of a number of problems. First and foremost, any such process should be thoroughly tailored to Ukraine's peculiarities so that it avoids creating institutional traps and critical societal tensions. So far, the Western advisors have too often misinterpreted local realities or imposed an agenda more appropriate to their own countries: from a fixed-exchange rate regime in 1996-98 to the treatment of corruption as "just a regular crime that should be simply punished". The country's sovereignty is an extremely fragile and subtle matter, so the scope for pressure of this sort is critically limited and should be precisely targeted. It should also be politically legitimate for the Ukrainian population, requiring effective feedback and correcting the program accordingly. Corrections are also necessary because no one can predict possible developments and problems *ex ante*. However, incumbent elites should not be allowed to capture these corrections, and these corrections should not go so far that they derail the whole program.

Then, the systemic transition is contingent upon peoples' beliefs and habits, if not cultural patterns and values, that are fundamental for a self-sustaining OAO. Although we observe some provisionally hopeful trends in recent years, the balance is still in the red. Hence, a powerful and permanent campaign for change at the societal level is a crucially important complementary component of the transformation program.

Last but not least, the political system should be able to conduct dramatic changes smoothly. This requires urgent and sound institutional reforms aimed at strengthening checks-and-balances, securing better representation, and improving trust in political institutions.

The main condition for smoothness is the cooperation of the incumbent elites. They formed under the LAO, which means that they were selected or self-selected accordingly, and further developed their competition by investing in the skills, connections, and other assets necessary for success in an LAO. Therefore, any direct attack on their privileges or, for instance, corruption, begets consolidated resistance that can be overcome only through violent revolution. The incremental changes they allow are reversible and can hardly cumulate into systemic ones unless they are made in spheres overseen by the incumbents.

Still, a closer look at these elites reveals that, despite all of them playing by essentially similar informal (and often illegal) rules, they display a variety of attitudes in the sphere of business and politics. Some of their members play by these "rules" willingly, and cannot imagine themselves doing anything else, as, for instance, in the case of many corrupt judges, police, or secret service officers. Some others, in contrast, are loath to do so, and impatiently wait for the moment they can start living and working as their Western peers do; many of them even move their businesses there. Most of the rest think that they could more or less conform to any kind of system, provided they are able to keep their wealth and not be persecuted for past sins. Respectively, one should expect that the first category of these elites would harshly resist the reforms, the second category would assist the reformers, and the third could be pacified or even engaged on certain conditions. The strategies of reforms should be such that elites are split along these lines, ideally creating more allies than harsh enemies at each step (the so-called subgame-perfect path). This is hardly possible in all cases, but the less the need to resort to brute force, the more efficient the process will be.

Game theory suggests the following conditions for such co-operation:

1. The elites should understand that transition is unavoidable, and the time of the LAO has come to an end. It is important for making the LAO's games finite,[183] thereby breaking the conspiracies and criminal ties and destroying corruption networks, rent-seeking cliques, and so on. This will force the players to revise their strategies and increase the demand for workable institutions. Ideally, there should be a firmly stipulated date set, as there was for the EU's new member states.

2. Those who agree to the transition do this because they rationally estimate their benefit from an OAO to be high, gaining from capitalization, secure property rights, etc. But these benefits work only when the majority play by the new rules, and the violators are punished. Therefore, the potential allies of reformers need a trustworthy arbiter that will enforce the rules, especially during the transition period. Importantly, a person can play this role only temporarily, and such an arrangement is not very credible. A duly operating court and law enforcement system needs to act as this institutional arbiter from a long-term perspective.

3. All participants need credibility and clarity from the rules. In the Ukrainian case, this can be achieved more easily than in many other examples because the country has an external existential threat, so every sane person understands that, for the reasons described above, there is no other way to proceed but fast modernization. This in turn can be largely facilitated and accelerated

---

183 The so-called "folk theorem" in game theory states that in an infinite game, the players use strategies different from the ones they use if they know that the game will end after a certain number of repetitions.

by the West. Stagnation will ultimately result in failure, and with it a new violent revolution.

At the societal level, this process requires the intense unity of the creative class and, especially, civil society that is the main, if not sole, consequent proactive driver of transformation. In practice, this means that all other goals (except, of course, national security) should be subsumed to the political nation's unity, at least for the period of this speedy transition. Obviously, language, ethnicity, confessional affiliation, and historical memory are not necessarily the factors that unite all Ukrainian citizens into one community. Therefore, the approaches to employing these indicators in the construction of a national project ought to be reconsidered, implemented with a lighter touch, or discarded in favor of embracing "value politics". This approach emphasizes combating "survival values", particularly zero-sum thinking, and prioritizes the adoption of values such as self-respect, respect for the rights and privacy of others, and fundamental "European values" like adherence to rules and their modification when needed, rather than circumventing them. It also promotes the appointment or hiring of individuals based on merit rather than kinship. In the economic sphere, further opening up both internally (for the development of domestic entrepreneurship) and externally for FDIs,[184] is vital. This is because it can also launch a virtuous cycle of other changes through the creation of payable demand for the rule-of-law, predictable democratic decision-making, and electoral reform. If the progress in these spheres is politically rewarded with an increase in economic growth, driven by unleashing the entrepreneurial potential of the Ukrainian nations along with FDI inflows, it will create sufficient incentives for politicians. And the new, growing entrepreneurial class, along with foreign investors, can further propel such policies. This, of course, depends on if they join efforts in this, rather than engaging in counterproductive

---

184 Here it is important to stress that in this regard only the investments made according to the equal rules of the game matter—as opposed to efforts at attracting foreign investors on an ad hoc basis, through special privileges and/or protections.

competition for privileges or policies subversive to each other, and, eventually, the country.

To sum up, the answers to our research questions are as follows:

Have the changes that occurred in the process of the Revolution of Dignity (including the Euromaidan uprising of 2013-14 and the following eight years full of dramatic and tragic events) already put Ukraine on a smooth evolutionary path towards an OAO?	Not yet: Ukraine remains predominantly an LAO, although competitive sectors in the economy have expanded, political competition has improved, and some other critical balances have shifted in the direction of an OAO.
If not, then, have they already created momentum that will soon complete the revolution process in the aforementioned direction?	Yes, provisional success has created such momentum, although the process will take time and effort and faces substantial risks. A return to the dual constitution and decentralization are likely to be important in securing further smooth progress. An ultimate and irreversible shift from the Russian political sphere to the European one can firmly anchor the vector of further developments, provided that Western assistance and pressure for modernization will be well-targeted and well-tailored to Ukrainian realities.
If not, what further changes, if any, should occur to give a positive answer to the previous question?	See Recommendations
Can such changes occur in an evolutionary way, or are further forceful transformations necessary (inevitable)?	These changes can hardly occur smoothly and, at the same time, sufficiently quickly as a natural endogenous evolution; but they can be accelerated and made manageable if conducted with the skillful help of external players and civil society.
Are the achievements listed above permanent/ sustainable, or could they be rolled back?	The main systemic change achieved in the previous years — the emergence of a largely prodemocratic and pro-EU Ukrainian political nation, including civil society — is irreversible unless some extreme events change this trajectory. The background societal and socioeconomic processes that led to the Revolution and were accelerated as a result of it are barely

	reversible, but could be disrupted by a major disaster like a full-fledged war.
	Progress in the RoL and the building of checks and balances is the most fragile link in this chain.
In the worst case, will the remaining permanent changes be sufficient to serve as a ground for further (r)evolutionary processes?	In the unlikely event of reversal in the country's nation-building and/or its European choice, any systemic transition will, at best, be put on hold for a long time. In case of reversal in the progress of political institution-building, this will likely result in a new revolution, with uncertain but possibly disastrous consequences.

Recommendations

The analysis provided above allows us to formulate some specific recommendations that are summarized below. We reiterate that they are by no means sufficient for turning Ukraine into an OAO the day after they are implemented; this process will still take no less than a decade or more, and there is no firm guarantee of success. However, such measures can at least create momentum for further changes and facilitate them, ideally making them self-sustainable and self-propelling. At the same time, they should be feasible at present or in the immediate future. According to our methodological approach, they should alter the main balances and create positive feedback for subsequent developments. Of course, this list is subject to further discussions and amendments. Here are our suggestions for what could and should be done to finalize the **political reforms**:

- Complete the partially accomplished electoral reform.
- Establish a workable mechanism for impeachment.
- Clear the remaining issues in the constitutional division of power and strengthen institutional accountability at all levels.
- Eliminate the informal instruments for blackmail that a President has at his disposal, as described before (influence on the SBU, SBI, ESBU, and PGO).

The aforementioned measures, when implemented, should ultimately lock in the checks-and-balances against the "vertical of power" and, at the same time, secure the smoothness of further changes, as the new system should be more representative and thus more legitimate. The demand for such reform is already there, but it is currently vested almost exclusively in civil society. Educating voters, particularly in the advantages of better-functioning representative democratic institutions, can have a systemic effect.

President Zelensky is well-positioned to drive these reforms forward, given his influential standing within all formal institutions, coupled with a Parliamentary majority. As a result, he is less likely to encounter the same level of apprehension towards checks and balances as his predecessors did. Furthermore, even if he is reluctant to strengthen these checks and balances right away for some good reasons, it is rational for him to introduce respective legislative changes by the end of his term, just as Kuchma did with constitutional changes that weakened the presidency. However, as of now he seems to be rather inclined to building his own political clan and mastering discretionary rule, including selective justice. These moves should be closely watched and politically punished.

With regards to establishing the rule-of-law, the paradox of the situation is the following: while we are convinced that for reforms to make an impact it is essential for the reformers to concentrate on a few key breakthrough interventions, the established multifold and often fragmented nature of reforms forces the situation to progress simultaneously in many areas. This situation arises from the lack of enthusiasm for reforms exhibited by both the present administration and the post-Euromaidan government, in contrast to the early Saakashvili administration. Thus, reforms have happened due to popular pressure and not via conscious design. Plus, the conceptual question that we mentioned above — the inclination of international friends of Ukraine to open too many fronts and always throw a new institution at a problem rather than reforming the existing ones — pushed towards this current fragmented, "many half-reforms" situation. This forces the observer to recommend finishing many of these reforms, achieving a critical mass. The greatest emphasis of donors and civil society alike is towards continuing the **judicial sector's reform**. Here the main issues are to:

- Continue reforming the High Council of Justice.
- Allow the Ethics Council to do its job and veto inappropriate appointments.
- Adopt legislative changes that open the path towards a competitive selection procedure for the Constitutional

Court to guarantee the integrity and competence of CCU judges.

- Enable "the selection process for the High Qualification Commission of Judges to work effectively, preparing the ground to re-launch the HQCJ in a way that it enjoys high public trust."[185]
- Liquidate the notorious District Administrative Court of Kyiv and transfer the most important administrative cases to a specialized court created following the model of the HACC selection.

Important work needs to be done to further weaken the principal agencies of the patronal model: prosecution and the SBU. These are the steps we recommend:

- Continue to implement the spirit of the law on prosecution, so the prosecution really becomes the overseer of the criminal procedure rather than the powerful arbiter of cases.
- For this purpose, the vetting process needs to be successfully concluded, and the counterattack of the fired prosecutors, with the help of pliant judges, should be resisted.
- The investigative institutions need to be strengthened, particularly the SBI and ESBU.
- The necessary legislative acts need to be taken and implemented so that the SBU is finally removed from the investigation of economic crimes. This will reduce the possibilities for corruption and allow the institution to concentrate on its vitally important mandate directly connected to national security.

These reform steps, if implemented, could further shift the balance towards the rule-of-law in Ukraine. Obviously, they need to be implemented in a politically feasible way as well as with due attention to national security interests. However, most of these re-

---

185 This and some further points come from the G7 ambassadors' recommendations. See: *07 Ambassadors' Support Group for Ukraine. Priorities for 2022*. Available at: https://twitter.com/G7AmbReformUA/status/1488086841857351682/photo/2

forms positively contribute to national security in multiple fashions.

Again, President Zelensky is in a good position to strengthen the RoL because he is the first President in Ukrainian history that has come to power from outside of traditional patronal politics. Therefore, he has much weaker conflicts of interest with respect to an independent judiciary and law enforcement than any of his predecessors, who needed selective justice to uphold their informal verticals. Regrettably, however, so far he has shown few signs of turning this advantage into real reforms that could be his most important legacy as president, with judicial reform being the main one. He should be strongly supported in this, but, at the same time, stimulated to complete this reform.

- Fight impracticable norms to the greatest possible extent, and dramatically reduce opportunities for blackmailing and extortion, especially with respect to business:

  1. Apply the "regulatory guillotine."
  2. Radically liberalize labor regulations for all firms except local monopolists in the labor market.
  3. Complete the already-commenced tax reform so that an honest taxpayer can "pay all taxes and sleep peacefully" (requires corporate taxation reform); eliminate the labor tax and partially substitute the PIT with land/real estate tax, abstain from curtailing and emasculating simplified taxation, and roll back the legislation that does so.
  4. Establish a permanent feedback hotline for the identification and elimination (to the greatest possible extent) of further corruption opportunities.

- Rein in the other rent-seeking opportunities by imposing further transparency, de-monopolization, along with opening up the land market, abolishing all subsidies to business firms, and otherwise encouraging the free entrepreneurship and competition.

There is not much new in these recommendations as such: respective draft laws are either already on the table or being developed. But the political-economic key to their implementation is coalition-building among predominantly profit-seeking businesses, as well as education of the population. Together, these recommendations will shift the balance between rent seeking and profit seeking towards the latter, while also positively affecting the RoL balance.

In the **societal sphere**, it is crucial to strengthen and maintain social cohesion:

- Recognize the significant social transformations and identity shifts that have taken place, and foster solidarity among the diverse segments of society while working together towards common goals and addressing shared challenges. This can be achieved through inclusive policies and initiatives that promote inter-group dialogue, tolerance, and cooperation.
- Foster a sense of belonging and emphasize the importance of a united political nation to sustain Ukraine's progress. Highlight the advantages of unity in the face of external challenges and actively work towards building consensus and common goals among citizens in all regions of Ukraine.
- Uphold and protect the rights of individuals, ensure transparency in governance, and communicate reforms initiatives effectively to maintain public trust.
- Capitalize on the influence and potential of the emerging creative class to promote values aligned with openness, accountability, and prosperity. Engage its active participation in shaping the future agenda of public dialogue regarding the future development of Ukraine.

To drive comprehensive and enduring **systemic change**, it is essential to undertake a multifaceted approach that encompasses the following measures:

- Run a broad information campaign to enlighten and educate voters addressing the most fundamental issues that hamper modernization: primarily, but not only, zero-sum thinking. "Value policies" can unite the Ukrainian political nation and make it more supportive to modernization.

- Equip voters with essential skills and knowledge to foster critical thinking and understanding of institutions and the market economy. Dispelling prevalent myths, illusions, and persistent misconceptions through the dissemination of factual information is imperative to empower them to make informed decisions.

- Coordinate the efforts of government, donors, and civil society in the shaping of reform strategies and tactics[186] according to the priorities and principles described above. This should be done within a new kind of strategic advisory project that should be inclusive, open to cooperation with civil society, holistic, and involve both institutional and educational components as described above.

- Prioritize projects which build on effective cooperation between the proactive population, civil society, and local and central authorities. Trust, transparency, and accountability are key for vertical and horizontal partnerships.

---

186 It is important to acknowledge the reasons behind the non-implementation of most reforms, particularly during the initial five years of the Revolution of Dignity. Simply attributing the lack of progress solely to a lack of political will provides an oversimplified explanation that fails to offer practical solutions. A closer examination reveals the following insights: many necessary reforms were not adequately prepared at the time of their presentation. Additionally, the prioritization of reforms differed. This was partly due to valid reasons (such as the importance of reforms like macroeconomic stabilization and army rebuilding for the country's survival). Part of the issue also arose from a lack of context-specific understanding, including on the part of international donors and creditors (for example, the creation of punitive anti-corruption institutions without sufficient emphasis on prevention). Furthermore, resistance from certain interest groups played a role in preventing reforms from taking place. These groups easily diverted attention to secondary issues, substituted the modernization agenda with other problems that cannot be quickly solved (such as identity cleavages), or even co-opted the reforms, as seen in the judicial case. Aside from countless, mostly powerless civil society activists and second-tier politicians, few made genuine efforts to garner public support for reforms. Lastly, conflicts of interest between the government and certain individuals in power hindered progress on at least some of the reforms, ranging from abolishing protectionism in the automotive industry to judicial reform.

Although these recommendations look ambitious and long-term, their strikingly advantageous feature is that none of them belong to so-called "unpopular reforms." They are, of course, highly unpopular in certain narrow but influential circles of oligarchs and other rent seekers. However, they could and should be popular among average Ukrainians, for whom they will bring greater justice, security, freedom, opportunities, and, finally, material wealth. It is true that currently people often fail to understand the links between, say, electoral reform and their own well-being: such links are, indeed, indirect and unclear, but can be popularly explained.

Previously, many observers and advisors lamented the lack of political leadership in Ukraine which, in their opinion, was the main culprit for the lack of speedy transformation. Now political authority in Ukraine, quite unexpectedly, has been consolidated, at least formally, in full. However, many drawbacks remain, and plenty of new risks arise. A more clearcut and comprehensive national strategy is essential, and sharper coordinated collective efforts are needed to make sure that this good chance pays off for Ukraine and its future.

Bibliography

Acemoglu, D., and Robinson, J. The Narrow Corridor: States, Societies, and the Fate of Liberty. New York: Penguin Publishers, 2019.

Acemoğlu, D., Robinson, J. Why Nations Fail: The Origins of Power, Prosperity, and Poverty. Crown Publishers, 2012.

Allen, K., "Shrinking Cities: Population Decline in the World's Rust-belt Areas." Financial Times, June 16, 2017. Available at: https://www.ft.com/content/d7b00030-4abe-11e7-919a-1e14ce4af89b.

Arel, D. "Language and Group Boundaries in the Two Ukraines." Paper presentation at the conference "National Minorities, Nationalizing States, and External National Homelands in the New Europe", Bellagio Study and Conference Center, August 1994.

Arendt, H. On Revolution. Penguin, 1963.

Babanin, O., Dubrovskiy, V. and Ivaschenko, O. "Ukraine: The Lost Decade ... and a Coming Boom?". Kyiv: Alterpress, 2002.

Brinton, C. The Anatomy of Revolution. First ed. 1938; revised ed. New York: Vintage Books, 1965.

Bystrytskyy, Y. et al. On the Equator of the New Government (the Years of 2019-2021): Achievements, Problems, Prospects, edited by Yakovlev, M., and Pekar, V. Kyiv: School for Policy Analysis NaUKMA, 2021. Available at: https://spa.ukma.edu.ua/analytics/na-ekvatori-novoi-vlady-2019-2021-dosiahnennia-problemy-perspektyvy/

Coynash, H. "New bill on the Security Service is in breach of Ukraine's Constitution and human rights standards." Kharkiv Human Rights Protection Group, September 28, 2021. Available at: https://khpg.org/en/1608809587

D'Anieri, P. "Introduction: Debating the Assumptions of State-led Nation Building in Ukraine." In Dilemmas of State-Led Nation Building in Ukraine, edited by T. Kuzio and P. D'Anieri, 1-17. Westport, CT: Praeger, 2002.

D'Anieri, P. "Societal Divisions and the Challenge of Liberal Democracy in Ukraine." Chap. 5 in Understanding Ukrainian Politics: Power, Politics, and Institutional Design. Armonk, NY: M.E. Sharpe, 2007.

Davies, J. "Towards a Theory of Revolution." American Sociological Review, No 27, 1962. 5-19.

Demsetz, H. "Toward a Theory of Property Rights." *The American Economic Review*, 1967, 374-359.

Dubrovskiy, V. "Patronalism and the Limited Access Social Order: The Case of Ukraine" in *Ukraine. Patronal Democracy and the Russian Invasion: The Russia-Ukraine War, Volume One*, edited by Madlovics, B. and Magyar, B. Budapest–Vienna–New York: CEU Press, 2023.

Dubrovskiy, V. "Political, Economic And Institutional Aspects Of Making Cuts To The Ukrainian Budget." *Vox Ukraine,* February, 2015. Available at: https://voxukraine.org/en/political-economic-and-instituti onal-aspects-of-making-cuts-to-the-ukrainian-budget/

Dubrovskiy, V. "The Main Driving Forces for De-Patronalization of Ukraine: The Role of Ukrainian business" in Ukraine. *Patronal Democracy and the Russian Invasion: The Russia-Ukraine War*, Volume One, edited by Madlovics, B. and Magyar, B. Budapest—Vienna—New York: CEU Press, 2023.

Dubrovskiy, V., Mizsei, K., Ivashchenko-Stadnik, K., and Wynnyckyj, M. *Six years of the Revolution of Dignity: what has changed?* CASE Ukraine, 2020. Available at: https://case-ukraine.com.ua/content/ uploads/2020/06/6-years-of-the-Revolution-of-Dignity_ENG.pdf

Dubrovskiy, V., Szyrmer, J., Graves, W., Golovakha, E., Haran', O., and Pavlenko, R. *The Driving Forces for Unwanted Reforms: Lessons from the Ukrainian Transition*, edited by Dubrovskiy V., Szyrmer J., and Graves W. CASE Ukraine, 2010.

Dunavova, D. et al. "Violent Conflict and Online Segregation: An Analysis of Social Network Communication Across Ukraine's Regions." *Journal of Comparative Economics*, No. 1, 2016.

Dzamukashvili, S. "Why is Ukraine's anti-oligarch bill so problematic?" *Emerging Europe*, November 21, 2021.

Faguet, J., Shami, M. "Instrumental Incoherence in Institutional Reform." London: *LSE Working Paper Series*, 2015.

Florida, R. "'Everything is gentrification now': but Richard Florida isn't sorry". Interview conducted by Oliver Wainwright. *The Guardian*, October 26, 2017. Available at: https://www.theguardian.com/citie s/2017/oct/26/gentrification-richard-florida-interview-creative-cla ss-new-urban-crisis

Florida, R. *The Rise of the Creative Class: And How it's Transforming Work, Leisure, Community and Everyday Life*. New York: Perseus Book Group, 2002.

Fukuyama, F. "Against Identity Politics. The New Tribalism and the Crisis of Democracy." *Foreign Affairs*, 2018. Available at: https://www.f oreignaffairs.com/articles/americas/2018-08-14/against-identity-p olitics-tribalism-francis-fukuyama

Gellner, E. *Nations and Nationalism*. Second edition. Blackwell Publishing, 2008.

Golovakha, E., Panina, N., Gorbachyk, A. "Measuring Index of Social Well-Being." *Sociology: Methodology, Methods, Marketing*, 1998. No.10, 47-71.

Golovakha, E. "The Changes of the Integral Indicator of Social and Psychological Well-being of the Ukrainian Population During the Years of Independence." In *Ukrainian Society: the Dynamics of Change*, edited by Vorona V. et al. Kyiv: Institute of Sociology NAS Ukraine, 2019, 300-308.

Golovakha, E., Ivashchenko-Stadnik, K., Mikheieva, O., and Sereda, V. "From Patronalism to Civic Belonging: The Changing Dynamics of the National-Civic Identity in Ukraine." In *Ukraine: Patronal Democracy and the Russian Invasion: The Russia-Ukraine War, Volume One*, edited by Madlovics, B., and Magyar, B. Budapest—Vienna—New York: CEU Press, 2023.

Hale, H. "Patronal Politics: Eurasian Regime Dynamics" in *Comparative Perspective (Problems of International Politics)*. Cambridge: Cambridge University Press, 2014.

Hawrylyshyn, O. *The Political Economy of Independent Ukraine: Slow Starts, False Starts, and a Last Chance?* London: Palgrave Macmillan, 2017.

Hellman, J. "Winners Take All: The Politics of Partial Reform in Post-Communist Transitions." *World Politics*, vol. 50, 1998, 203-234.

Hrycak, A. "Institutional Legacies and Language Revival in Ukraine." In *Rebounding Identities: The Politics of Identity in Ukraine and Russia*, edited by Arel, D. and Ruble, B. Baltimore: The Johns Hopkins University Press, 2006.

Hrytsak, Y. "Understanding Ukrainian history." Interview conducted by Yermolenko, V. *Ukraine/World*, 2019. Available at: https://ukrainew orld.org/articles/ukraine-explained/history-hrytsak?fbclid=IwAR2 DqIFafNJ96GpmQkXHWpJsryfntlKAEBoiG-u2qATiIk5lWQn-mto7 AB4

Hrytsak, Y. "Overcoming the Past. The Global History of Ukraine." *Kyiv: Portal*, 2021.

Hrytsak, Y. "Selected Issues of European History." Series of online lectures. *PROMETHEUS*, 2017. Available at: https://prometheus.org.ua/

Hulli, E. "Ukraine: The Next Startup Nation." *Medium*, August, 2017. Available at: https://medium.com/startup-grind/ukraine-the-next -startup-nation-d81e0b7cffcc.

Ivashchenko-Stadnik, K. "What's Wrong With the Donbas? The Challenges of Integration Before, During and After the War." in *Ukraine in Transformation*, edited by Veira-Ramos, A., Liubiva, T., and Golovakha, E. London: Routledge, McMillan, 2020.

Lane, D. "The Orange Revolution: 'People's Revolution' or Revolutionary Coup?" *The British Journal of Politics & International Relations*, vol. 10, 2008, 525–549.

Lenard, P. "Trust Your Compatriots, but Count Your Change: The Roles of Trust, Mistrust, and Distrust in Democracy." *Political Studies*, Vol. 56 issue 2 2008. Available at: https://onlinelibrary.wiley.com/doi/abs/10.1111/j.1467-9248.2007.00693.x

Levy, B. "Governance Reform: Bridging Monitoring and Action." *World Bank*, 2007. Available at: http://documents.worldbank.org/curated/en/276631468328173186/Governance-reform-bridging-monitoring-and-action

Lough, J., Dubrovskiy, V. *Are Ukraine's Anti-corruption Reforms Working?* Chatham House, 2018.

Lunina, I., and Vincetz, V., "The Subsidisation of Ukraine's Enterprises." In *Ukraine at the Crossroads: Economics Reforms in International Perspective*, edited by Axel Siedenberg and Lutz Hoffmann, 118–32. Berlin—Heidelberg: Springer-Verlag, 1999.

Magyar B., Madlovics B. *The Anatomy of Post-Communist Regimes. A Conceptual Framework.* Budapest: Central European University Press, 2020.

Mashtaler, O. "The 2019 Presidential Election in Ukraine: Populism, the Influence of the Media, and the Victory of the Virtual Candidate" in *The Politics of Authenticity and Populist Discourses*, edited by Christoph Khol et al. Palgrave Macmillan, 2021, 127-160. Available at: https://link.springer.com/book/10.1007/978-3-030-55474-3

Matsiyevsky, Y. *Has Ukraine's Regime Changed Since the 2014 Revolution? EU-Eurasian Relations at the Crossroads.* Montreal: The EU Centre of Excellence; PONARS Eurasia, December, 2016.

Mattli W. *The Logic of Regional Integration: Europe and Beyond.* Cambridge: Cambridge University Press, 1999.

Minakov, M. "Reconstructing the Power Vertical: the Authoritarian Threat in Ukraine." *Open Democracy*, June, 2017. Available at: https://www.opendemocracy.net/en/odr/reconstructing-power-vertical-authoritarian-threat-in-ukraine/

Mizsei, K. "The New East European Patronal States and the Rule-of-Law." in *Stubborn Structures: Reconceptualizing Post-Communist Regimes*, edited by Magyar, B. Budapest-New York: CEU Press, 2019.

North, D., Wallis, J. et al. "Limited Access Order in the Developing World: A New Approach to the Problem of Development." *Policy Research Working Paper.* The World Bank, Independent Evaluation Group, 2007.

North, D., Wallis, J., and Weingast, B. Violence and Social Orders: A Conceptual Framework for Interpreting Recorded Human History. Cambridge: Cambridge University Press, 2009.

Olson, M. The Rise and Decline of Nations: Economic Growth, Stagflation, and Social Rigidities. New Haven: Yale University Press, 1982.

Ostrom, E. Governing the Commons: The Evolution of Institutions for Collective Action. Cambridge: Cambridge University Press, 1990.

Party Systems and Voter Alignments: Cross-National Perspectives, edited by Lipset, S. and Rokkan, S. New York: The Free Press, 1967.

Pehlivanova P. "The Decline in Trust in Post-Communist Societies: The Case of Bulgaria and Russia." Contemporary Issues, No.1, 2019, 32–47.

Petrenko, I. "State Bureau of Investigations: will it be possible to create an independent and transparent authority?" in Inside Ukraine. Independent Centre for Policy Studies, January 31, 2018. Available at: http://icps.com.ua/assets/uploads/files/IU_75_ENG_2018_01_31_co l%20(1)_2103.pdf

Plokhy, S. The Gates of Europe: A History of Ukraine. Basic Books, 2015.

Popova, M. "Ukraine's Judiciary after Euromaidan." *Comparative Politics Newsletter*, Volume 25, Issue 2, Fall.

Putnam, R., Leonardi, R., and Nanetti, R. *Making Democracy Work: Civic Traditions in Modern Italy*. Princeton: Princeton University Press, 1993.

Rachok, A. et. al. *Middle Class in Ukraine: Prevalence and Relevance of the Notion*. Kyiv: Razumkov Center, 2016. Available at: http://razumko v.org.ua/uploads/article/2016_Seredn_klas.pdf

Riabchuk, M. "Two Ukraines Reconsidered: The End of Ukrainian Ambivalence?" *Studies in Ethnicity and Nationalism*, vol. 15, no. 1, 2015.

Romanov, R. *Study Report: The Role of the Public Prosecutor at the Pre-Trial Stage of Criminal Proceedings*. The Renaissance Foundation, 2015.

Sasse, G. "Who Is Who in the Ukrainian Parliament?". *Carnegie Europe*, September, 2019.

Shveda, Y., and Ho Park, J. "Ukraine's Revolution of Dignity: The Dynamics of Euromaidan." *Journal of Eurasian Studies*, November 2015. Available at: https://doi.org/http://dx.doi.org/10.1016/j.euras. 2015.10.007.

Sviatnenko, S., Vynogradov, O. "Euromaidan Values from a Comparative Perspective." *Social, Health, and Communication Studies*, 2014, No. 1(1), 41-61.

Ukraine in World Values Survey. World Values Survey, NGO Ukrainian Centre for European Policy, 2020. Available at: http://ucep.org.ua/ wp-content/uploads/2020/11/WVS_UA_2020_report_ENG_WEB. pdf

Todorova, M. *"What is useful about the 'post-' in East European Studies? On post-colonialism, post-socialism, and historical legacies."* Public lecture given at Charles University, Prague, May 2019.

Tregubov, V. "Old problems threaten Ukraine's new Bureau for Economic Security." Atlantic Council. *Ukraine Alert*, October 14, 2021. Available at: https://www.atlanticcouncil.org/blogs/ukrainealert/old-pr oblems-threaten-ukraines-new-bureau-of-economic-security/

Veira-Ramos, A., et al. *Ukraine in Transformation.* London: Routledge, McMillan, 2020. Available at: https://www.palgrave.com/gp/book /9783030249779.

Vinnichuk, I., Ziukov, S., "Shadow Economy in Ukraine: Modelling and Analysis." *Business Systems and Economics*, No. 2, 2013, 141–152.

Wilson, A. *Ukraine Crisis: What It Means for the West.* New Haven: Yale University Press, 2014.

Wynnyckyj, M., *Institutions and Entrepreneurs: Cultural Evolution in the 'De Novo' Market Sphere in Post-Soviet Ukraine.* University of Cambridge, 2003.

Zhernakov, M. "Judicial Reform in Ukraine: Mission Possible? Policy Report." *International Renaissance Foundation,* 2017. Available at: http s://rpr.org.ua/wp-content/uploads/2017/02/Renaissance_A4_5J URIDICIAL-REFORM.pdf

Zimmerman, W. "Is Ukraine a Political Community?". *Communist and Post-Communist Studies*, no. 1 (1998).

Дубровський В., Черкашин В., Порівняльний аналіз фіскального ефекту від застосування інструментів ухилення/уникнення оподаткування в Україні. Київ, Інститут соціально-економічної трансформації, 2017. Available at: https://rpr.org.ua/wp-content /uploads/2018/02/Instrumenty-uhylyannya-vid-splaty-podatkiv-2 017-1.pdf .

Іващенко К. Динаміка міграційних настроїв населення України: що змінилось за 30 років? Українське суспільство: моніторинг соці-альних змін. 30 років незалежності. Київ: Інститут соціології НАН України, 2021, Випуск 8 (22), 169–184.

Середній клас в Україні. Критерії ідентифікації. Razumkov Centre & Friedrich Naumann Stiftung, Kyiv, 2014. Available at: https://razu mkov.org.ua/uploads/article/2014_ser_klass_kryterii_ident.pdf

Українське суспільство: моніторинг соціальних змін. 30 років Неза-лежності. Випуск 8(22). Київ: Національна Академія Наук Укра-їни, Інститут соціології, 2021, с.630. Available here: https://i -soc.com.ua/ua/edition/ukrainske-suspilstvo/issues/

SOVIET AND POST-SOVIET POLITICS AND SOCIETY

Edited by Dr. Andreas Umland | ISSN 1614-3515

1   *Андреас Умланд (ред.)* | Воплощение Европейской конвенции по правам человека в России. Философские, юридические и эмпирические исследования | ISBN 3-89821-387-0

2   *Christian Wipperfürth* | Russland – ein vertrauenswürdiger Partner? Grundlagen, Hintergründe und Praxis gegenwärtiger russischer Außenpolitik | Mit einem Vorwort von Heinz Timmermann | ISBN 3-89821-401-X

3   *Manja Hussner* | Die Übernahme internationalen Rechts in die russische und deutsche Rechtsordnung. Eine vergleichende Analyse zur Völkerrechtsfreundlichkeit der Verfassungen der Russländischen Föderation und der Bundesrepublik Deutschland | Mit einem Vorwort von Rainer Arnold | ISBN 3-89821-438-9

4   *Matthew Tejada* | Bulgaria's Democratic Consolidation and the Kozloduy Nuclear Power Plant (KNPP). The Unattainability of Closure | With a foreword by Richard J. Crampton | ISBN 3-89821-439-7

5   *Марк Григорьевич Меерович* | Квадратные метры, определяющие сознание. Государственная жилищная политика в СССР. 1921 – 1941 гг | ISBN 3-89821-474-5

6   *Andrei P. Tsygankov, Pavel A.Tsygankov (Eds.)* | New Directions in Russian International Studies | ISBN 3-89821-422-2

7   *Марк Григорьевич Меерович* | Как власть народ к труду приучала. Жилище в СССР – средство управления людьми. 1917 – 1941 гг. | С предисловием Елены Осокиной | ISBN 3-89821-495-8

8   *David J. Galbreath* | Nation-Building and Minority Politics in Post-Socialist States. Interests, Influence and Identities in Estonia and Latvia | With a foreword by David J. Smith | ISBN 3-89821-467-2

9   *Алексей Юрьевич Безугольный* | Народы Кавказа в Вооруженных силах СССР в годы Великой Отечественной войны 1941-1945 гг. | С предисловием Николая Бугая | ISBN 3-89821-475-3

10 *Вячеслав Лихачев и Владимир Прибыловский (ред.)* | Русское Национальное Единство, 1990-2000. В 2-х томах | ISBN 3-89821-523-7

11 *Николай Бугай (ред.)* | Народы стран Балтии в условиях сталинизма (1940-е – 1950-е годы). Документированная история | ISBN 3-89821-525-3

12 *Ingmar Bredies (Hrsg.)* | Zur Anatomie der Orange Revolution in der Ukraine. Wechsel des Elitenregimes oder Triumph des Parlamentarismus? | ISBN 3-89821-524-5

13 *Anastasia V. Mitrofanova* | The Politicization of Russian Orthodoxy. Actors and Ideas | With a foreword by William C. Gay | ISBN 3-89821-481-8

14 *Nathan D. Larson* | Alexander Solzhenitsyn and the Russo-Jewish Question | ISBN 3-89821-483-4

15 *Guido Houben* | Kulturpolitik und Ethnizität. Staatliche Kunstförderung im Russland der neunziger Jahre | Mit einem Vorwort von Gert Weisskirchen | ISBN 3-89821-542-3

16 *Leonid Luks* | Der russische „Sonderweg"? Aufsätze zur neuesten Geschichte Russlands im europäischen Kontext | ISBN 3-89821-496-6

17 *Евгений Мороз* | История «Мёртвой воды» – от страшной сказки к большой политике. Политическое неоязычество в постсоветской России | ISBN 3-89821-551-2

18 *Александр Верховский и Галина Кожевникова (ред.)* | Этническая и религиозная интолерантность в российских СМИ. Результаты мониторинга 2001-2004 гг. | ISBN 3-89821-569-5

19 *Christian Ganzer* | Sowjetisches Erbe und ukrainische Nation. Das Museum der Geschichte des Zaporoger Kosakentums auf der Insel Chortycja | Mit einem Vorwort von Frank Golczewski | ISBN 3-89821-504-0

20 *Эльза-Баир Гучинова* | Помнить нельзя забыть. Антропология депортационной травмы калмыков | С предисловием Кэролайн Хамфри | ISBN 3-89821-506-7

21 *Юлия Лидерман* | Мотивы «проверки» и «испытания» в постсоветской культуре. Советское прошлое в российском кинематографе 1990-х годов | С предисловием Евгения Марголита | ISBN 3-89821-511-3

22 *Tanya Lokshina, Ray Thomas, Mary Mayer (Eds.)* | The Imposition of a Fake Political Settlement in the Northern Caucasus. The 2003 Chechen Presidential Election | ISBN 3-89821-436-2

23 *Timothy McCajor Hall, Rosie Read (Eds.)* | Changes in the Heart of Europe. Recent Ethnographies of Czechs, Slovaks, Roma, and Sorbs | With an afterword by Zdeněk Salzmann | ISBN 3-89821-606-3

24 *Christian Autengruber* | Die politischen Parteien in Bulgarien und Rumänien. Eine vergleichende Analyse seit Beginn der 90er Jahre | Mit einem Vorwort von Dorothée de Nève | ISBN 3-89821-476-1

25 *Annette Freyberg-Inan with Radu Cristescu* | The Ghosts in Our Classrooms, or: John Dewey Meets Ceauşescu. The Promise and the Failures of Civic Education in Romania | ISBN 3-89821-416-8

26 *John B. Dunlop* | The 2002 Dubrovka and 2004 Beslan Hostage Crises. A Critique of Russian Counter-Terrorism | With a foreword by Donald N. Jensen | ISBN 3-89821-608-X

27 *Peter Koller* | Das touristische Potenzial von Kam"janec'–Podil's'kyj. Eine fremdenverkehrsgeographische Untersuchung der Zukunftsperspektiven und Maßnahmenplanung zur Destinationsentwicklung des „ukrainischen Rothenburg" | Mit einem Vorwort von Kristiane Klemm | ISBN 3-89821-640-3

28 *Françoise Daucé, Elisabeth Sieca-Kozlowski (Eds.)* | Dedovshchina in the Post-Soviet Military. Hazing of Russian Army Conscripts in a Comparative Perspective | With a foreword by Dale Herspring | ISBN 3-89821-616-0

29 *Florian Strasser* | Zivilgesellschaftliche Einflüsse auf die Orange Revolution. Die gewaltlose Massenbewegung und die ukrainische Wahlkrise 2004 | Mit einem Vorwort von Egbert Jahn | ISBN 3-89821-648-9

30 *Rebecca S. Katz* | The Georgian Regime Crisis of 2003-2004. A Case Study in Post-Soviet Media Representation of Politics, Crime and Corruption | ISBN 3-89821-413-3

31 *Vladimir Kantor* | Willkür oder Freiheit. Beiträge zur russischen Geschichtsphilosophie | Ediert von Dagmar Herrmann sowie mit einem Vorwort versehen von Leonid Luks | ISBN 3-89821-589-X

32 *Laura A. Victoir* | The Russian Land Estate Today. A Case Study of Cultural Politics in Post-Soviet Russia | With a foreword by Priscilla Roosevelt | ISBN 3-89821-426-5

33 *Ivan Katchanovski* | Cleft Countries. Regional Political Divisions and Cultures in Post-Soviet Ukraine and Moldova | With a foreword by Francis Fukuyama | ISBN 3-89821-558-X

34 *Florian Mühlfried* | Postsowjetische Feiern. Das Georgische Bankett im Wandel | Mit einem Vorwort von Kevin Tuite | ISBN 3-89821-601-2

35 *Roger Griffin, Werner Loh, Andreas Umland (Eds.)* | Fascism Past and Present, West and East. An International Debate on Concepts and Cases in the Comparative Study of the Extreme Right | With an afterword by Walter Laqueur | ISBN 3-89821-674-8

36 *Sebastian Schlegel* | Der „Weiße Archipel". Sowjetische Atomstädte 1945-1991 | Mit einem Geleitwort von Thomas Bohn | ISBN 3-89821-679-9

37 *Vyacheslav Likhachev* | Political Anti-Semitism in Post-Soviet Russia. Actors and Ideas in 1991-2003 | Edited and translated from Russian by Eugene Veklerov | ISBN 3-89821-529-6

38 *Josette Baer (Ed.)* | Preparing Liberty in Central Europe. Political Texts from the Spring of Nations 1848 to the Spring of Prague 1968 | With a foreword by Zdeněk V. David | ISBN 3-89821-546-6

39 *Михаил Лукьянов* | Российский консерватизм и реформа, 1907-1914 | С предисловием Марка Д. Стейнберга | ISBN 3-89821-503-2

40 *Nicola Melloni* | Market Without Economy. The 1998 Russian Financial Crisis | With a foreword by Eiji Furukawa | ISBN 3-89821-407-9

41 *Dmitrij Chmelnizki* | Die Architektur Stalins | Bd. 1: Studien zu Ideologie und Stil | Bd. 2: Bilddokumentation | Mit einem Vorwort von Bruno Flierl | ISBN 3-89821-515-6

42 *Katja Yafimava* | Post-Soviet Russian-Belarussian Relationships. The Role of Gas Transit Pipelines | With a foreword by Jonathan P. Stern | ISBN 3-89821-655-1

43 *Boris Chavkin* | Verflechtungen der deutschen und russischen Zeitgeschichte. Aufsätze und Archivfunde zu den Beziehungen Deutschlands und der Sowjetunion von 1917 bis 1991 | Ediert von Markus Edlinger sowie mit einem Vorwort versehen von Leonid Luks | ISBN 3-89821-756-6

44 *Anastasija Grynenko in Zusammenarbeit mit Claudia Dathe* | Die Terminologie des Gerichtswesens der Ukraine und Deutschlands im Vergleich. Eine übersetzungswissenschaftliche Analyse juristischer Fachbegriffe im Deutschen, Ukrainischen und Russischen | Mit einem Vorwort von Ulrich Hartmann | ISBN 3-89821-691-8

45 *Anton Burkov* | The Impact of the European Convention on Human Rights on Russian Law. Legislation and Application in 1996-2006 | With a foreword by Françoise Hampson | ISBN 978-3-89821-639-5

46 *Stina Torjesen, Indra Overland (Eds.)* | International Election Observers in Post-Soviet Azerbaijan. Geopolitical Pawns or Agents of Change? | ISBN 978-3-89821-743-9

47 *Taras Kuzio* | Ukraine – Crimea – Russia. Triangle of Conflict | ISBN 978-3-89821-761-3

48 *Claudia Šabić* | „Ich erinnere mich nicht, aber L'viv!" Zur Funktion kultureller Faktoren für die Institutionalisierung und Entwicklung einer ukrainischen Region | Mit einem Vorwort von Melanie Tatur | ISBN 978-3-89821-752-1

192 *Aleksandr Burakovskiy* | Jewish-Ukrainian Relations in Late and Post-Soviet Ukraine. Articles, Lectures and Essays from 1986 to 2016 | ISBN 978-3-8382-1210-4

193 *Natalia Shapovalova, Olga Burlyuk (Eds.)* | Civil Society in Post-Euromaidan Ukraine. From Revolution to Consolidation | With a foreword by Richard Youngs | ISBN 978-3-8382-1216-6

194 *Franz Preissler* | Positionsverteidigung, Imperialismus oder Irredentismus? Russland und die „Russischsprachigen", 1991–2015 | ISBN 978-3-8382-1262-3

195 *Marian Madeła* | Der Reformprozess in der Ukraine 2014-2017. Eine Fallstudie zur Reform der öffentlichen Verwaltung | Mit einem Vorwort von Martin Malek | ISBN 978-3-8382-1266-1

196 *Anke Giesen* | „Wie kann denn der Sieger ein Verbrecher sein?" Eine diskursanalytische Untersuchung der russlandweiten Debatte über Konzept und Verstaatlichungsprozess der Lagergedenkstätte „Perm'-36" im Ural | ISBN 978-3-8382-1284-5

197 *Victoria Leukavets* | The Integration Policies of Belarus and Ukraine vis-à-vis the EU and Russia. A Comparative Analysis Through the Prism of a Two-Level Game Approach | ISBN 978-3-8382-1247-0

198 *Oksana Kim* | The Development and Challenges of Russian Corporate Governance I. The Roles and Functions of Boards of Directors | With a foreword by Sheila M. Puffer | ISBN 978-3-8382-1287-6

199 *Thomas D. Grant* | International Law and the Post-Soviet Space I. Essays on Chechnya and the Baltic States | With a foreword by Stephen M. Schwebel | ISBN 978-3-8382-1279-1

200 *Thomas D. Grant* | International Law and the Post-Soviet Space II. Essays on Ukraine, Intervention, and Non-Proliferation | ISBN 978-3-8382-1280-7

201 *Slavomír Michálek, Michal Štefansky* | The Age of Fear. The Cold War and Its Influence on Czechoslovakia 1945–1968 | ISBN 978-3-8382-1285-2

202 *Iulia-Sabina Joja* | Romania's Strategic Culture 1990–2014. Continuity and Change in a Post-Communist Country's Evolution of National Interests and Security Policies | With a foreword by Heiko Biehl | ISBN 978-3-8382-1286-9

203 *Andrei Rogatchevski, Yngvar B. Steinholt, Arve Hansen, David-Emil Wickström* | War of Songs. Popular Music and Recent Russia-Ukraine Relations | With a foreword by Artemy Troitsky | ISBN 978-3-8382-1173-2

204 *Maria Lipman (Ed.)* | Russian Voices on Post-Crimea Russia. An Almanac of Counterpoint Essays from 2015–2018 | ISBN 978-3-8382-1251-7

205 *Ksenia Maksimovtsova* | Language Conflicts in Contemporary Estonia, Latvia, and Ukraine. A Comparative Exploration of Discourses in Post-Soviet Russian-Language Digital Media | With a foreword by Ammon Cheskin | ISBN 978-3-8382-1282-1

206 *Michal Vít* | The EU's Impact on Identity Formation in East-Central Europe between 2004 and 2013. Perceptions of the Nation and Europe in Political Parties of the Czech Republic, Poland, and Slovakia | With a foreword by Andrea Petö | ISBN 978-3-8382-1275-3

207 *Per A. Rudling* | Tarnished Heroes. The Organization of Ukrainian Nationalists in the Memory Politics of Post-Soviet Ukraine | ISBN 978-3-8382-0999-9

208 *Kaja Gadowska, Peter Solomon (Eds.)* | Legal Change in Post-Communist States. Progress, Reversions, Explanations | ISBN 978-3-8382-1312-5

209 *Pawel Kowal, Georges Mink, Iwona Reichardt (Eds.)* | Three Revolutions: Mobilization and Change in Contemporary Ukraine I. Theoretical Aspects and Analyses on Religion, Memory, and Identity | ISBN 978-3-8382-1321-7

210 *Pawel Kowal, Georges Mink, Adam Reichardt, Iwona Reichardt (Eds.)* | Three Revolutions: Mobilization and Change in Contemporary Ukraine II. An Oral History of the Revolution on Granite, Orange Revolution, and Revolution of Dignity | ISBN 978-3-8382-1323-1

211 *Li Bennich-Björkman, Sergiy Kurbatov (Eds.)* | When the Future Came. The Collapse of the USSR and the Emergence of National Memory in Post-Soviet History Textbooks | ISBN 978-3-8382-1335-4

212 *Olga R. Gulina* | Migration as a (Geo-)Political Challenge in the Post-Soviet Space. Border Regimes, Policy Choices, Visa Agendas | With a foreword by Nils Muižnieks | ISBN 978-3-8382-1338-5

213 *Sanna Turoma, Kaarina Aitamurto, Slobodanka Vladiv-Glover (Eds.)* | Religion, Expression, and Patriotism in Russia. Essays on Post-Soviet Society and the State. ISBN 978-3-8382-1346-0

214 *Vasif Huseynov* | Geopolitical Rivalries in the "Common Neighborhood". Russia's Conflict with the West, Soft Power, and Neoclassical Realism | With a foreword by Nicholas Ross Smith | ISBN 978-3-8382-1277-7

215 *Mikhail Suslov* | Geopolitical Imagination. Ideology and Utopia in Post-Soviet Russia | With a foreword by Mark Bassin | ISBN 978-3-8382-1361-3

241 *Izabella Agardi* | On the Verge of History. Life Stories of Rural Women from Serbia, Romania, and Hungary, 1920–2020 | With a foreword by Andrea Pető | ISBN 978-3-8382-1602-7

242 *Sebastian Schäffer (Ed.)* | Ukraine in Central and Eastern Europe. Kyiv's Foreign Affairs and the International Relations of the Post-Communist Region | With a foreword by Pavlo Klimkin and Andreas Umland| ISBN 978-3-8382-1615-7

243 *Volodymyr Dubrovskyi, Kalman Mizsei, Mychailo Wynnyckyj (Eds.)* | Eight Years after the Revolution of Dignity. What Has Changed in Ukraine during 2013–2021? | With a foreword by Yaroslav Hrytsak | ISBN 978-3-8382-1560-0

244 *Rumena Filipova* | Constructing the Limits of Europe Identity and Foreign Policy in Poland, Bulgaria, and Russia since 1989 | With forewords by Harald Wydra and Gergana Yankova-Dimova | ISBN 978-3-8382-1649-2

245 *Oleksandra Keudel* | How Patronal Networks Shape Opportunities for Local Citizen Participation in a Hybrid Regime A Comparative Analysis of Five Cities in Ukraine | With a foreword by Sabine Kropp | ISBN 978-3-8382-1671-3

246 *Jan Claas Behrends, Thomas Lindenberger, Pavel Kolar (Eds.)* | Violence after Stalin Institutions, Practices, and Everyday Life in the Soviet Bloc 1953–1989 | ISBN 978-3-8382-1637-9

247 *Leonid Luks* | Macht und Ohnmacht der Utopien Essays zur Geschichte Russlands im 20. und 21. Jahrhundert | ISBN 978-3-8382-1677-5

248 *Iuliia Barshadska* | Brüssel zwischen Kyjiw und Moskau Das auswärtige Handeln der Europäischen Union im ukrainisch-russischen Konflikt 2014-2019 | Mit einem Vorwort von Olaf Leiße | ISBN 978-3-8382-1667-6

249 *Valentyna Romanova* | Decentralisation and Multilevel Elections in Ukraine Reform Dynamics and Party Politics in 2010–2021 | With a foreword by Kimitaka Matsuzato | ISBN 978-3-8382-1700-0

250 *Alexander Motyl* | National Questions. Theoretical Reflections on Nations and Nationalism in Eastern Europe | ISBN 978-3-8382-1675-1

251 *Marc Dietrich* | A Cosmopolitan Model for Peacebuilding. The Ukrainian Cases of Crimea and the Donbas | With a foreword by Rémi Baudouï | ISBN 978-3-8382-1687-4

252 *Eduard Baidaus* | An Unsettled Nation. Moldova in the Geopolitics of Russia, Romania, and Ukraine | With forewords by John-Paul Himka and David R. Marples | ISBN 978-3-8382-1582-2

253 *Igor Okunev, Petr Oskolkov (Eds.)* | Transforming the Administrative Matryoshka. The Reform of Autonomous Okrugs in the Russian Federation, 2003–2008 | With a foreword by Vladimir Zorin | ISBN 978-3-8382-1721-5

254 *Winfried Schneider-Deters* | Ukraine's Fateful Years 2013–2019. Vol. I: The Popular Uprising in Winter 2013/2014 | ISBN 978-3-8382-1725-3

255 *Winfried Schneider-Deters* | Ukraine's Fateful Years 2013–2019. Vol. II: The Annexation of Crimea and the War in Donbas | ISBN 978-3-8382-1726-0

256 *Robert M. Cutler* | Soviet and Post-Soviet Russian Foreign Policies II. East-West Relations in Europe and the Political Economy of the Communist Bloc, 1971–1991 | With a foreword by Roger E. Kanet | ISBN 978-3-8382-1727-7

257 *Robert M. Cutler* | Soviet and Post-Soviet Russian Foreign Policies III. East-West Relations in Europe and Eurasia in the Post-Cold War Transition, 1991–2001 | With a foreword by Roger E. Kanet | ISBN 978-3-8382-1728-4

258 *Paweł Kowal, Iwona Reichardt, Kateryna Pryshchepa (Eds.)* | Three Revolutions: Mobilization and Change in Contemporary Ukraine III. Archival Records and Historical Sources on the 1990 Revolution on Granite | ISBN 978-3-8382-1376-7

259 *Mikhail Minakov (Ed.)* | Philosophy Unchained. Developments in Post-Soviet Philosophical Thought. | With a foreword by Christopher Donohue | ISBN 978-3-8382-1768-0

260 *David Dalton* | The Ukrainian Oligarchy After the Euromaidan. How Ukraine's Political Economy Regime Survived the Crisis | With a foreword by Andrew Wilson | ISBN 978-3-8382-1740-6

261 *Andreas Heinemann-Grüder (Ed.)* | Who are the Fighters? Irregular Armed Groups in the Russian-Ukrainian War in 2014–2015 | ISBN 978-3-8382-1777-2

262 *Taras Kuzio (Ed.)* | Russian Disinformation and Western Scholarship. Bias and Prejudice in Journalistic, Expert, and Academic Analyses of East European, Russian and Eurasian Affairs | ISBN 978-3-8382-1685-0

263 *Darius Furmonavicius* | LithuaniaTransforms the West. Lithuania's Liberation from Soviet Occupation and the Enlargement of NATO (1988–2022) | With a foreword by Vytautas Landsbergis | ISBN 978-3-8382-1779-6

264 *Dirk Dalberg* | Politisches Denken im tschechoslowakischen Dissens. Egon Bondy, Miroslav Kusý, Milan Šimečka und Petr Uhl (1968-1989) | ISBN 978-3-8382-1318-7

ibidem.eu